— GUNS, DRUGS, AND DEVELOPMENT IN COLOMBIA —

T0340641

GUNS, DRUGS, AND DEVELOPMENT IN COLOMBIA

JENNIFER S. HOLMES
SHEILA AMIN GUTIÉRREZ DE PIÑERES
KEVIN M. CURTIN

UNIVERSITY OF TEXAS PRESS
Austin

Requests for permission to reproduce material from this work
should be sent to Permissions, University of Texas Press, Box 7819,
Austin, TX 78713-7819.

♾ The paper used in this book meets the minimum requirements of
ANSI/NISO Z39.48-1992 (R1997) (Permanence of Paper).

Library of Congress Cataloging-in-Publication Data
Holmes, Jennifer S.
Guns, drugs, and development in Colombia / Jennifer S. Holmes,
Sheila Amin Gutiérrez de Piñeres, Kevin M. Curtin.
p. cm.
Includes bibliographical references and index.
ISBN 0-292-72154-4
1. Political violence—Colombia. 2. Cocaine industry—Colombia.
3. Colombia—Economic conditions—1970- I. Amin Gutiérrez
de Piñeres, Sheila. II. Curtin, Kevin M., 1967- III. Title.
HN310.Z9V5345 2008
303.6'20986109045—dc22
2008006632

To our families

CONTENTS

LIST OF FIGURES

LIST OF TABLES

ACKNOWLEDGMENTS

Guns, Drugs, and Development in Colombia began in 1999. It started with an innocent question from Jennifer Holmes: "I study violence and terrorism and I know you do work on Colombia. By chance do you have any violence data?" This book has withstood two infants, one toddler, three moves, a divorce, two administrative positions, and countless other distractions. It survived because of our dedication to the project and our fundamental belief that development whether economic, political, or physical transcends disciplinary boundaries and demands a broad approach to capture the rich dynamics at play.

There are many people we need to thank and without whom this project would not have been possible. Victor Gutiérrez de Piñeres, Sheila Amin Gutiérrez de Piñeres's husband, made it possible for us to travel to Colombia to collect data and meet with our contacts. Without his support and patience we could have never completed this project. Jennifer and Sheila must acknowledge that without grandparents this project would have been impossible. Rupa and Jay Amin; Diane and Lyell Holmes; and Carolyn and Ted Smith watched their grandchildren, Victor, Sebastian, and Trevor, so we could meet deadlines and travel.

Without CINEP, this project would have evolved down an inferior path. To the many people in Colombia, Luis Fernando Jaramillo, Aurelio Mora, Hernan Avendaño Cruz, Oscar Huertas Diaz, Alejandro Cadena, and Fabio Sanchez to name a few, from all walks of life who answered our calls for assistance, we express our deepest gratitude. Others, including Henry Gamboa Castañeda, Transito Porras Garzón, Jenny Fagua Duarte, Karolina Gudmundsson, Luz Deyanira Mateus P., Martha Paredes R., William Jiménez, and Carlos Velasqués also provided clarification and insight. Over the eight years of this project they have been invaluable in answering questions and helping us acquire some of the most obscure data. We greatly appreciate their generosity, diligence, and service to their country. The conclusions of this project should be attributed to the authors only and in no way assigned to any of those named above.

A special thanks to Theresa May, editor-in-chief, who never gave up on us and the importance of this project. We also want to thank the anonymous reviewers for their constructive criticism.

This book embodies the interdisciplinary essence of the School of Economic, Political, and Policy Sciences at The University of Texas at Dallas. The book is multidisciplinary, qualitative, quantitative, and collaborative. There are very few in the School who we did not at one time or another consult. When we started this project we only anticipated using the simplest of econometric tools; yet, the field has advanced over the years and we advanced with it. We must also acknowledge our colleagues who endured as we sought advice while learning new methodological techniques: Kurt Beron, Patrick Brandt, Chetan Dave, Roxanne Ezzet-Lofstrom, Magnus Lofstrom, Jim Murdoch, Clint Peinhart, and Carole Wilson. Brian JL Berry provided general support for the project over the years. Todd Sandler introduced us to a series of new literature that enriched the analysis of violence. Richard Scotch read the entire manuscript. Then, there are all the occupants of the south hallway of Cecil Green Hall who tolerated our very unorthodox and cacophonous way of working.

Sheila would also like to thank Provost B. Hobson Wildenthal for his support and patience as she worked to meet the final deadline. Valerie Williams deserves a special mention because without her it would have been impossible to leave the office for three weeks to finish the book.

Jennifer thanks Richard Millett for all the introductions, encouragement, and constructive criticism during this project and others.

Then, there are the two professors who have been our mentors and biggest supporters through the years, always encouraging us to reach our potential and push the boundaries of our fields: Robert T. Holt and Steve Pejovich, without whom we would not be who we are.

— GUNS, DRUGS, AND DEVELOPMENT IN COLOMBIA —

ONE

INTRODUCTION

Mired in a conflict in which the lines among the different violent actors are not always clear, Colombia struggles for control of its territory. Typically, Colombia is considered a deviant democracy, characterized by chronic insurgency and a seemingly stable political system. The country has enjoyed exceptional regime stability but is racked by internal conflict. Although constitutional rule has been uninterrupted since Rojas Pinilla seized power and imposed a military dictatorship from 1953 to 1957, the veneer of sovereignty is thin: numerous armed groups effectively rule parts of the country where central-government control is weak or nonexistent. Since the 1960s, Colombia has faced a rebel insurgency, which has led to the rise of many active paramilitary groups formed to counter the insurgency. The paramilitaries, essentially private armies, have varying degrees of loyalty to the Colombian government and military. Compounding the insurgency problem is the illegal-drug industry, which started in the 1970s and has created expansive networks within Colombian politics and society. As violence increased and the illegal drug trade began to take hold, the traditionally stable Colombian economy began to falter in the 1990s. This project examines the multiple connections among violence, coca, and the economy in an attempt to explain how these factors interact and react to one another.

Colombia is a country of contradictions. Compared to its Latin American peers, Colombia remains relatively poor as measured by per capita gross domestic product (GDP) and poverty rates, but its economic policy has been generally considered successful. It was the sole Latin American country to escape the debt crisis of the 1980s, yet violence restrains economic growth and drugs distort the economy. Its homicide rates and levels of political violence set it apart from the other countries.

The guerrilla groups, drug-related violence, and paramilitaries have made Colombia one of the most violent nations in the world. Approximately two million Colombians have fled the country since 1985. This is a significant number in a country with a population of less than 44 million. During the rebel conflict and the drug war from 1985 to 2000, hundreds of bombs exploded in Colombian cities; the Unión Patriótica, a left-wing political party of former guerrillas, had over 3,500 members murdered or disappeared by paramilitaries; and four presidential candidates, half of the Supreme Court justices, over 1,200 police officers, 200 journalists and judges, and more than 300,000 ordinary Colombians have been murdered (Pardo 2000, 65). In 2002 alone, 144 politicians and public officials were assassinated by armed illegal groups, 124 were kidnapped (including 1 presidential candidate, 19 mayors, 25 councilmen, 1 governor, 19 deputies, and 3 members of congress), and more than 600 mayors were threatened with death. In 2001, one oil pipeline was attacked 170 times, costing $520 million (monetary figures are in U.S. dollars unless otherwise indicated). From 2000 to 2002, more than 1,200 electrical towers were attacked (Ministerio de Defensa Nacional 2003, 25). In 2002, 412,553 people were displaced (CODHES), up to 8 journalists were killed for political reasons (Committee to Protect Journalists 2003), and from January through November, 184 trade unionists and 17 human rights activists were murdered (CINEP). This book examines the multiple forms of Colombian violence and cycles of violence (drug, guerrilla, paramilitary, and state) at the subnational level and investigates how economic performance and coca cultivation affect trends in violence.

While Colombia survived the debt crisis of the 1980s relatively unscathed, the drug crisis and guerrilla violence handicapped the economy in the 1990s. Violence made Colombia a less attractive destination for both domestic and foreign investment. According to Arbelaez, Echavarria, and Gaviria (2002, 41), the growth of per capita GDP fell from 2.3 percent in 1985–1994 to −1.5 percent in 1995–1999. Beginning in 1993, growth rates of per capita GDP declined until 2000, and it was not until 2002 that Colombia experienced positive growth. Some may blame coca cultivation for the pervasive violence, but Colombia was violent before coca, and not all other coca producing countries have experienced internal conflict to this extent. In 2001, Colombia had an estimated 145,000 hectares (358,000 acres) of coca cultivated, down from 163,000 in 2000. Its Andean neighbors, Peru and Bolivia, also grow coca. Peru cultivated 46,200 hectares (114,000 acres), down from a peak of 115,300 in 1995, and Bolivia cultivated 19,900 hectares (49,000 acres), a 59 percent reduction from the 1995 peak of 48,600 hectares (120,000 acres) (UNDCP 2005). Other countries have experienced entrenched civil violence, without coca, including El Salvador, Guatemala, and Nicaragua. Argentina

1.1 COLOMBIA COMPARED TO OTHER MAJOR LATIN AMERICAN COUNTRIES

Country	GDP (per capita, 1999)	Gini 1999	Homicides (per 100,000)	Poverty (%)	Schooling (mean years)
Argentina	7,435	.53	4.8 (1996)	17.8 (1997)	9.4
Brazil	4,225	.64	23.3 (1995)	35.8 (1996)	6.0
Chile	5,129	.55	2.9 (1994)	23.2 (1996)	9.8
Colombia	2,266	.55	60.8 (1995)	50.9 (1997)	5.6
Mexico	4,577	.57	17.1 (1995)	52.1 (1996)	5.9
Venezuela	3,037	.49	16.8 (1994)	48.1 (1997)	7.1

Sources: Yunes and Zubarew 1999, ECLAC 2002, UNDP 2004

Note: GDP is measured in 1999 U.S. dollars. The Gini coefficient is a measure of inequality: the higher the figure, the greater the inequality in the country.

had revolutionary groups, such as the Montoneros, and counterrevolutionary groups, such as Mano, without any coca cultivation. Peru experienced coca cultivation in addition to violence from the Shining Path and the MRTA. What is the relationship between violence and coca?

Traditional economic analysis of the Colombian economy has failed to study the connection between illegal drugs, violence, and political variables as they relate to the economy and sources of growth. How do different types of violence affect the economy? Does coca cultivation add to the economy or harm it? We examine the influence of both coca cultivation and different types of violence on the economy. Since violence and coca production are not uniformly dispersed across the country, data aggregated at the national level are unlikely to reveal the true underlying relationships. This project uses subnational data to more accurately discern the impact of coca and violence on the economy. The econometric analysis is supplemented with other types of quantitative and qualitative analysis to provide a more comprehensive examination of the issue.

A survey of the costs of the conflict reveals the importance of understanding the evolution and dynamics of the conflict. Nonetheless, some still ask, why Colombia? Substantively, questions of violence, development, and stability are of fundamental importance to U.S. foreign policy. Specifically,

Colombia shares borders with Panama, Venezuela, Brazil, Ecuador, and Peru, so Colombian security problems can cross borders and lead to regional instability. The main foreign policy aims of the United States in relation to Colombia are to reduce the flow of drugs from Colombia to the United States and to quell the forty-year insurgency. Establishing the extent of connections between drug production and political violence is essential to crafting an appropriate policy. Finally, lessons learned in Colombia can produce guidelines for policy creation in other countries facing violent insurgency, lacking a strong governmental presence, and struggling to achieve development.

The policy implications of these issues will become clear as we attempt to answer the following questions. What is the role of Colombian geography and political development in the conflict? Who are the main violent actors? What is the most appropriate unit of analysis for examining the Colombian conflict and economy? What factors facilitate different types of violence? How do violence and the drug trade affect the economy? What general lessons can a study of Colombia provide other countries facing entrenched and seemingly intractable conflicts?

This project began as a simple collaboration between a political scientist and an economist trying to answer questions about the nexus between violence and the economy. The complexities of these questions quickly overwhelmed disciplinary boundaries. Violent groups need to fund themselves. Different groups have distinct origins and aims. Specific indicators of violence and economic well-being should be chosen that are appropriate for the historical evolution of the group in question. Poverty and inequality may encourage economic grievances. Paramilitary groups may form to protect economic assets. Issues of governability and stability affect economic growth and development. We needed a geographer to help us grasp the physical constraints to development, the geographic proclivities toward violence, and the subnational nature of Colombian society. After making numerous trips to Colombia, where we talked with diverse groups, ranging from the human rights community to the military and the business community, we realized that the project required a book-length treatise to capture the multiplicities of the Colombian situation.

The Colombian conflict can be understood as containing elements of terrorism, vigilantism, state repression, revolution, insurgency, guerrilla violence, and civil war, among others. However, instead of being a deviant case, in many ways the Colombian example is representative of the study of political violence, which tends to be disjointed, conceptually muddled, handicapped by a lack of data, and troubled by political connotations in the definitions given for different types of violence and the relationships among them.

Because of this, we have taken an extensively broad approach to the study of Colombian violence. Significant variations of violence, economic performance, and political factors within the country make Colombia an ideal test case for examining theories of civil war and nonstate violence. First, we use multiple forms of investigation. In most of the literature on conflict, there is a "troubling lack of cross-method communication" (George and Bennett 2005, 4). Scholars have noted a lack of "theoretically grounded case studies" in terrorism and conflict (F. Schultz 2004, 183–184). To more fully illustrate causal mechanisms, studies should focus on cases that statistical analyses identify either as deviant or representative. This is a best practice in comparative politics, a field in which "scholars routinely go back to a small number of cases to assess the validity of conceptualization and measurement, as well as to refine causal inferences" (D. Collier 1998a, 2).

Additionally, relevant historical and contextual factors are difficult to appropriately include in many large cross-national, quantitative models. Longstanding concerns regarding the comparability of indicators and concepts remain controversial. Moreover, issues of approach aside, severe data constraints in many developing countries preclude certain types of study. Since it is difficult to compensate for omitted variables through statistical analysis alone, other analytical tools must be utilized to fully understand the impact of violence. Moreover, unmodeled heterogeneity creates inefficient estimates. Since important factors cannot be incorporated into the statistical models, we complement the statistical analyses with other tools, such as cartographic visualization and qualitative analysis, and contextualize the conclusions. Synergetic studies that integrate findings from works with different methodologies are particularly useful when there are apparent multiple causal pathways and potentially probabilistic causation (D. Collier 1998a, 4).

Second, we use the theoretical literature from Colombia specialists, area specialists, and generalists to grapple with the multiple forms of Colombian violence and their effects. Third, given the nature of types of political violence, it is best to incorporate insights from multiple disciplines, such as geography, history, economics, sociology, and psychology (Holmes, forthcoming). To research these issues in the Colombian context, we have used insights from geography, history, political science, and economics. Fourth, we use multiple levels of analysis. In general, Della Porta (2003, 388) calls for a multilevel analysis (macro-, meso-, and micro-) because of the complex nature of political violence. We examine trends at both the national and subnational level. While most of the research on Colombia is conducted at the national level, a subnational study offers a unique opportunity to incorporate many of the theoretically important factors into analyses, and avoids questions of the comparability of indicators common to cross-national studies.

The book is composed of eight chapters, including the introduction. Traditionally, the introduction sets out the main question and provides a literature review. Since each chapter focuses on a different aspect of violence or development, relevant literature reviews are included throughout the book. The last chapter draws upon all of the substantive chapters to provide an overall, integrated conclusion.

Chapter Two, "Historical and Geographical Propensities to Violence," examines how the geography of Colombia creates challenges for state building and nurtures guerrilla conflict. The land is inhospitable for nation building. Instead of inspiring integration, it fosters fragmentation. The Colombian state has consistently struggled to achieve a monopoly of legitimate force; historically, challengers have ranged from numerous rebellions to two armies claiming to represent the nation. Classic theories of state building provide insight into the evolution of the Colombian state, explaining how it has become one of "permanent and endemic [internal] warfare" (Sanchez and Bakewell 1985, 789). Colombian regionalism has its roots in the colonial period, independence, and a lack of external wars. Historical settlement patterns, the distribution of the population, and the physical geography hindered centralization and provided opportunities for rebellion. These factors have contributed to a weak Colombian national state and created a proclivity toward violence.

Chapter Three, "Colombian Economic History: Regional Context and Colombian Policies," examines Colombia's economic performance within the regional context of Latin America, focusing on the six larger economies of Argentina, Brazil, Chile, Mexico, Peru, and Venezuela. This overview of Colombia's relative position in Latin America from the 1970s through the early 2000s reveals that Colombia has not yet reached its potential, which is a likely result of violence, weak state control, and the illegal drugs that permeate its economy. The Colombian economy has experienced long-term positive growth punctuated by periods of crisis. By the 1990s, the main focus of this book, the national government had not overcome the economic insecurity. However, since the election of President Uribe, the Colombian economy has improved and is showing signs of potentially reaching the next level of development. In 2005, foreign direct investment had grown dramatically, and Colombia was the third choice for foreign investment in the region. Foreign investment is an independent, market-driven indicator of confidence in the long-term growth potential of the country. While President Uribe appears to have begun to address the issues of economic insecurity, the lack of a concurrent focus on improvements in infrastructure, education, and unemployment diminishes hopes that Colombia will move out of the bottom tier of this group of Latin American countries.

Chapter Four, "The Main Actors in the 1990s and into the Twenty-first Century: Guerrillas and Paramilitaries," provides a general overview of the origins, organization, and actions of the different violent groups in Colombia. Groups discussed include major guerrilla groups (FARC, the ELN, the ELP, etc.) and the paramilitaries (the AUC). To understand the current Colombian challenge, it is important to study the historical context in which these groups emerged. *La violencia,* a bloody ten-year civil war in which the Liberals and Conservatives fought against each other, is discussed along with the National Front pact that reconciled them; the aim is to provide an understanding of the shared inspiration of many of the guerrilla groups.

Chapter Five, "Differences within Colombia and Available Subnational Data," establishes the best level of analysis with which to examine the relationships among violence, coca, and the economy. There have been considerable regional differences since the time of the original Spanish colonization. Today, those differences involve the intensity of violence, level of development, and amount of coca cultivation throughout the country. So instead of conducting a national-level analysis, with an embedded assumption of homogeneity, we have chosen to examine the country subnationally. This chapter provides an overview of the great diversity within the country and a discussion of the data used in the book. As Thoumi (2005, 14) highlights, "Since colonial times Colombia has been a collection of diverse regions with little communication and trade among them. Physical barriers are so great that many regions remained very isolated and self-sufficient." A subnational analysis provides greater rigor because of the increased sample size, allowing us to conduct statistical analyses to probe the differences among departments in what would otherwise be extremely short national time series.

Chapter Six, "Guns and Protection: Guerrillas and Paramilitaries," examines the factors contributing to guerrilla and paramilitary violence. Since these violent groups have very different origins and aims, it is important to examine different types of violence separately. Additionally, it is vital to acknowledge that factors encouraging the emergence of violent groups during such a protracted conflict may not be the same as those that explain the persistence of conflict. Daniel Pécaut (1997) states that the pervasive Colombian violence has created its own influences, regardless of the original causes of the violence. Understanding old and new dynamics is essential to crafting an appropriate and effective policy response to the challenge of insurgency. This chapter focuses on the time period of 1990–2001 to understand the contemporary evolution of the Colombian conflict.

Chapter Seven, "The Effects of Illegal Drugs and Violence on the Colombian Economy," examines the economic consequences of coca and violence. According to many scholars, pundits, and diplomats, the illegal-drug industry harms the Colombian economy. For example, Thoumi (1995a) states that "the drug trade has in fact weakened the country's economy by fostering violence and corruption, undermining legal activity, frightening off foreign investment, and all but destroying the social fabric." Moreover, Colombia suffers from high rates of political violence and violent criminal activity, which may also have corrosive economic effects. The violence is estimated to cost the economy at least two percentage points of growth every year (Arbelaez, Echavarria, and Gaviria 2002, 38). Although these two issues are interrelated, we attempt to differentiate them. As background for a department-level analysis, a brief overview of the relationship at the national level is provided.

Chapter Eight, "Acknowledging Constraints to Find Comprehensive Peace: The Four Cornerstones of Pacification," concludes with a Colombian policy solution as well as generalizable recommendations. Because of the decades-long conflict, only a sustained commitment and a coordinated strategy will successfully calm the country. In the Colombian case, historical, geographic, and economic constraints affect policy choices and the likelihood of success. Moreover, specific relationships uncovered within the empirical chapters can similarly inform policy choices, identify constraints, and influence the likelihood of success. In general, we identify four cornerstones of a successful pacification strategy: military dominance, economic reform, increased state capacity, and a strong political community. Each of the four is necessary, but there are multiple feedbacks and overlaps among them. Moreover, it is important that policy makers have both a long- and a short-term perspective on the conflict so that they do not set immediate goals that might hinder progress on a long-term goal.

This project extends beyond a simple study of Colombian violence and drugs to one of appropriate level of data choice and type of analysis. We examine the relationships among illegal drugs, violence, and the economy at the national and subnational levels. We do not assume homogeneity of departments and, therefore, use subnational data to capture the underlying relationships. To assume that illegal drugs or violence has a pervasive negative effect on the economy without first determining if the effects are consistent across the country would be misleading. Finally, the very nature of illegal drugs and insurgent violence leads to unobserved variables that cannot always be captured in statistical analysis. To address this, we complement our statistical analysis with other qualitative and quantitative methodologies. The aim of this project is not only to shed more light on the dynamic relationships among illegal drugs, violence, and the economy in Colombia, but also to encourage other scholars to diversify their methodological and disciplinary approaches.

TWO

HISTORICAL AND GEOGRAPHICAL
PROPENSITIES TO VIOLENCE

M ajor theories of political development and conflict predict instability and fragmentation for Colombia. If a state can be understood as having a monopoly of legitimate force, Colombia has consistently struggled to achieve this status. The historical settlement pattern, the distribution of the population, and the physical geography hinder effective central governmental control and provide opportunities for rebellion. These factors, in combination, have contributed to a weak Colombian national state and created a proclivity toward violence. The geography of Colombia provides a strategic landscape ripe for guerrilla conflict and has created challenges for state building as well. This chapter examines how Colombia's historical development has been influenced by both its physical geography and the human dimensions of the landscape.

GEOGRAPHY AND PATTERNS OF DEVELOPMENT

The physically imposing Colombian landscape facilitated internal fragmentation and rebellion. As seen in Figure 2.1, the northernmost extension of the Andes, running north-northeast from the southern boundary with Ecuador to the northern boundary with Venezuela, dominates the Colombian landscape. This mountain range, divided into three nearly parallel chains, or *cordilleras*—simply referred to as the Western, Central, and Eastern Cordilleras—have peaks as high as 5,500 meters (18,000 feet). Just beyond the northern extent of the Andes lies the low-lying Caribbean coastal region, and to the southwest lies the Pacific coastal region. To the east of the Andean cordilleras lies a vast area (253,000 square kilometers, or 97,700 square miles) of tropical plains known as the Llanos, or Llanos Orientales (Rausch 1984). Although the topography, vegetation, and climate are fairly consistent through-

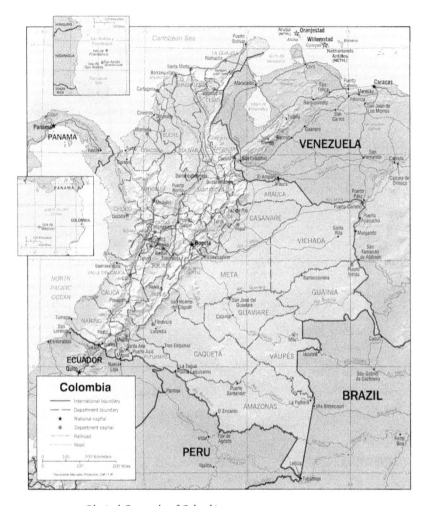

FIGURE 2.1 *Physical Geography of Colombia*

out this low-lying region, as one moves to the south the Llanos become more tropical as the region blends into greater Amazonia.

The rugged topography of Colombia has often been cited as both a barrier to effective national integration, and an aid to the development and persistence of dominant regional centers (Hartlyn 1989; Helmsing 1986). Population settlement in Colombia has been historically clustered in relatively independent areas and dispersed throughout the region in small agricultural communities connected by only limited communication. Figure 2.2 shows

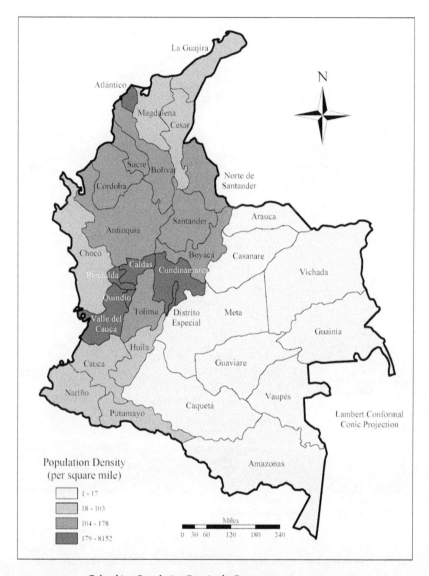

FIGURE 2.2   *Colombian Population Density by Department*

how this pattern of population density has persisted into the modern era (Safford and Palacios 2002). The regions with greater concentrations of population are those with either a more temperate climate or with greater access to lands outside Colombia. Therefore, the Andean cordilleras and the coastal regions have a greater population density than the Llanos and Amazonia. Figure 2.3 demonstrates the clustering of population in the major cities.

The historically limited communication between settlements was reinforced by the absence of an effective transportation network. More accurately, the lack of transportation infrastructure has been a substantial hindrance to economic expansion and state cohesion (Safford and Palacios, 2002). The "backwardness of travel" (Eder 1913) has been noted in nearly every historical account of the exploration of the country. One report claimed

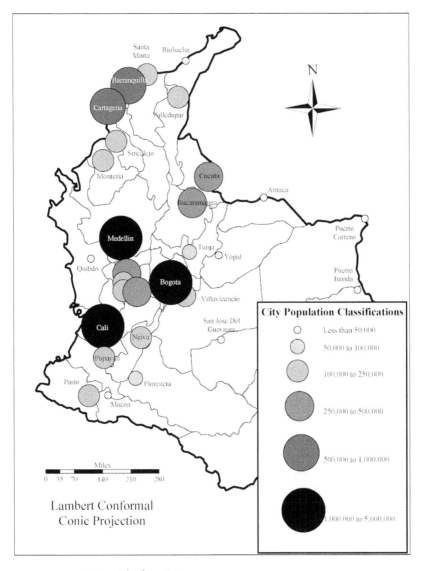

FIGURE 2.3 *Major Colombian Cities*

that at the end of the nineteenth century only seventy-five miles of roads existed in the whole country (Galbraith 1966). The road system is so poorly developed that Colombia has been referred to as "a country without roads" and has been said to have "neither a single road system radiating from the nation's capital . . . nor any integrated road system from any other point" (Stokes 1967). Throughout Colombia's history, road transportation in general has been a problem due to the rough topography and the wet weather that dominates several months of each year (A. C. Smith 1930; Renner 1927).

Moreover, the railroad system is similarly underdeveloped. During the nineteenth century, several attempts were made to build railroads in order to encourage economic activity. These developments were plagued by natural barriers (mountains, swamps) and human error in judgment, including decisions to change rail gauges and to attempt false economies in construction that necessitated substantial rebuilding (James 1923). At the end of the nineteenth century, Colombia only had 565 kilometers (350 miles) of functioning track—compared to 20,000 (12,400 miles) in Argentina (Henderson 2001, 10). At the end of the nineteenth century, "virtually all inland population centers were reached (reachable) only by horse- or muleback, or on foot" (10). The fragmented rail system resulted in many broken journeys between the major interior and coastal cities, where freight and passengers were forced to change their mode of travel from water to rail or from rail to road. By the end of 1930, after a $280,000 investment in transportation, Colombia still only had 1,211 kilometers (750 miles) of rail and 6,000 kilometers (3,700 miles) of highways (239).

Given the lack of roads and rails, it is not surprising that the economy has historically been dependent on river transportation (Posada-Carbó 1996), although even modern river transport is plagued by low water levels during the dry season. The only mode of transport that can reliably offer connections between all parts of Colombia is air transport (Stokes 1967; Galbraith 1966; Posada-Carbó 1996). Even in 2007, although a flight from Bogotá to Medellín takes only half an hour, the drive takes almost seven hours. Similarly, a flight from Bogotá to Barranquilla lasts only one hour, but the drive requires fourteen.

The rugged geography and history of sporadic settlement have also impeded state building. According to Bushnell, "No part of Spanish America had so many obstacles to unity, so many obstacles to transportation and communication per square kilometer—as New Granada, with a population scattered in isolated clusters in various Andean ranges, not to mention other settlements along the coast. Geographic separation thus came to reinforce all the basic socioeconomic and cultural differences among major regions, and the result was an intense sectionalism that vastly complicated the first efforts at political organization" (1993, 36). This geographically reinforced regionalism "has hampered the ability of any government in Bogotá to create the notion of a nation" (Watson 2000, 530). The topography and historical settlement pattern created conditions ripe for the emergence of internal conflict.

Historically, the Colombian state has been weak and continues to be plagued by rebellion. Classic theories of state building provide insight into how the Colombian state has become one plagued by "permanent and endemic [internal] warfare" (Sanchez and Bakewell 1985, 789). According to Charles Tilly's classic theory of state building, to create a strong, coherent state, it is necessary to eliminate internal rivals (Tilly 1985, 182). In the cases upon which Tilly based his study, "European governments reduced their reliance on indirect rule by means of two expensive but effective strategies; (a) extending their officialdom to the local community and (b) encouraging the creation of police forces that were subordinate to the government rather than to individual patrons, distinct from war-making forces, and therefore less useful as the tools of dissident magnates. In between, however, the builders of national power all played a mixed strategy: eliminating, subjugating, dividing, conquering, cajoling, buying as the occasions presented themselves" (175). This process of subordination of internal rivals has not occurred uniformly in Colombia.

Tilly's work is the basis for the bellicist, or predatory, model of state building, in which external wars serve as the impetus to increase the power of the national state via the building and support of a national military. Numerous scholars have applied Tilly's general theory to Latin America. Some have argued that Latin American geography limited the number of major wars between nations. For example, López Alves argues that "for the most part state building in Latin America also took place in the absence of interstate conflict. . . . Geography—mountain chains, jungles, deserts, poor roads, treacherous rivers—and Indian resistance also impeded the types of wars that provoked the well-studied bloodbaths in the Old World" (2001, 168). In other words, geography discouraged the type of interstate conflict that builds nations while it also increased the chances of internal conflict.

Understanding political development from this perspective leads to a prediction of a weak state and internal conflict for Colombia. In fact, Colombia has suffered many internal conflicts and few external wars. This persistent instability and weakness of the state is due to a failure, since independence, to create an effective national movement. Contemporary Colombian regionalism has its roots in the colonial period, independence, and a lack of external wars. Inside Colombia, there were regional desires for autonomy not only from Spain but from the other Colombian regions as well. This urge for regional self-government contributed to the movement for independence. During the opening years of the wars for independence (1810–1815), the political expression of Colombian regionalist sentiment erupted into violence. This early period has been called the foolish state, or *patria boba,* because of the failure to centralize power and create a coherent nation. Moreover, "the regions fought amongst themselves instead and failed to provide a united front against Spain. . . . serious difficulties in centralizing power, remained a defining feature of state making until the twentieth century" (López Alves 2000, 96).

At independence, central authority had all but disappeared with the elimination of Spanish authority, leaving only local governments capable of exerting control (Park 1985). Centeno discusses the historical weakness of Latin American states as being partially a reflection of their independence: "The stunted development of Latin American states and the frailty of their respective nations reflect the key, but too often underemphasized, aspect of the development of the continent's nation-states. The wars of independence produced fragments of empire, but not new states. There was little economic or political logic to the frontiers as institutionalized in the 1820s—they merely were the administrative borders of the empire. The new countries were essentially mini-empires with all of the weaknesses of such political entities" (2002, 25).

At independence, within the province of Bogotá (modern-day Colombia), the territory was divided into departments by "The Colombian Territorial Division Law" of June 25, 1824 (Ireland 1938). There were nine original departments (then called sovereign states) in what is today the north of Colombia and Panama (Antioquia, Bolívar, Cauca, Cundinamarca, Magdalena, Panama, Santander, and Tolima; see Figure 2.4).

When Simón Bolívar died, in 1830, the common bond of liberation among Bogotá, Caracas, and Quito was sundered and the short-lived grouping of states fragmented into its original constituent parts—Venezuela, New Granada, and Ecuador (del Río 1965). Bolívar was succeeded in New Granada by General Francisco de Paula Santander, who had been the vice president of the province (Jones 1899). During the following two decades, New Granada was simply an abstract entity for purposes of identification; the people felt allegiance to the provinces or regions where they conducted their business and professional affairs (Bushnell 1993). There were numerous internal conflicts between partisan factions. These conflicts were both electoral and military, and concerned control over local, state, and federal governments.

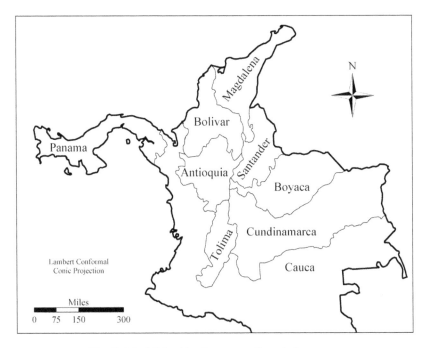

FIGURE 2.4   *Nine Original Colombian Department Boundaries*

The ability of politicians to maintain authority rested in part on their ability to harness a sense of regional allegiance. Since these conflicts often required the conscription of citizens into military units, resistance to the nation-state was often seen as a means of avoiding military conscription. Additionally, resistance to a central government and its laws was seen by some as a means to ensure continued protection for the smuggling of contraband and other illegal activities (Posada-Carbó 1996). As an example, Cartagena and Bogotá often had separate interests: the port city concentrated on maritime activities, whereas the capital focused on the development of resources in the interior. There was no effective central government that could unite these disparate regions and separate interests under a single state bureaucracy (Kline 1999).

This trend toward regional expression and national disintegration continued well beyond the wars of independence. Over the next several decades, regional politicians with local military forces attempted several times to sever all ties with the central government. Potential unifying forces within the nation, such as the Catholic Church, were denigrated, and its power waned. From the beginning of Colombian independence, there was a rejection of centralized power. According to Rochlin, "Dominant political and economic

elites in Colombia could not relate to centralized power arrangements. . . .
Part of this may be due to the strong geographic obstacles in Colombia that
isolated various regions of the country" (2003, 89).

Although these feelings of national disunity did not ultimately result in
any regions obtaining absolute political autonomy (with the exception of
Panama, which gained its independence in 1903 with the help of the United
States), there were several informal groupings of departments that formed
around geographic unity, economic interests, and political identification.
Defined in this way, the four primary regions of Colombia were Cauca; the
north coast (Panama, Bolívar, and Magdalena); the Cordillera Central, occu-
pied by Antioquia and Tolima; and the eastern mountain region of Santander, Boyacá, and Cundinamarca (Park 1985). In this period, around 1830–1831,
there were early threats of secession of Casanare to Venezuela, and Cauca to
Ecuador, and ideas of Panamanian independence (Safford and Palacios 2002,
132). In response to the regionalism, national resources and power were decentralized in 1850 with the aim of undermining "the chief cause of partisan
strife—the passion to get control of the offices and patronage of the national
government" (204). Similarly, the next three Colombian constitutions (1853,
1858, and 1863) were also decentralized. Instead of an emphasis on national
armies, there were department-level armies, in addition to numerous private
armies (Rochlin 2003, 90). The result was a drop in national services, such as
the military, and a loss of tax receipts. For example, in the 1850s the central
government had fewer than 375 soldiers under its control (Osterling 1989,
66). Instead of reducing regional conflict, this early federalism appeared to
intensify and spread it (Safford and Palacios 2002, 221), as seen in the civil
war of 1859–1863. This early period of nation building, 1858–1885, has been
described as an unstable federalism in which "rival city-states controlled their
hinterlands and clashed with one another" (López Alves 2000, 97). The state
was weak, the military small, and local elites relied upon the strength of local
caudillos in case of conflict (98).

In the late nineteenth century, efforts at recentralizing power were made
under President Nuñez (1884–1889) and during the time known as the *regen-
eration* of 1878–1900. After 1886, *estados* became *departamentos*. The change
in name reflected a shift from federalism to hopes for a more centralized nation. The change was more than symbolic, since now governors and political
chiefs were both appointed by the president (López Alves 2000, 102; Safford
and Palacios 2002, 239). Despite these efforts, military power was not completely centralized: "In Colombia, even under the centralizing policies of the
regeneración in the 1880s and 1890s, at least two 'armies' claimed to embody
the legitimate government" (López Alves 2001, 163). This persistent regional-

ism made the nation vulnerable to internal conflicts as conflicts among local areas escalated nationally (López Alves 2000, 99). Although efforts to centralize power did somewhat strengthen the state—the number of governmental employees increased from 4,500 in the late nineteenth century to 42,700 in 1916—there was an insufficient number of functionaries to efficiently administer the country. Moreover, there was not a sufficient state presence in many municipalities (Safford and Palacios 2002, 243).

In general, the state was weak and parties were strong (see Leal Buitrago 1984; Deas 1973). The organization of the two-party political system (Conservatives and Liberals) dates from 1848–1849 (Martz 1992), and this development divided the population less on regional preferences and more on national social issues. Nonetheless, the country retains significant regional division: "Unlike many other Latin American nations, Colombia never overcame the nineteenth-century political divisions between Conservatives (clericals) and Liberals (anticlericals); never resolved the nineteenth-century issues of centralism versus federalism; never established a national government that truly forged and administered a nation; never replaced personalism, factionalism, and the quest for partisan hegemony with a modern political agenda" (Guevara 1985, 266). Although this regional identification has in many cases persisted to the present day, political developments on the federal level are slowly working to integrate the nation into its present form.

Colombian civil strife is both a reflection of a weak state and a persistent challenge to the strengthening of the nation. Although it is recognized as one of the longest-surviving democracies of the Western Hemisphere, with the exception of the Rojas Pinilla government (1953–1957) and the following military junta, it has also suffered from frequent internal conflict and violent regionalism. According to López Alves (2000, 119), there were eleven significant uprisings in the nineteenth century (1826, two in 1828, 1830, 1831, 1839–1842, 1851, 1859–1862, 1876–1877, 1885, 1895) and three coups (1854, 1867, 1900). Major civil wars occurred in 1839, 1854, 1876, 1884, and 1899, in addition to the War of Cauca (1859), and the secession of Panama (1903), which followed the War of a Thousand Days (Centeno 1997).

This early period of violence suggests a historical inability of the central government to create or maintain a monopoly of legitimate force. Unlike other Latin American countries, such as Mexico during the Porfiriato, Colombia never had a unifying dictatorship (Waldmann 1997, 415n2). Although many of the conflicts occurred in remote countryside regions, where the central government had little impact, some conflicts were devastating nonetheless. For example, the War of a Thousand Days (1899–1902) resulted in the deaths of up to 2 percent of the population; most of the 80,000 victims were noncombatants (Bushnell 1992, 14). Additionally during this conflict, dissident Liberals invaded Panama in order to take advantage of the conflict. The Colombian government, too weak to directly respond, requested assistance from the United States. Although the U.S. Marines ended the rebellion, another group declared Panama independent shortly after. This time, instead of aiding the Colombian national government, the United States recognized Panama as an independent nation (Osterling 1989, 74–75). Exhaustion from this conflict resulted in a relative peace that lasted until the long-standing battle between the Liberals and Conservatives over control of the presidency (Maullin 1973) erupted into *la violencia,* which claimed as many as 200,000 lives from the 1940s to the 1960s (Henderson 1985). This splintered, regional, and largely unorganized civil war has been described as "an inextricable mixture of political confrontations and social conflicts, of repression led by Conservatives and fratricidal peasant warfare, of collective strategies and individual actions, of self-defense and large-scale social disorganization, of deliberate acts, and of great fear" (Pécaut 1992, 222). This outbreak was the result of an incremental chain of retaliation between the Liberal and Conservative populations. In addition to the hundreds of thousands killed, *la violencia* resulted in massive destruction, especially in areas of relatively recent settlement or land conflict. For example, more than 360,000 people fled the department of Tolima, where over 34,000 homes were burned and at least 40,000 properties were abandoned (Sánchez 1992, 105).

In response to the violence of this period, the central government attempted to increase the size of the national military. Before the start of the conflict in 1949, the national military had only about 15,000 soldiers. During the presidency of Rojas Pinilla (1953–1957), it increased to 42,000, still a relatively weak force (Ortiz Sarmiento 1990–1991, 253–254). Despite a strengthened national identity in Colombia, regional calls for autonomy have persisted: for example, during the 1970s the department of Antioquia demanded greater departmental power (Park 1985). Clearly, the combination of a strong regionalism, a weak federal state, and a weak military has had a sustained impact on the country's historical evolution (Hartlyn 1989); namely, it has aggravated the lack of political order throughout the country, "confirmed the atomization of local authority, which was in the hands of an autonomous political personnel . . . [and] left the field open for local and private power relationships to manage local tensions" (Pécaut 1992, 223). In the words of López Alves, "Colombia comes close to a Tillean revolutionary situation, where the state cannot efficiently deal with contenders or effectively undermine the commitment of a sizeable part of the population to the contender's claims" (2001, 163).

Two scholars argue for adapting Tilly's theories to Latin America. First, according to Centeno, in addition to outlining the number and intensity of wars, one should identify a driver for state building: "The machine of the state needs a 'driver' able to use the stimulus provided by war to expand its reach and power. Without such a driver, whether it be state personnel, a dominant class, or even a charismatic individual, the political and military shell of the state has no direction. Without this direction, wars do not present opportunities for growth, but mere challenges to survival" (2002, 166). Either the external conflicts and rivalries were not serious enough to force the Colombian elite to unite, or the elites were too factionalized to take advantage of such opportunities. Second, Thies argues that interstate rivalry should also be considered: "Interstate rivals, whether operationalized as 'enduring' or 'strategic' rivals, have a positive effect on the state's extractive capacity. Intrastate rivals, on the other hand, have the expected negative effect on state building" (2005, 451). Internal rivals reduce state capacity "whether through the damage they cause to the economy's productive capacity, the bargaining they conduct with the state to reduce their share of the tax burden, or their temporary occupation of territory that places productive wealth beyond the state's grasp" (463).

Colombian history is marked more by interstate rivalries than outright wars. Many of these rivalries were border disputes. The current boundaries of Colombia were formally defined in 1863, when New Granada became the Estados Unidos de Colombia, or the United States of Colombia. However, the national and internal boundaries have changed numerous times. Colombia has at one time or another been at odds with each of its neighbors regarding their common boundaries. Although the Treaty of San Ildefonso (October 1, 1777) was meant to provide for the boundary line between Spanish and Portuguese possessions, the remote location of the boundary line has been a source of contention between successive governments of Colombia and Brazil. The Colombian government has protested what it believes to be encroachments by Brazil on many occasions (Ireland 1938). The boundary between Peru and Colombia along the Putumayo River (which provides river access to the Amazon) has historically been a source of dispute. Relations between Colombia and Peru are described as a strategic rivalry, i.e., a competition with overtones of actual or latent threats (Thies 2005; Thompson 2001). In the early twentieth century, boundary disputes in this region became intertwined with commercial interests (particularly in the rubber trade), deplorable working conditions, and crimes committed against the native population (Markham 1913). The region of Leticia was later the source of a dispute that was resolved only by military action in 1932–1933 (Rausch 1999). Other boundary disputes include those with Venezuela over the Guajira, Guainía, and Arauca-Yavita regions (Safford and Palacios 2002, 266–296), and those with Ecuador over the naturally defined (and rugged) border formed by the convergence of the three Andean cordilleras (James 1923). This strategic rivalry has continued since 1831 (Thompson 2001; Thies 2005).

Finally, Colombia's borders were changed dramatically with the creation of the "sovereign federal state" of Panama in 1903. The secession of this region was due to the growing importance of the Isthmus of Panama. Colombia simply could not retain possession of Panama in the face of the growing interest of world powers such as Great Britain, France, and the United States (Safford and Palacios 2002, 188–238). However, none of these conflicts—the Leticia war with Peru or the strategic rivalries with Ecuador, Peru, and Venezuela—served as a stimulus to state building.

STRATEGIC ASPECTS OF COLOMBIAN GEOGRAPHY

Besides negatively affecting early political development and national cohesion, the geography continues to pose a challenge for the successful resolution of contemporary guerrilla conflict. The Colombian landscape provides the basic conditions for successful irregular warfare as outlined by Clausewitz.

1. The war must be carried out in the interior of the country.
2. It must not be decided by a single stroke.
3. The theater of operations must be fairly large.
4. The national character must be suited to that type of war.
5. The country must be rough and inaccessible, because of mountains or forests, marshes, or local methods of cultivation. (Clausewitz 1976, 480)

There are geographic aspects of the country that are strategically important in a conflict: "The physical terrain of many parts of Colombia . . . offered numerous opportunities for guerrilla *focos*. In fact, politically inspired guerrilla bands and 'independent republics' of peasantry operated for decades outside the control of the national government before the Cuban revolution. Jungles, mountains, and isolated *llanos* separated from urban centers by difficult terrain and poor transportation systems were ideal centers of guerrilla operations" (Guevara 1985, 273).

The rugged Colombian landscape is hard to control and may be relatively susceptible to insurgency. According to the conventional understanding of guerrilla warfare and geography:

Areas with lots of cover, i.e. jungle canopy or rainforests and rugged terrain, are good for hiding guerillas, for providing bases, hideouts, and arms caches that are difficult to find on the ground and difficult to see from the air. Such terrain . . . renders airpower (including the use of attack helicopters) virtually useless. Altogether, such terrain conditions tend to raise the ratios of counterinsurgency forces to insurgents required for victory for the former, and vice versa, also making more like a protracted, indeterminable, stalemated conflict that, more often than not, will be to the political detriment of an incumbent regime on the defensive. (Harkavy and Neuman 2001, 79)

Harkavy and Neuman recognize that real-world scenarios often involve combinations of these factors. Colombian geography provides such "cover" for hiding guerrillas. Mountains, for example: "Larger forces cannot bring their superior numbers to bear against well chosen positions in narrow passes. Mountains have been a traditional haven for lightly armed forces opposing a heavily armed foe" (O'Sullivan and Miller 1983, 65). Traditionally, the mountainous areas of Colombia have housed rebels.

A prime requirement of guerrilla activity is the "availability of cover to fade into" (O'Sullivan 1983, 147). This cover can be dense terrain or areas of high population density. The main urban centers in Colombia are concentrated in the Andean cordilleras and along the Caribbean coast (see Figure 2.4). Parts of the mountainous interior are also areas with the highest population density, such as the departments of Cundinamarca, Caldas, and Bogotá. More than a third of the nation's people live in the departments of Cundinamarca, Antioquia, and Valle del Cauca, forming a triangle of the major cities of Bogotá, Medellín, and Cali (Dambaugh 1959). In 1993, these three departments accounted for 28 percent of the population, 31 percent of the attributed human rights violations, 21 percent of the homicides, and 45 percent of the unattributed human rights violations. O'Sullivan refines the conventional understanding to include urban landscapes: "The shift of insurrectionary movements into the cities of the world in the last decade takes advantage of the intensity of the urban fabric," which provide sources of support, ample targets, and sufficient cover (O'Sullivan 1983, 147).

Expectations derived from major theories of political development, geography, and economic development suggest that Colombia is ripe for conflict. Its geography and historical heritage have influenced both the contemporary conflict and the available responses to it. By the 1990s, the main focus of this book, the national government had not succeeded in unifying the country and eliminating competing claims to authority or force. Max Manwaring states, "Virtually anyone with any kind of resolve can take advantage of the instability engendered by the ongoing Colombian crisis. The tendency is that the best armed organization on the scene will eventually control that instability for its own narrow purposes" (2002, 3). The next chapter provides a historical discussion of the Colombian economy and its relative position in Latin America.

THREE

COLOMBIAN ECONOMIC HISTORY

Regional Context and Colombian Policies

This chapter examines Colombia's development relative to those of the six larger economies of Latin America in order to better understand the relationships among illegal drugs, violence, and the economy. This brief overview will help clarify how the Colombian economy differs from the others and perhaps shed light on the causes and economic consequences of violence and the illegal drug trade. While liberalization began under President Gaviria, the Colombian economy did not take off in the same way that the Chilean economy did when it liberalized and embraced the policies of the Washington consensus, i.e., free market policies coupled with directives designed to reduce governmental intervention. A possible explanation is that economic uncertainty caused by violence and illegal drugs hampered growth potential in Colombia. While data limitations restrict the models presented in this text to the 1990s, this comparative analysis of Colombia's relative position extends from the 1970s through early 2000. This chapter highlights conditions or policies unique to Colombia that affected its performance relative to its peer economies in the region.

Within Latin America, the seven largest economies are those of Brazil, Mexico, Argentina, Venezuela, Colombia, Chile, and Peru. These seven differ in size and development. Measured by GDP in constant billions of U.S. dollars (see Figure 3.1), in 1960 there were two distinct groups of countries: the larger economies of Brazil, Mexico, and Argentina, and the smaller economies of Venezuela, Colombia, Chile, and Peru. In the early 1970s, Brazil and Mexico moved to outperform and separate themselves from the rest of the countries. The Venezuelan economy is unique due to its heavy reliance on the petroleum industry and lack of economic diversification. Venezuela would have a much smaller economy if oil revenues were removed. Among the smaller economies, Colombia's has been the largest since the early 1980s.

The gap between the Colombian and the other larger economies has grown dramatically over time as the Argentine, Brazilian, and Chilean economies

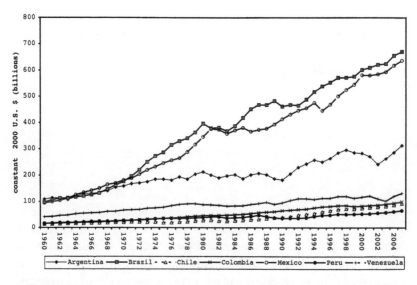

FIGURE 3.1   *GDP*

have prospered. Purchasing power parity GDP provides a clearer picture of Colombia's relative position. By this measure, Colombia consistently ranks as the fourth-largest economy in Latin America, behind Brazil, Mexico, and Argentina (see Figure 3.2).

Except in 1999, Colombia escaped the economic contractions common to many other developing economies in the region. Colombian GDP growth rates varied, but remained within a 1 percent to 3 percent range (see Figure 3.3). When compared to average growth in Latin America and the Caribbean, Colombian growth exhibits less volatility. It grew faster than the average during good times and declined by less than the average during bad times. While other Latin American countries experienced periods of negative growth throughout the 1990s, Colombia suffered negative growth only in 1999. The question remains: how has Colombia maintained stable and positive growth in the face of rising violence in the country? A secondary question is whether the violence has had a dampening effect on Colombian economic growth. In Chapter Seven, we examine the effects of violence and coca cultivation on the Colombian economy. Measured in constant U.S. dollars, however, Colombia had the lowest per capita GDP among the largest Latin American economies in 1960 and remained the lowest in 2004. Interestingly, real GDP per capita generally increased, although only slightly, during the National Front period of governance (see Figure 3.4). By the 1980s, GDP per capita throughout Latin

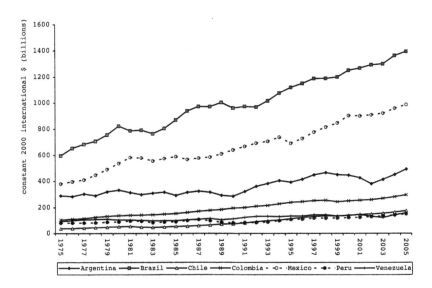

FIGURE 3.2   *GDP, PPP*

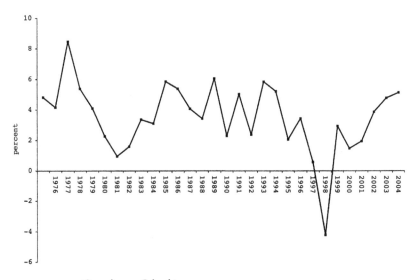

FIGURE 3.3   *Growth rate, Colombia*

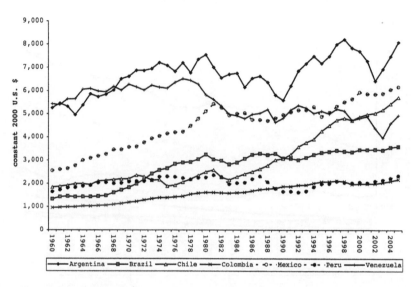

FIGURE 3.4   *GDP per capita*

America was stagnating as a result of the debt crisis; Colombia was the only exception to this trend.

To examine Colombia's relative position it is important to examine per capita GDP as measured in purchasing power parity. Purchasing power parity allows for a per capita comparison of relative living standards. Constant dollar per capita values have potential measurement errors, since values are first converted to dollars using official exchange rates, which may not accurately reflect the currency's purchasing power. Purchasing power parity (PPP) comparisons are relative, so if per capita PPP GDP in one country is twice that of another, then a person in the first country is twice as well off as a person in the second. In per capita PPP GDP, Colombia lags behind Argentina, Brazil, Chile, and Mexico (see Figure 3.5). Other than Chile and Mexico, Colombia is the only country whose relative per capita PPP GDP has improved. The ability of Colombia to grow consistently even in the face of violence leads one to wonder what might have happened if the country had suffered less conflict.

Despite this slow economic progress, other factors indicate the possibility of strong future growth. For example, Colombia's age-dependency ratio has dropped dramatically (see Table 3.1). The age-dependency ratio measures the ratio of dependents to the working-age population. In 1965, Colombia had one of the highest age-dependency ratios—approximately 100 percent. By 2005, it had dropped to 56 percent. As the number of dependents to income

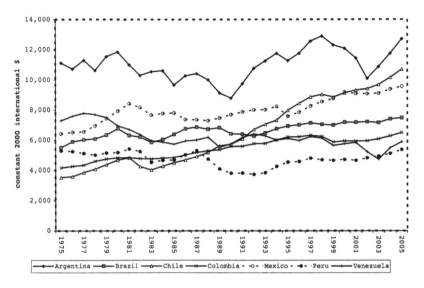

FIGURE 3.5   *GDP per capita (PPP)*

earners falls, the standard of living increases, since income is not spread as thinly. Additionally, as families have fewer children, the quality of care per child improves and a country's human capital investment and return increases. As the number of dependents to the working-age population falls, the future quality of life tends to improve, since there is an increase in human capital investment.

Another positive indicator is the decline in the rural population and the shift out of the agricultural sector into manufacturing and service-related sectors. Colombia's rural population has fallen from 47 percent to 27 percent, while there has been a simultaneous increase in rural population density (Table 3.2). Colombia has the highest rural population density among the seven Latin American countries examined, and it continues to increase. The creation of rural development centers and small cities increases the potential for agricultural development over that possible with a dispersed rural population. It is easier for the state to provide services to a dense rural population, which does not suffer from many of the problems common to large urban centers. The urban population has grown also, although Colombia continues to have the lowest percentage of urban residents among large Latin American countries. This indicates that the population is not concentrated in one or two large cities. In fact, there are three cities with populations larger than 500,000, and six cities with populations of between 250,000 and 500,000. Perhaps reflecting the strong historical trends of regionalism discussed in

3.1 POPULATION DISTRIBUTION IN SEVEN LARGE LATIN AMERICAN COUNTRIES

Country	Age-dependency ratio			Rural population (% of total)			Urban population (% of total)		
	1965	1985	2005	1965	1985	2005	1965	1985	2005
Argentina	57.3	65.3	57.8	23.6	15.0	9.9	76.4	85.0	90.1
Brazil	89.3	69.8	51.5	49.7	28.7	15.8	50.3	71.3	84.2
Chile	83.3	57.9	49.2	28.3	17.4	12.4	71.7	82.6	87.6
Colombia	99.7	71.9	56.5	47.2	34.8	27.3	52.8	65.2	72.7
Mexico	102.1	87.2	57.1	45.1	30.4	24.0	54.9	69.6	76.0
Peru	91.0	78.0	60.0	48.1	33.1	27.4	51.9	66.9	72.6
Venezuela	96.3	73.8	56.9	33.3	18.1	6.6	66.7	81.9	93.4

Note: Age-dependency ratio is the ratio of dependents to the working-age population.
Source: World Development Indicators (World Bank)

3.2 RURAL POPULATION DENSITY IN SEVEN LARGE LATIN AMERICAN COUNTRIES

Country	1965	1985	2003
Argentina	25.7	16.8	14.0
Brazil	149.7	82.6	52.3
Chile	65.8	61.1	105.3
Colombia	259.7	290.7	545.0
Mexico	88.1	98.5	99.9
Peru	219.7	191.3	204.1
Venezuela	104.0	108.3	74.3

Note: Rural population density is the rural population per square kilometer of arable land.
Source: World Development Indicators (World Bank)

Chapter Two, Colombia is the only Latin American country to have more than two large urban centers that are geographically dispersed. This minimizes the problems of megacities, such as São Paulo and Mexico City, and the concentration of financial resources and governmental services in metropoles such as Buenos Aires and Santiago.

A sectoral analysis reveals that Colombia is still one of the smaller economies in Latin America as measured by value added in agriculture, manufacturing, and industry (Table 3.3). However, since 2000 there has been an increasing trend in each sector, indicating that Colombia is moving toward closing the gap.

Gross capital formation saw a significant upward trend in 2001, after falling between 1995 and 2000. While gross capital formation in Colombia remains one of the lowest in Latin America, it more than doubled from 1985 to 2005.

Inflation has been the bane of most Latin American economies. The Colombian economy outperformed the average Latin American economy on measures of inflation throughout the twentieth century (see Table 3.4). Colombian inflation is clearly less volatile compared to the leading economies of the region.

Throughout the last forty years, Colombia maintained a more or less stable inflation rate, while the other countries experienced episodes of hyperinflation. Volatile inflation rates make long-term investments difficult and hinder economic growth. Historically, countries faced with civil strife tend to experience high rates of inflation. Yet Colombia has not.

Unemployment and labor-force participation are also indicators of the health of an economy. Colombia has the highest labor-force participation rate (Table 3.5) in Latin America in all categories. The high participation rate could be a result of young people moving into the labor force rather than pursuing further educational opportunities. Another reason: since 1980, many women have entered the workforce. By 2005, Colombian women were more likely to work outside the home than their counterparts in the rest of the countries. Moreover, even the male labor-force participation rate was higher in Colombia than in the rest of the countries studied. If, however, there are not jobs to absorb the growing labor pool, higher unemployment will occur. Given the high labor participation rate, it is not surprising that Colombia has the third-highest unemployment rate in Latin America (see Table 3.6).

Additionally, Colombia has lagged behind in attracting foreign direct investment (FDI). An examination of FDI as a percentage of GDP shows that Colombia attracts less investment than the other industrializing economies of Latin America (Table 3.7). The current changes in the business climate in

3.3 VALUE ADDED IN THREE SECTORS OF THE ECONOMY AND GROSS CAPITAL FORMATION IN SEVEN LARGE LATIN AMERICAN COUNTRIES

Country	Agriculture			Industry			Manufacturing			Gross capital formation		
	1965	1985	2005	1965	1985	2005	1965	1985	2005	1965	1985	2005
Argentina	7,405	9,319	15,357	42,155	53,841	85,842	30,710	37,499	53,959	24,751	27,126	56,206
Brazil	11,995	23,624	42,234	25,794	102,037	145,862	n/a	n/a	n/a	24,474	80,906	128,684
Chile	1,259	2,119	5,583	8,043	11,735	31,474	4,745	6,178	15,828	3,292	3,730	25,503
Colombia	4,797	9,910	11,819	5,995	15,465	29,288	4,291	10,824	14,747	3,451	9,280	21,814
Mexico	10,762	18,965	23,947	30,161	88,050	150,623	21,773	59,868	106,449	36,650	71,963	134,958
Peru	1,728	2,401	4,787	5,663	9,485	18,721	3,655	5,937	9,677	6,851	5,023	12,704
Venezuela	1,690	3,526	5,836	—	38,486	56,748	5,960	13,165	23,215	9,876	13,090	32,067

Note: Figures are in constant 2000 U.S. dollars.
Source: World Development Indicators (World Bank)

3.4 INFLATION IN CONSUMER PRICES IN SEVEN LARGE
LATIN AMERICAN COUNTRIES (ANNUAL % CHANGE)

Country	1965	1975	1985	1995	2005
Argentina	28.6	182.9	672.2	3.4	9.6
Brazil	n/a	n/a	226.0	66.0	6.9
Chile	28.8	374.7	29.5	8.2	3.1
Colombia	3.5	22.9	24.0	21.0	5.1
Mexico	3.6	15.2	57.8	35.0	4.0
Peru	16.4	23.6	163.4	11.1	1.6
Venezuela	1.7	10.2	11.4	59.9	16.0

Source: World Development Indicators (World Bank)

3.5 LABOR-FORCE PARTICIPATION RATE IN SEVEN
LARGE LATIN AMERICAN COUNTRIES

	Female			Male			Total		
Country	1980	1990	2005	1980	1990	2005	1980	1990	2005
Argentina	30.9	43.5	61.1	83.1	84.7	82.4	56.7	63.8	71.7
Brazil	40.5	47.6	61.0	88.7	88.8	83.6	64.5	68.0	72.1
Chile	31.0	35.2	40.9	76.6	80.9	76.0	53.5	57.9	58.4
Colombia	26.4	48.5	65.9	82.6	85.0	85.2	54.1	66.5	75.4
Mexico	31.1	36.2	42.6	84.2	85.5	83.0	57.2	60.2	62.1
Peru	30.3	48.6	61.2	82.7	82.0	83.6	56.6	65.4	72.4
Venezuela	32.3	39.8	61.9	81.9	82.4	85.7	57.4	61.3	73.8

Note: Figures represent the percentage of each cohort population in the age range 15–64.
Source: World Development Indicators (World Bank)

Colombia, however, have resulted in significant increases in FDI. In 2005, Colombia had the highest FDI (net inflows as a percentage of GDP) among its peers. In absolute terms, Colombia historically has had the lowest net inflows in FDI; yet by 2005 it had the third-highest inflow, behind only Mexico and Brazil. Increases in FDI are a signal that foreign markets have confidence in Colombia's future.

Colombia's economy has been improving since the early 2000s; however, it is also important to gauge the standard of living in Colombia compared

3.6 UNEMPLOYMENT IN SEVEN LARGE
LATIN AMERICAN COUNTRIES
(% OF TOTAL LABOR FORCE)

Country	1980	1992	2003
Argentina	2.3	6.7	15.6
Brazil	—	6.4	9.7
Chile	10.4	4.4	7.4
Colombia	3.8	9.4	14.1
Mexico	—	3.1	2.5
Peru	—	9.4	10.3
Venezuela	5.9	7.7	16.8

Source: World Development Indicators (World Bank)

3.7 FOREIGN DIRECT INVESTMENT IN SEVEN LARGE
LATIN AMERICAN COUNTRIES

Country	Net inflow (% of GDP)			Net inflow (BOP)		
	1980	1990	2005	1980	1990	2005
Argentina	0.88	1.30	2.58	678	1,836	4,730
Brazil	0.81	0.21	1.91	1,911	989	15,193
Chile	0.77	2.10	5.78	213	661	6,667
Colombia	0.47	1.24	8.48	157	500	10,375
Mexico	1.08	0.97	2.44	2,090	2,549	18,772
Peru	0.13	0.16	3.17	27	41	2,519
Venezuela	0.08	0.96	2.11	55	451	2,957

Note: "BOP" = balance of payments; net inflow (BOP) measured in millions of current U.S. dollars.
Source: World Development Indicators (World Bank)

to those in the rest of Latin America. Colombia's average life expectancy has increased along with those throughout Latin America, but remained the third lowest from 1960 until 2005 (Table 3.8). Many scholars blame ongoing security concerns and civil strife for the relative lag (Caballero Argaez 2003, 8). However, Colombia fares well in other measures. Sanitation facilities are a proxy for development, since most fatal diseases in developing countries are a result of contaminated water supplies. Colombia ranks at the top for improved sanitation facilities between 1990 and 2004. Colombia ranks at the top for the percentage of urban population with access to sanitation, third for rural, and third overall (Table 3.9). These rankings are consistent with the expectation that Colombia has the potential to break away and experience accelerated growth and increases in standard of living.

Violence and illegal drugs have had an impact on the Colombia economy

3.8 LIFE EXPECTANCY AT BIRTH IN SEVEN
LARGE LATIN AMERICAN COUNTRIES
(YEARS)

Country	1960	1985	2005
Argentina	65.2	70.7	74.8
Brazil	54.8	64.4	71.2
Chile	57.3	71.9	78.2
Colombia	56.8	67.5	72.8
Mexico	57.3	69.0	75.4
Peru	48.0	63.2	70.7
Venezuela	59.8	69.8	74.2

Source: World Development Indicators (World Bank)

3.9 IMPROVED SANITATION FACILITIES IN
SEVEN LARGE LATIN AMERICAN COUNTRIES
(% OF POPULATION WITH ACCESS)

Country	Total		Rural		Urban	
	1990	2004	1990	2004	1990	2004
Argentina	81	91	45	83	86	92
Brazil	71	75	37	37	82	83
Chile	84	91	52	62	91	95
Colombia	82	86	52	54	95	96
Mexico	58	79	13	41	75	91
Peru	52	63	15	32	69	74
Venezuela	n/a	68	n/a	48	n/a	71

Source: World Development Indicators (World Bank)

3.10 HEALTH EXPENDITURES IN SEVEN LARGE
LATIN AMERICAN COUNTRIES (% OF GDP)

Country	Private		Public		Total	
	2000	2004	2000	2004	2000	2004
Argentina	3.97	5.25	4.93	4.35	8.90	9.60
Brazil	4.48	4.04	3.12	4.76	7.60	8.80
Chile	3.28	3.23	3.02	2.87	6.30	6.10
Colombia	1.47	1.09	6.23	6.71	7.70	7.80
Mexico	2.99	3.48	2.61	3.02	5.60	6.50
Peru	2.21	2.18	2.49	1.92	4.70	4.10
Venezuela	2.83	2.73	3.37	1.97	6.20	4.70

Source: World Development Indicators (World Bank)

and so should have an effect on the Colombian standard of living. In health expenditures as a percentage of GDP, Colombia ranks third overall, first in public, and last in private (Table 3.10). For a country with such internal strife, health expenditures are high. This could be a result of caring for victims of violence and crime. High health expenditures in developing countries frequently indicate a crisis rather than a healthy population and high quality care (as one would expect in a more developed country).

Statistics on the status of Colombian children, however, indicate problems. Colombia has the second-highest prevalence of undernourishment (Figure 3.6). Despite significant improvement since 1971, approximately 15 percent of Colombian children are still malnourished. Similarly, educational persistence to the fifth grade in Colombia is the lowest for females and males (Table 3.11). While 80 percent of the cohort did persist to the fifth grade, this rate is substantially lower than in other Latin American countries. Given that such a large percentage of children do not stay in school through the fifth grade, it is not surprising that Colombia's labor-force participation rate is so high compared to other countries in the region.

Although in general the percentage of governmental spending on education has been decreasing for the last decade throughout the region, the Colombian decline has been steeper. Moreover, Colombia's percentage of total governmental expenditures on education in 2004 was the lowest in Latin America (Figure 3.7). Investment in education is important for future economic growth, since human capital is a key source of growth. High health-care expenditures coupled with increased military spending have come at the cost of lower investment in education. Although some may argue that Colombia's military spending is low for a country facing multiple insurgencies and paramilitary violence, years of conflict may have taken a toll on investment in education.

The Colombian economy has experienced long-term positive growth punctuated by periods of crisis.[1] Scholars have noted that Colombia avoided many of the typical development mistakes of the era, such as generalized import-substitution policies at the expense of their export sector, high debt burdens, and arbitrary spending. For example, Bruce Bagley notes that the "overall quality of economic decision making in Colombia compares well with virtually any other Latin American country. The growth performance during the late 1960s and most of the 1970s was not an accident, but rather the result of technically sound, macroeconomic decisions made by successive National Front and post-Front governments in the context of a regime that freed them from the imperative of responding directly to lower-class demands for a more equitable share of the benefits of economic growth" (Bagley 1984, 136). This failure to address the needs of the lower class, however, had implications for the civil strife in Colombia.

From the mid-twentieth century until 1967, Colombia followed a mixed policy: import substitution to support domestic capitalists, and export promotion to favor the coffee sector. Unlike trade policies in most of Latin America, Colombia's has always included export promotion, because of the strong influence of the coffee sector. Historically, coffee was a major force in integrating the Colombian economy into the world market. While coffee early on was seen as a luxury product, its growing popularity in the United

3.11 PERSISTENCE TO FIFTH GRADE
IN SEVEN LARGE LATIN AMERICAN
COUNTRIES (% OF COHORT)

Country	1991	1998	2003
Argentina	n/a	94.7	n/a
Brazil	72.8	n/a	n/a
Chile	92.3	99.8	99.0
Colombia	76.3	63.4	77.5
Mexico	79.5	88.9	92.6
Peru	n/a	87.9	89.7
Venezuela	86.0	n/a	91.0

Source: World Development Indicators (World Bank)

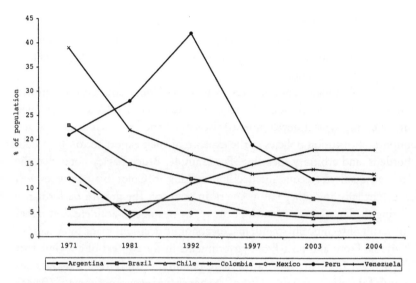

FIGURE 3.6   *Prevalence of Undernourishment*

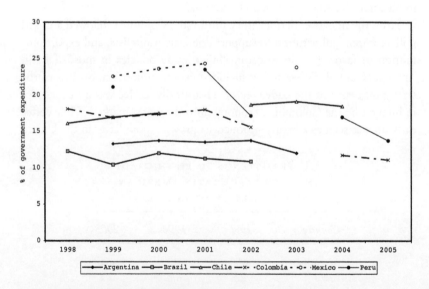

FIGURE 3.7   *Public Spending on Education*

States created a large market for Colombian exports. The revenues from these exports allowed for the development of badly needed transportation and communications infrastructure. This development is likely one of the major forces that acted against regionalization and supported a growing national identity (Helmsing 1986). Because coffee was such a dominant export crop throughout much of the twentieth century, the Colombian economy has often been tied directly to the market for coffee. For example, when world coffee prices fell sharply after 1896, national revenues were dramatically reduced. It has been suggested that this contributed significantly to an upsurge in regional separatist feeling, leading to the One Thousand Days War and the eventually to the secession of Panama (Bergquist 1978). Conversely, during the "coffee bonanza" of 1975–1977, coffee prices reached record levels (Berry 1992). However, as the Colombian economy has diversified over time, coffee's relative importance has declined (Helmsing 1986). For example, the ratio of coffee exports to total exports throughout the twentieth century fell from 83 percent in 1955 to 17 percent in 1995 (Lieberman and Hanna 1992; Dambaugh 1957). The focus on coffee exports created a disincentive to implement comprehensive import substitution policies, even when they were very popular and widely enacted throughout Latin America.

National Front economic policies resulted in stable growth and moderate rates of inflation (Edwards and Steiner 2000). From 1950 to 1966, the Colombian economy was characterized by some import-substitution policies and a fixed exchange rate. This was also the period of *la violencia*. Inflation was high and economic growth moderate. In August 1966, President Lleras Restrepo took office. Lleras began an austerity program that included trade and exchange-rate controls, tight credit policies, tax reforms, a balanced budget, and an emphasis on export expansion and import substitution (*Worldmark* 1984). Aided by favorable world economic conditions and moderate fiscal and monetary policies, the Colombian economy showed stable and consistent growth. From 1966 until 1974, annual growth rates of real GDP averaged 6.57 percent. In 1975, however, policies of export promotion and import substitution were reversed (Garcia Garcia and Montes Llamas 1988).

During the coffee bonanza, governmental spending increased dramatically as economic growth decelerated. The first coffee bonanza period (1976–1977) was characterized by sharply rising coffee prices. Yet GDP growth decelerated to 4.05 percent annually. The influx of coffee export revenues hid a number of policy mistakes, such as an unsustainable growth of governmental expenditures. The increased revenues of the late 1970s tempered the impact of the debt crisis of 1982–1983. However, the relief was temporary: it was still necessary to implement a macroeconomic stabilization program in 1984. The stabilization program included a drastic reduction in the fiscal deficit and the devaluation of the Colombian peso. While there was modest liberalization, the inward orientation of the trade regime was not fundamentally altered. During 1986–1987, there was another small and short-lived coffee bonanza. However, faced with falling coffee prices in 1988, the government was forced to enact a serious stabilization program. In 1990, influenced by the Washington consensus, the Colombian government began a comprehensive liberalization program. The commitment to liberalization began in the late 1980s under President Barco's administration and was further supported in the early 1990s by President Gaviria. The trade liberalization program eliminated most nontariff barriers and dramatically reduced tariffs. The government also implemented a program of financial liberalization, eliminating the previous system of exchange rate controls and permitting free flows of foreign exchange and international capital. To make Colombia more attractive to foreign investment, restrictions on direct foreign investment were reduced, and labor laws were rewritten to provide for increased flexibility in hiring and firing. Were these reforms effective in improving Colombian economic development and its relative position in Latin America?

While the economy did grow in the early 1990s, the average growth rate was still only around 4 percent (see Figure 3.3). The early 1990s was a time of major reform in Colombia, as leaders responded to an economic slowdown, stubborn inflation, and growing inefficiencies (Edwards 2001, 33). President Gaviria came to power in 1990 and embarked on a reform package that included both economic and political changes. The trademark of his reform policies was called *apertura,* economic opening. The broad-based changes included privatization of major sectors, such as banking and telecommunications, and trade liberalization, and required support from often competing groups (Knoester 1998, 87–91). Concurrently, major political and drug-related programs were announced; Gaviria was granted more autonomy to craft economic policies, including labor, financial, and tax reforms (Edwards 2001, 65). New tax reforms were introduced in 1990, 1992, and 1995 in the middle of a marked decentralization process (Arbelaez, Echavarria, and Gaviria 2002, 19). While Congress and the public were focused on the constitutional reforms and the drug war, Gaviria quietly implemented a major economic-reform package. It included relaxation of import barriers, reduction and rationalization of reserve requirements, the freeing of most (but not all) interest rates, abolition of exchange controls, liberalization of imports, reform of labor legislation, relaxation of controls over foreign direct investment, deregulation of the financial sector, modification of legislation governing port operations, liberalization of the insurance industry, and modernization of the tax system (Edwards 2001, 51).

Apertura was consistent with neoliberal economic policies. In theory, export promotion would generate foreign exchange, while reducing import tariffs would force domestic industries to become more efficient and competitive. Resources would be allocated to their most efficient use, and, consequently, the economy would grow. The aim was to expand external markets, increase capital accumulation, and facilitate technological improvements through a four- to five-year period, allowing domestic firms to restructure and prepare for import competition. However, as imports fell and foreign capital inflows increased faster than expected, the original time line was compressed. The reform process was to be completed over four years, 1990–1994; yet by late 1991 it was clear that the government would need to speed up the implementation to reduce inflationary pressures. National tariffs were to be reduced gradually from 40 percent to 11 percent over a four-year period; instead, the scheduled 1995 tariffs were in place by 1992. The economy was in the midst of a macroeconomic crisis as inflation increased, the currency appreciated, and capital inflows grew: "Both exporters and the import competing sector began to lose competitiveness" (Edwards 2001, 72). Raw materials and foreign-produced capital goods had a 5 percent tariff, intermediate goods 10 percent and 15 percent, and finished consumer goods 20 percent, creating an average tariff of 11.5 percent. As a result, exports grew from 20.7 percent of GDP in 1990 to 32.6 percent in 1997, but less rapidly than imports, which grew from 15 percent of GDP in 1990 to almost 50 percent in 1997 (Jaramillo 2001, 823–828). This led to a widening trade deficit as imports grew faster than exports. Although the economic reforms continued to be influential in later years, some argue that they were incomplete, contributing to continuing economic problems (Edwards 2001, 83).

Capital inflow increased as investors took advantage of interest-rate differences and Law 9, which facilitated the movement of capital by permitting the legal exchange of up to $20,000. Law 9 provided a legal means for narco-trafficking groups and others to repatriate their profits. These profits could then be used legally in the domestic economy to purchase consumer goods and services and investments, allowing illegal money to be integrated into the legal economy. The large inflows of capital forced the central bank, which gained autonomy in 1991, to institute sterilization policies. Sterilization policies attempt to reduce the inflationary effect that large inflows of capital have on the economy. Large capital inflows during the early 1990s caused the peso to appreciate by more than 20 percent from 1992 to 1998 (Arbelaez, Echavarria, and Gaviria 2002). The appreciation of the peso hurt domestic import substitution industries and the export sector, weakening growth and employment. An appreciated peso made imported consumer goods and capital cheaper. Globalization requires industries to compete and be efficient, but domestic Colombian industry was not prepared to compete, and many businesses fell victim to globalization. The inability to be competitive in a global marketplace led to industry failures. Globalization policies by Gaviria set the stage for an economic downturn.

Concurrent political reforms were more successful, although they had some long-term negative implications for the economy. In 1991, a new constitution and Congress were approved. The first civilian defense minister was appointed, and peace negotiations with the guerrilla movement were moving forward. The country was also basking in newfound international credibility. But even these accomplishments were not enough to mask the economic problems. Moreover, some analysts blame the political reforms for later economic ills: "In fact, with the benefit of hindsight it is possible to argue that many of Colombia's current ills have their origins in this frustrated reform initiative. In particular a number of provisions in the Constitution enacted in 1991 as part of the overall reform program, have generated serious fiscal imbalances and important rigidities and distortions" (Edwards and Steiner 2000). A number of spending provisions and promises of social services were included in the constitution without regard to how they would be funded or implemented. This reduced the central government's fiscal discretion and ability to influence the economy.

Trade liberalization had its effect as domestic production fell. Industry was substituting capital for labor. The less-skilled worker had fewer legitimate employment opportunities. By 1998, economic crisis had occurred. The crisis reflected the open-market policies of President Gaviria and the failure of institutions to adapt to the changing economic and political environment in both Colombia and the rest of the world. The recession of 1999, the worst on record since 1930, was fueled by a doubling of labor costs in the 1990s and a mismatch of workers' skills and employers' needs, which created a dramatic rise in unemployment. An examination of economic data clearly reveals that 1999 was a turning point: unemployment was at its highest, while per capita GDP and the growth rate of GDP were at their lowest.

Employment conditions deteriorated rapidly. Unemployment increased to 20 percent in 2000, the highest on record, compared to 7.5 percent in 1994, the lowest on record (Iregui and Otero 2003). Iregui and Otero noted that since the 1990s, wages were above the "steady-state level," which may have contributed to the increase in unemployment (2003, 896). Wages higher than equilibrium wages lead to relatively expensive labor. Labor is expensive because employers are forced to pay workers more than they are worth or what the market supports. When workers must be paid more than they are worth, firms tend to reduce their hiring and substitute capital for labor. Iregui and Otero found that wages in the public sector respond more to institutional, noneconomic factors than to productivity changes (2003). Furthermore, they found that wages above equilibrium levels result in higher unemployment. However, reducing wages below that level does not increase employment: just lowering wages would not necessarily lead to a higher demand for labor and lower unemployment. The institutional rigidity in the Colombian labor markets, such as complex rules for employee termination, means that it would take more than wage reductions to convince firms to hire more labor.

In response, the Colombian government attempted to address labor-market rigidity. Reforms designed to increase flexibility in hiring and firing practices should have helped reduce unemployment and improve firm efficiency. Labor-market reforms "introduced more flexibility in labor markets, as they decreased firms' hiring and firing costs, and very likely affected firms' incentives to employ informal workers" (Goldberg and Pavcnik 2003, 465). Unemployment did not decline, since there were other factors, such as institutional and legal restrictions, that effected productivity and growth. For example Arbelaez, Echavarria, and Gaviria argue that the "exchange rate appreciation and labor reforms of the early 1990s increased the relative cost of labor with respect to capital and made it more difficult to create jobs for less skilled workers" (2002, 20). An appreciated exchange rate further reduces the relative cost of imported capital. This encourages capital-intensive production, which tends to employ more skilled and fewer unskilled workers. Additionally, labor participation fell in agriculture and industry as investment moved into the more capital-intensive mining and financial sectors. Agriculture fell from almost 20 percent of GDP in 1970 to just less than 15 percent in 1999. Industry's share fell from 17 percent to 13.5 percent during the same period (Paredes 2001). Firms in Colombia responded to high wages and institutional rigidity by moving away from hiring labor and moving into more capital-intensive production.

This overview of Colombia's relative position in Latin America reveals that Colombia has not yet reached its potential, which is a likely result of weak state control along with the violence and illegal drugs that permeate its economy. By the 1990s, the main focus of this book, the national government had not succeeded in gaining control over the economic insecurity. In general, Colombia's economy did not begin to show signs of taking off until after President Uribe began to restore confidence in the economy through his aggressive stance on security issues. The reforms under President Gaviria may have laid the groundwork for growth, but without a clear and comprehensive plan to deal with the violence, sustained and substantial growth was unlikely. In 2005, FDI had grown dramatically and Colombia was the third choice for foreign investment in the region. As mentioned, foreign investment is an independent market-driven indicator of confidence in the long-term growth potential of the country. For Colombia to grow, private sector and foreign investment must increase so that opportunities for the labor force are created. Furthermore, to achieve sustainable development, Colombia must address its unemployment and educational problems along with the violence and illegal drugs. If Colombia's youth come to prefer economic opportunities in the illegal sector, then education rates will decline, a result with long-term consequences for human capital growth. Without growth, economically viable alternatives are limited—further undermining policies to encourage Colombians to reenter the legal workforce. Additionally, without an educated workforce, reaching higher levels of economic growth becomes difficult.

Another long-term challenge to growth is the lack of transportation infrastructure, as outlined in Chapter Two. Resources used to fight the guerrilla conflict and combat illegal drugs are not being used to improve infrastructure. Without infrastructure development, the potential for growth is further hampered. However, since infrastructure is targeted in the conflict, without improved security, these investments can be destroyed. In Chapter Seven, we examine the impact of justice and security spending on the economy. While President Uribe appears to have begun to address the issues of insecurity, education, and unemployment, these issues must be part of any long-term development plan if Colombia has any hope of moving out of the bottom tier of this group of Latin American countries. The next chapter provides a historical discussion of the main violent groups active in the late twentieth and early twenty-first centuries.

FOUR

THE MAIN ACTORS IN THE 1990S AND INTO THE TWENTY-FIRST CENTURY

Guerrillas and Paramilitaries

This chapter focuses on the main violent groups active in Colombia since the 1990s. To understand the current Colombian challenge, it is important to understand the historical context in which these groups emerged. Although the focus will be on the main violent groups of the 1990s (FARC, the ELN, and the paramilitaries), other groups, such as the EPL and M-19, deserve mention.[1] Despite decades of rebellion, Colombian democracy has, by Latin American standards, enjoyed exceptional stability.

Two notable exceptions to Colombia's political stability are *la violencia* and the subsequent military dictatorship. *La violencia* was a bloody ten-year (1948–1958) civil war between the two main political parties, the Liberals and Conservatives. Following this conflict, Rojas Pinilla seized power and imposed a military dictatorship from 1953 to 1957. Rojas became repressive, targeting self-defense groups and the communists in 1954, thereby creating a new conflict between the state and rebels. Rojas was removed by a military junta in 1957, and a political agreement called the National Front soon followed. This agreement facilitated reconciliation of the Liberals and Conservatives, including an amnesty offer to the mostly Liberal and communist guerrilla groups and to military and police officers accused of political crimes before the 1944 coup attempt. This amnesty benefited approximately 20,000 Colombians. Although the National Front settled the disagreements between the Liberals and Conservatives, it also sowed discontent among those who did not benefit from it.

Many Colombian guerrilla groups share an origin in resistance to the National Front power-sharing agreement. After the National Front (1958–1974) was established, President Alberto Lleras Camargo (1958–1962, Liberal Party) announced an amnesty, of which few rebels took advantage (Osterling 1989, 277–279). However, despite this early conciliatory gesture, the National Front, which prevented political participation by groups other than the official Liberal and Conservative parties, helped inspire early revolutionary movements.

The National Front's rigidity "gave rise to an opposition that, lacking a means of expression, turned toward a plan of radical rupture" (Pécaut 1992, 227). During this time, structural problems in the countryside were maintained, and the institutional presence was mainly repressive as opposed to consensual (Ortiz Sarmiento 1990–1991, 254). Before the political reforms that began in 1982, no local or departmental elections were held, despite significant rural, regional, and urban protest in addition to guerrilla activity throughout the country (Romero 2003, 63). Moreover, until 1972, "all parties had to propose rosters on Liberal or Conservative tickets. Thus the Communist party presented its candidates on the Liberal ticket and General Rojas Pinilla's populist movement presented its candidates on both the Conservative and Liberal tickets" (Pécaut 1992, 238n3). Alternation of Liberal and Conservative candidates for president and the guarantee of equal numbers of seats for the two parties ended in 1974.

During the National Front and the transition to more open elections, others were committing themselves to revolutionary activity. Some groups were inspired by Che Guevara's *foco* route, and others wanted to replicate the example of the Chinese Revolution. After the Colombian Communist Party endorsed a resolution of the 20th Congress of the Communist Party of the Soviet Union (1956), calling for a peaceful path to revolution, some of its members left to pursue revolution more directly and violently. Moreover, patterns of violence from *la violencia,* such as banditry and guerrilla activity, continued: "There is no doubt that in the nuclei of survivors of the old Liberal guerrilla groups there was enormous frustration. They joined the Movimiento Revolucionario Liberal (Revolutionary Liberal Movement, MRL) in massive numbers and, in many cases, allied themselves with new revolutionary groups" (Pizarro 1992, 175).

Some former guerrilla groups have been successfully integrated into the legitimate Colombian political system. Before its 1990 demobilization and integration into the political process, the M-19 (Nineteenth of April Movement) had been one of Colombia's main guerrilla groups. Its formation was in response to contested elections in 1970, in which the independent Alianza Nacional Popular (ANAPO) had its victory stolen. The allegations of fraud cost the National Front legitimacy.[2] Unlike the origins of traditional guerrilla groups, its roots were urban. M-19 learned about the importance of a political emphasis from the example of another Latin American urban guerrilla group, the Uruguayan Montoneros (Alape 1985, 324). M-19 committed many high-profile symbolic acts. For example, it stole Bolívar's sword (Pizarro 1992,

183). Other notable actions included the seizure of the Dominican embassy in 1980 and a successful raid on an urban weapons depot. These successes of M-19 raised tensions within the armed forces, which demanded that President Turbay allow military trials of civilians (Safford and Palacios 2002, 360). One of the most infamous M-19 acts was the seizure of the Palace of Justice in Bogotá in November 1985. The entire Supreme Court was held hostage. Eventually, the building was stormed by the military, resulting in the death of most of the M-19 leadership and half of the justices. After that debacle, the remaining M-19 leaders signed an agreement with President Virgilio Barco Vargas in 1989 to abandon their armed struggle and become a political party, which is today known as the Democratic Alliance/M-19. It remains part of the legal left in Colombia. In contemporary Colombia, three leftist guerrilla groups and one main paramilitary coalition are active.

EPL (EJÉRCITO POPULAR DE LIBERACIÓN)

Another group, the EPL (Ejército Popular de Liberación, or Popular Army of Liberation), is the guerrilla arm of the Colombian Communist Party (PCML). According to EPL leader William Calvo, the group was founded in 1967 and was self-identified as the armed wing of the party (Alape 1985, 303). According to Pizarro, the EPL was the Colombian reflection of the "Chinese-Soviet rupture during the first years of the 1960s and the subsequent division of the pro-Soviet Communist parties into two wings" (1992, 172). EPL founders were inspired by foco theory. According to Ernesto Rojas, who was imprisoned for two years because of his involvement in the EPL, the group originally focused on peasants, who could be recruited because of the failure of the Liberal Party and the Communist Party to absorb their participation (quoted in Behar 1985, 43). Its origins were in the northwest Antioquia (Pizarro 1992, 172) and in rural areas, and its general plan was to direct the guerrilla campaign principally in rural zones, on the model of a people's war. By 1976, the EPL had changed its focus to include other regions and the workers. According to Francisco Caraballo of the EPL, group members are both political and military combatants. The EPL is an organization directed by the ideology of the proletariat (Alape 1985, 303–313).

The group was remarkably unsuccessful in the 1960s, and was almost eliminated. Rebuilding began in the early 1980s with a movement away from a traditionally Maoist prolonged popular war, which is peasant dependent. Instead, the movement reached out to the cities, urban working classes, and receptive intellectuals (Pizarro 1992, 179n25). Much of the group accepted a truce agreement in 1984 with the Betancur government. Others demobilized in 1991 under President Gaviria. A small number of EPL members remained outside of the peace process. The group lost most of its remaining leadership by 2000. In 1994 Francisco Caraballo was arrested, and in 2000 Luis Alberto Carvajal, "Caliche," was captured. In 2000, the remaining leader, Hugo Carvajal Mosquera, "El Nene," was killed in a clash with the military (*Semana* 2000). By 2000, most of the remaining militant members had joined either FARC or the ELN.

ELN (EJÉRCITO LIBERACIÓN NACIONAL)

Ni un paso atrás . . . liberación o muerte
Not one step back . . . liberation or death

A group of sixteen youths gathered in 1962, creating what would become the core of the ELN (Army of National Liberation). These Colombian students visited Cuba on scholarship during the Cuban missile crisis. They asked for military training in the hopes of transplanting Che Guevara's focoista tradition in Colombia (de la Torre 1980). The recruits focused their early actions in areas of traditional social conflict by targeting "militant petroleum workers and peasant land colonizers" (Pizarro 1992, 177–178). In the view of the ELN, its origin is the result of the maturation of the conflict in Colombian society (Alape 1985, 279). Its first major action occurred the next year, when the ELN attacked the police station in the town of Simacota, Santander, and released its "Manifesto of Simacota." Most of the first members were university students. The nascent ELN was initially successful because it operated among angry petroleum workers and peasants, who were ready recruits (Pizarro 1992, 177–178; Alape 1985, 282).

The group was also influenced by some militant strains of liberation theology. In 1965, the group attracted the support of a Catholic priest, Camilo Torres, and his group, the Frente Unido. Despite being quickly killed in the conflict, he became an important symbol to the group (Pécaut 1997, 12). Manuel Pérez Martínez, in addition to Spaniards José Antonio Jiménez and Domingo Lain, was a member of the group of reformist, opposition priests called Golconda, which wanted more radical reform than that recommended by the Latin American bishops who met in Medellín in 1968 (Pécaut 1997, 11). Pérez Martínez was a key leader in the ELN from 1973 until his death in 1998. He was instrumental in increasing the number of ELN forces from less than 100 to more than 5,000.

The ELN's stated goals include popular power, elimination of the powerful oligarchy, and the end of U.S. imperialism (Sánchez Torres, Díaz, and Formisano 2003, 12; Medina 2001).[3]

The ELN initially operated in northern Colombia, specifically in Santander, Antioquia, and Bolívar. The military almost succeeded in eliminating the ELN in the 1970s. The group suffered the loss of an entire column in an attack against a police post in Anorí (Alape 1985, 287). Additionally, severe internal conflicts resulted in executions within the group and expulsions. Despite these setbacks, the group recovered, and currently has approximately 3,500 to 5,000 fighters. Since 1986, much of its activity has been concentrated on bombing the Caño Limón Coveñas oil pipeline, which runs from the eastern plains to the Caribbean (Bagley 2001; Offstein 2002, 4). The oil industry was a target of extortion as well as attacks. Increased funding from the extortion of the oil companies in northeastern Colombia helped the group rebound (Maullin 1973, 41–48; Echandía Castilla 2000, 51–57; Offstein 2002).

The ELN began peace talks in 1991 and 1992 along with the other guerrilla groups, but did not continue. In 1998 and 1999, the ELN met with business and civic leaders and agreed to begin discussions about possible peace talks. The ELN reached an agreement with the government in Maguncia in July 1998. This was a procedural agreement as opposed to a substantive peace agreement; it created a framework for a series of peace conventions the following year. On April 25, 2000, the Colombian government announced the creation of a zone for the ELN.[4] However, the creation of this zone was resisted from the beginning by groups within the government, by the population, and by the paramilitaries. The process was attempted again in January 2001, again with many proposed rules, but was suspended in August. However, this accord, which granted the ELN a demilitarized area called the *zona de encuentro* (meeting zone), was not consecrated, because of nationwide roadblocks, the resistance of local officials, and general paramilitary resistance to the plan. As the military moved out, the paramilitaries moved in to prevent implementation of the zone (*Semana* 2001).

As peace talks and the implementation of the zone failed, the ELN was involved in some high-profile incidents. In April 1999, the ELN hijacked an Avianca airplane and kidnapped the majority of the passengers. In May 1999, the ELN attempted another mass kidnapping in an attempted show of strength. The *pesca milagrosa* (fishing for miracles) at a church in Cali led to the kidnapping of 143 parishioners. In August 1999, peace talks began again, but no real progress was made. The ELN continues to kidnap civilians and to damage the oil infrastructure.

FARC (FUERZAS ARMADAS
REVOLUCIONARIAS DE COLOMBIA)

FARC, the Revolutionary Armed Forces of Colombia, is the dominant guerrilla group in Colombia, with approximately 17,000 members. FARC, a dominant force in much of rural Colombia, is currently making inroads into the main cities (Petras 2000, 134). Formally, FARC originated out of peasant self-defense groups in the 1960s. However, its deeper historical roots lie in the agrarian revolt of poor agricultural workers against the large landed estates in the 1920s and 1930s (Pizarro 1992, 180n26).

FARC itself recognizes this early historical antecedent. In its document "The self-defense forces: There's a big difference between the one and the other," it states: "The notion of self-defense has its historical antecedents in the agrarian struggles developed in the twenties and thirties by pockets of peasants who organized themselves in some regions of the country (e.g., Sumapaz and Tequendama) to defend what they had won against the continuous aggression of the public forces, which was instigated by the big landowners" (FARC 2002).

By the 1940s, the Communist Party had started recommending the formation of peasant self-defense groups in response to governmental repression, strengthening ties between the peasant groups and the communists (Rangel Suárez 1999; Pizarro 1992; Rochlin 2003, 97). Although FARC is Marxist, it would be a mistake to view it as simply another foco inspired by the example of the Cuban Revolution: "On the contrary, as had happened in 1949 and 1955, the FARC emerged as a people's response to official violence and militarist aggression" (Pizarro 1992, 181).[5] In fact, the Colombian Communist Party, despite being illegal in the 1956 and 1958 elections and being repressed by the Colombian government, had endorsed the idea of peaceful change as opposed to revolution. In 1958, the Communist Party proposed working toward a democratic popular front and suspended its mobilization of peasant groups (Pizarro 1992). The absence of a broad political solution led to the evolution of Liberal guerrilla groups of the 1940s and 1950s into FARC.[6] According to Pizarro (1992), there was a persistence of the old type of violence. During the government of Rojas Pinilla and the National Front, increasing attacks by the police, military, and irregular governmental forces caused these groups to evolve from spontaneous peasant organizations into guerrilla groups. This transformation is dramatically exemplified by the situation in Marquetalia (FARC 2002).

Parts of the country with concentrations of old guerrillas became targets of military action. Guerrilla activity continued in areas such as Marquetalia, in southern Tolima; the region of Aríari, in the Llanos Orientales; and in Sumapaz, in the central part of the state. For example, in December 1963, FARC founder Pedro Antonio Marín, a.k.a. Manuel Marulanda Vélez "Tirofijo," attacked a supply column, killing soldiers, confiscating arms, shooting down a plane, and kidnapping the pilots (Vélez 2000, 3). Conservative congressman Álvaro Gómez Hurtado called those areas "independent republics." The air force and army attacked the independent republics. An attack on Marquetalia on May 27, 1964, set the stage for the current guerrilla conflict with FARC. According to FARC, this attack was pure governmental repression against local peasants: "This 'subversive centre' was composed of peasants who had settled in the region of Marquetalia, Tolima Department after surviving the calamities of the war between the traditional political parties. . . . Of the state, they only demanded roads to transport their products, schools for the education of their children and guarantees against the activities of the 'pajaros,' the paramilitary gangs of that time" (FARC 2000a).

Although the government dislodged the peasants in approximately three weeks, the attack provided pregnant symbolism for the birth of FARC.

48 men, poorly armed and with insufficient resources, commanded and oriented by Comrade Manuel Marulanda Vélez, turned into an armed revolutionary nucleus infused by our people's tradition of struggle . . .

The Revolutionary Armed Forces of Colombia—People's Army, FARC-EP, arose in the course of the confrontation, with a revolutionary programme calling together all the citizens who dream of a Colombia for Colombians, with equality of opportunities and equitable distribution of wealth and where among us all we can build peace with social equality and sovereignty (FARC 2000a).

According to Pizarro, the "result was truly a Pyrrhic military victory with tremendous implications. The use of thousands of soldiers to dislodge a few hundred peasant families resulted in a situation, twenty years later, in which the Communist-inspired guerrilla groups of the FARC had a network of twenty-seven armed fronts" (1992, 181). In the words of FARC founder Manuel Marulanda Vélez, "Marquetalia was the spark that set a fire in a crucial moment in history that is now impossible to extinguish" (Alape 1985, 266).[7]

At the end of 1965 in Marquetalia, the first guerrilla conference was held and the Southern Block was officially formed, incorporating guerrillas, agrarian movements, and self-defense groups from Riochiquito, Natagaima ("26 de Septiembre"), El Pato, Guayabero, and Marquetalia (Vélez 2000, 3). Despite losing the conflict in Marquetalia, the guerrillas were able to meet there for their conference, since the government did not follow through with promised investments in infrastructure improvements after the conflict. Subsequently, the continued lack of governmental presence allowed the guerrillas to return permanently.[8] According to the newly invigorated guerrillas, the military action at Marquetalia revealed that the government preferred repression to reform (FARC 1999). For FARC, the attack on Marquetalia demonstrated disregard for the citizens of the area: instead of spending money to improve the lives of the peasants, the government instigated a new chapter of violence.

At the first guerrilla conference, the guerrillas drafted an agrarian reform plan, with eight main points.

1. Demand structural change in the countryside, including land reform, expropriations, and technical and infrastructure assistance to the peasants to improve their lives.
2. Depending on land quality, create new plots of 10–20 hectares to be distributed, usurious peasant debts abolished, while respecting the rights of non-absentee landowners.
3. Respect the rights of rich peasants, who directly work the land.
4. Create a new system of peasant credit and assistance. Pursue specific projects of irrigation, education, sanitation, and electrification. Leave large farms and factories intact, for the public good, but all must include rural development plans in their operations.
5. Create a system of agricultural price supports.
6. Protect indigenous communities, granting cultural and political autonomy.
7. Recognize the need for a worker-peasant alliance.
8. Invite cooperation from a broad spectrum of the left and center in support of a national revolution to achieve a democratic program of national liberation. (adapted from FARC 1993)

In conclusion, the origin of FARC should be understood within the context of state repression and the failure of the Liberal Party to achieve significant social, agrarian, or economic reform (Rochlin 2003, 97). The geographic location of early FARC support reflects this. The early FARC was concentrated in areas with a history of strong peasant movements and land conflict (Pizarro 1991; Sánchez Torres, Díaz, and Formisano 2003).

Two years after the first guerrilla conference, FARC officially formed out of the Southern Block. According to Manuel Marulanda Vélez, "the Southern Block precisely signified the beginning and the extension of the guerrilla conflict" (Alape 1985, 276).[9] During the second guerrilla conference, a FARC constitution was written, and the movement changed from self-defense groups to revolutionary groups eager to go on the offensive. According to FARC ideologue Jacobo Arenas, "No longer do we only fight for a little piece of land or to retake our farms but to become revolutionaries, until the triumph of the revolution" (Alape 1994; Vélez 2000, 4).[10] FARC has continued to evolve from a primarily localized movement based on peasant support to a revolutionary movement of national breadth, with fronts in both rural and urban areas. For example, when three IRA (Irish Republican Army) members were arrested in Colombia, many became concerned that the Europeans were in Colombia to offer their expertise and experience in urban guerrilla warfare to help FARC's desires to further urbanize the conflict. It should be noted that the "Colombian Three"—James Monaghan, Martin McCauley, and Niall Connolly—were acquitted on charges of training FARC rebels and were released with credit for time served (Murphy 2005).

Table 4.1 provides an overview of the main developments in FARC strategy and organization.

From its founding through the 1970s, FARC could still be considered a peasant movement within a limited geographic area. FARC support was based on its providing basic order in parts of the country that did not have a significant governmental presence (Rangel Suárez 1999; Vélez 2000; Medina Gallego 1990; Cubides 1998). Some scholars, such as Pizarro (1992), recognize a geographic overlap among successive Colombian conflicts: "The map of the old violence and the map of the new had no substantial differences; both coincide with the map of the MRL and the Communist enclaves, forming the map of the resistance and of the national rebellion" (175; see also Ortiz Sarmiento 1990–1991, 255).

During *la violencia* and its aftermath (1948–1963), as shown in Figure 4.1, the departments of Tolima, Meta, Vichada, and Vaupés suffered more than other departments. However, Figure 5.4 shows a concentration of FARC violence in Antioquia and Bolívar in 1991, 1995, and 1999, with a general prevalence of violence in the central part of the country. From this rough comparison, it appears that the theater of the conflict has shifted since its beginning.

After a period of stagnation in the 1970s, the guerrilla movements began to expand. Scholars have theorized that a combination of factors led to the growth of FARC, including an increase in the price of coffee, drug production, macroeconomic austerity measures, popular effects of the neoliberal reforms of López Michelsen (Liberal, 1974–1978) and Turbay Ayala (Liberal, 1978–1982), and the rise of the underground economy (Pécaut 1992, 229; Pizarro

Guerrilla conference	Major points and achievements of conference	Approximate strength of FARC and major strategic events
2nd (1966)	• Emergence from the Southern Block to the FARC • First FARC constitution • Strategic change from self-defense groups to offensive guerrilla movement	• Spread to Huila, Caldas, northern Tolima, and possibly Caquetá, while maintaining influence in Marquetalia
3rd (1969)	• Creation of fourth front, in Magdalena Medio • Examination of ways to increase public support	• Part of FARC located in Quindio lost 70% of arms and many men
4th (1971; El Pato)	• Strategic coordination among fronts, initial organization of detachments and columns	• Approximately 780 men
5th (1974; Meta)	• Change from a guerrilla movement to a revolutionary army	• Recovered from losses at Quindio; expansion to Meta, Huila, Caquetá • Cundinamarca y Tolima and expansion to the north
6th (1978; Duda)	• Priority: increase soldiers' abilities and leadership structure • New coordination among fronts to coordinate attacks	• Aim: double the number of fronts, to at least one front per department
7th (1982; Yacopí)	• Elaboration of a strategic plan • Clear strategic and operational coordination • Mandated expansion to at least 48 fronts with a national presence • Plans to urbanize the conflict • Discussed plans for the dissemination of FARC documents, bulletins, etc. to communicate aims and motivations	• Expansion from 10 fronts at the end of the '70s to 20 fronts by the beginning of the '80s • By 1987, 35 fronts with a presence in almost all departments
8th (1993)	• Restatement of the 1982 commitment to urbanize the conflict • Acknowledgment of necessity of violence to gain cooperation of the bourgeoisie • Revision of strategic plan and agrarian program, modification of self-governance	• By the end of the 20th century, 67 rural and 4 urban fronts

Sources: Vélez 2000, Alape 1994, Sánchez Torres, Díaz, and Formisano 2003, Marks 2005, FARC documents

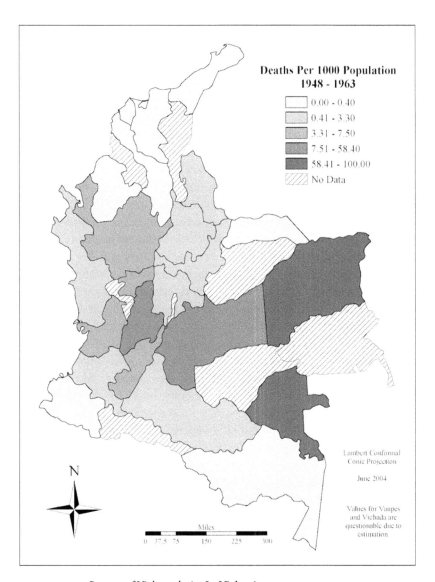

FIGURE 4.1 *Patterns of Violence during* La Violencia
Data Source: John A. Booth, "Rural Violence in Colombia: 1948–1963,"
Western Political Quarterly 27 (4): 657–679, Appendix Table A.

1992, 189). By the 1980s, the group had expanded from its peasant base. In 1985, leaders of FARC met to put into motion the plans of the seventh guerilla conference. According to Rangel Suárez (1999), there are three phases in the plan: first, growth of the organization and the creation of additional fronts; second, control of the Cordillera Central, with the aim of isolating the eastern plains and Bogotá; and third, the creation of a provisional government in the southern jungles and a national offensive to topple the government.

FARC has grown considerably, changed its strategy, and modified its rhetoric. To communicate its goals, FARC created a political wing, the Movimiento Bolivariano, in 2000 to fight against "state terrorism, the injustices, inequalities, unemployment, and the humiliation before US imperialism" (FARC 2000a). This document affirms FARC's position that military success will lead to political success (FARC 2000b). Despite the constitutional reforms of 1991, FARC still views the government as exclusionary and illegitimate. In its "Manifiesto del movimiento Bolivariano por la nueva Colombia," it states, "Colombia is gravely ill because the governing class of liberals and conservatives have taken advantage of their positions for personal gain and to favor the rich; because the governments have only served to defend the insatiable voracity of the large capitalists, of the landowners, and of the drug cartels; and because they have handed our sovereignty over to the United States of America, contrary to our patriotic traditions, the economy and the dignity of the entire country" (FARC 2000c).[11] The group builds on its original basis of demands for land reform, but adds to its motivations charges of corruption, the perversion of capitalism, and U.S. imperialism. Pécaut argues that the motivations of the young guerrillas are very different from those of the older ones, in that the younger guerrillas tend to look at being a guerrilla as merely one potential job among many (1997, 915). Whether the group has become less ideological and more bureaucratized is not the subject of this study.

By the 1990s, FARC had been completely transformed. By the end of the twentieth century, it had sixty-seven rural and four urban fronts, composed of the Caribbean Block (Costa Atlántico), the Central Block (Tolima, Huila, and Cundinamarca), the Southern Block (Nariño, Putumayo, and Caquetá), the Eastern Front (Meta, Vichada, and Guaviare), and the José María Córdoba Block (Urabá and Antioquia) (Vélez 2000, 6–9; Marks 2005).[12]

AUC (AUTODEFENSAS UNIDAS COLOMBIANAS)

Decree 3398 of 1965 and Law 48 of 1968 legalized the creation of Colombian civil-defense groups as a way to confront the guerrillas and support army counterinsurgency efforts (Cubides 2001, 127–150). Landowners, and, later, drug traffickers, formed paramilitary groups to fight guerrillas. Paramilitary violence increased in the 1980s because of deepening links between paramilitaries and narco-traffickers. Paramilitary leaders have acknowledged that proceeds from taxing the drug trade finance their operations. The increased violence led the government to aggressively target drug cartels and some paramilitary groups (Pérez 1999, 667). Because of the increasing number of human rights violations, paramilitary groups were made illegal in 1989. There are well-documented ties of military-paramilitary cooperation during the 1980s and 1990s (Jiménez-Gomez 1986, 112–120; Vásquez Carrizosa 1986, 121–125; Chernick 1988, 58).

Despite their illegality, these groups continue to operate and to retain some support, ranging from the tacit approval of governmental or military agencies' reliance on the paramilitaries for intelligence on guerrillas (CIA 1997, 10) to direct support from people in the military and government (Amnesty International 2000, 2002a, 2002b). Romero (2003) argues that the emergence of Colombian paramilitaries must be understood in the context of military resistance to peace talks with the guerrillas; ongoing decentralization, which undermined presidential reform initiatives; and the land conflict having changed as a result of narcos' converting themselves into large landowners with private armies (18). As Chernick points out, the peace agreements of the 1980s were "negotiated without the support or the participation of party leadership or of the armed forces" (1988, 73). There was substantial resistance among military officers, who rejected negotiations and political concessions unless the guerrillas first surrendered their weapons.

Although there are numerous factions of Colombian paramilitary groups, a confederation among them has emerged. An understanding of this—at times tenuous—alliance has important implications for the dynamics of Colombian paramilitary violence. In an attempt to increase coordination among paramilitary groups, Carlos Castaño founded the AUC (United Self-Defense Groups of Colombia) in 1996. Previously, after the kidnapping and murder of his father by FARC, Castaño had created the ACCU (Autodefensas Campesinas de Córdoba y Urabá, or Peasant Self-Defense Groups of Córdoba and Urabá), which, although officially founded in 1994, could trace its origins to groups active since the 1980s (Romero 2000, 52–69). Fidel Castaño, a prominent ACCU leader and brother of Carlos Castaño, disappeared in 1994.

According to an account in the Colombian newspaper *El Tiempo* (June 20, 2002), the AUC is composed of approximately 15,000 active paramilitaries from groups such as the ACCU and is funded by landowners, businesses, and drug dealers. By 2001, it was estimated that the AUC had an armed presence in approximately 40 percent of all municipalities (Manwaring 2002, 6). By 2004, another estimate counted forty-nine paramilitary blocks in twenty-six departments (Camacho 2004).

In the view of the AUC, it is a legitimate group, founded to fight the Colombian leftist insurgents.[13] Its members view themselves as patriots defending the country. In a 2003 letter, they state, "The historic military role assumed by the self-defense forces has been a necessary and determinant factor that has allowed Colombia to sustain its fragile and threatened democracy and to develop its budding economic capacities in the context of the indecision and incongruence of the political system" (Mancuso and Castaño 2003a).[14] According to its leaders, the AUC "has a political project of a democratic nature with the ultimate goal of a completely legal political activity with the aim of collaborating to eliminate the weaknesses and deficiencies of the state" (Mancuso and Castaño 2003b).[15]

Since the paramilitaries were declared illegal, the official position of the government, however, has been that paramilitary groups are criminal organizations to be pursued with "equal or greater vigor than other violent groups" (Ministerio de Defensa Nacional 2000b, 5). The Colombian Defense Ministry has also documented a strong correlation nationally between the growth of the number of paramilitary soldiers and the level of coca cultivation from 1996 to 1999 (Ministerio de Defensa Nacional 2000b, 11). In response to criticism from foreign governments and human rights groups, the Colombian government has repeatedly claimed that there are no ties between the government and paramilitary groups and that people who support them are vigorously prosecuted.

This independence of the government from the paramilitaries has been contested. For example, Salazar Pérez (2002) claims that their recent growth was intended to facilitate the protection of investments and to serve a social-cleansing function. Human rights groups such as Amnesty International and Human Rights Watch also document persistent ties between the government and paramilitary groups. Human Rights Watch, in its *World Report* for 2000, documents specific ties between the Colombian Army's Fourth Brigade and the AUC, alleging that Castaño's men exchanged civilian corpses for weapons from the army. The army would then claim that the dead civilians were guerrillas who had been killed in combat. The U.S. State Department has also found military complicity with the paramilitaries. Its *1999 Country Reports on Human Rights* documents collaboration, intelligence sharing, and the provision of military supplies (U.S. Department of State 2000).

There have been attempts to reform the judicial system and the armed forces to reduce human rights violations. For example, in November 1998 the *procurator* delegate for human rights tallied fifty dismissals and disciplinary sanctions against 126 military officers and police personnel for violations of human rights since mid-1997 and the opening of hundreds of new cases (Amnesty International 1998). In 1999, President Pastrana removed four generals from service for allegedly having links to the paramilitaries; one went to trial. In 2000, to further purge the military of paramilitary sympathizers, Pastrana delegated to the armed forces the authority to directly dismiss offending personnel; 89 officers and 299 others were dismissed, but none of them were officially charged. Many human rights organizations charge that officials and officers complicit in rights violations remain in their jobs (Amnesty International 2001). Other attempts at reform continue.

The AUC claims to be an alternative to the guerrilla groups and to be assuming the traditional counterinsurgency role of the military. Carlos Castaño stated that the AUC "was born from the union of diverse groups with dissimilar interests, all similarly oriented toward the legitimate defense of life and the rewards of citizenship before the weakness and lack of political will of the state to combat the Marxist guerrillas" (Castaño 2001a).[16] In the view of the AUC, the guerrillas are not truly interested in peace and the government is unable to provide security. Consequently, it stepped in where the government failed (Mancuso 2002). Responsibility for the infamous massacres at Mapiripán in July 1997, Barrancabermeja in May 1998, and La Gabarra-Tibú in August 1999 has been attributed to the paramilitaries. In fact, Castaño admitted in 2001 that at first he was motivated solely by the desire to kill guerrillas: "I remember, many years ago, when I began my fight against the subversives, how I only thought of executing guerrillas. . . . I thought of nothing else, it was my whole world, I didn't know another" (Castaño 2001b).[17] Castaño justified killing noncombatants, since the AUC was fighting "guerrillas dressed as peasants" (Bagley 2001). In an interview with Castro Caycedo, he stated, "In this war much of the civilian population dies. Do you know why? Because two-thirds of the effective forces of the guerrillas do not have weapons and are acting as part of the civilian population" (Castro Caycedo 2001). In response to criticism of the massacres, Castaño announced in an open letter to Defense Minister Marta Lucía Ramírez that the AUC would no longer commit massacres (Castaño and Mancuso 2002a). Many analysts suggest that the AUC continues to kill en masse, but disperses the bodies to avoid the appearance of a massacre (Martinez 2002).

In regard to allegations of drug trafficking, Castaño has denied that paramilitary members are involved for personal enrichment, and affirmed that members would cooperate with foreign and domestic courts investigating drug-trafficking charges: "With respect to narco-trafficking, our organization has been clear and realistic since its formation: those members who commit such crimes will have to respond to the Colombian or foreign courts and in no moment may their personal activity involve the organization, which does not participate in this type of business. In this sense, our statutes provide for maximum punishment for those who try to use the organization for personal enrichment, just like those who try to use it for particular interests" (Castaño 2001a).[18] However, he has publicly acknowledged drug funding of the AUC. In an interview with Cecilia Orozco on October 10, 2002, Castaño clarified how drug dollars fund paramilitaries: "Our declarations that the AUC collects 'taxes' on the coca producers should not be interpreted as evidence of trafficking or exporting of drugs to the United States. The taxes on production are necessary to maintain the fight against the FARC, but are not evidence of personal enrichment. Not in my case. I can prove it" (Orozco 2002; see also Aranguren Molina 2005).[19] The official position of the AUC toward the drug trade is to attack every link in the chain, from production to consumption.

The AUC actively promoted candidates in the 2002 elections and seemed to support the candidacy of Uribe, the current president. Nonetheless, in an interview in 2002, Castaño denied having direct influence over lawmakers: "Thirty-five percent of the Congress is elected from our zones of influence, but this is not to say that we have a legal political base, that we direct these congressmen as our allies. It would be an error to appraise the situation in this way, just as it would be an error to label as guerrillas congressmen from guerrilla zones, or congressmen from drug zones as narcos" (Orozco 2002).[20] Although Castaño denies efforts to support certain candidates, the organization has a clear interest in assuming a political role. Later, in 2005, José Vicente Castaño, brother of Fidel and Carlos Castaño, announced that they still had 35 percent of Congress as friends and would gain more in the next election (*El Nuevo Herald*, June 7, 2005). In response, some members of Congress requested that José Vicente Castaño release the names of the supportive members.

The group recently moved toward the goal of participating in government peace talks. To do this, the AUC needed to appear less involved in drug trafficking and human rights violations. In August 2001, Castaño released a letter, "Today's AUC," in which he described the organization and its functioning. He confirmed that he resigned his leadership role of the AUC in May 2001 because of the excesses and deviations from his command decisions. According to Castaño, his aim had been to make the AUC a true national self-defense force. A new collective command was created, and the individual responsibilities of AUC members were publicly delineated. According to this reorganization, the AUC was to function as a decentralized confederation of antisubversive groups, each individual commander being responsible for his own organization. Castaño retained control of the ACCU. New staff leadership positions were created, including the Estado Mayor, to represent the confederation, and the Dirección Política Nacional, led by Castaño and Ernesto Báez. The new commander general was Salvatore Mancuso (Castaño 2001). On July 6, 2002, Castaño released a letter, "¿Así nos ve el mundo?" in which he stated the breaking of all ties between the AUC and drugs was progressing, in order to advance the political process of legitimation, reinsertion, and national defense. He also claimed that the AUC had never been involved in poppy production and that the legitimate economy was recovering in areas wrested from control of the guerrillas (Castaño 2002a).

Later that month, in response to unpopular actions by some paramilitaries, such as the kidnapping of Venezuelan businessman Richard Boulton, Castaño began to distance himself publicly from the AUC. In the view of Castaño, these controversial and unpopular actions were part of a plot to undermine the AUC by narco-traffickers and enemies in Colombia and Venezuela. In his July 17, 2001, letter, "Notificación pública a secuestradores," he stated, "The narco-traffickers have tried to slowly appropriate the different groups of the AUC, and the ACCU has always been its major obstacle. Now they must be celebrating the possible disintegration of the AUC . . . Because of this, I call on all of the groups of the AUC not to fall into the hands of the narco-traffickers, which would transform us into their mercenaries, closing future doors" (Castaño 2002b).[21] Castaño retained the role of political commander until July 2002, when he stated that the AUC was out of control and too involved in drug trafficking. The AUC formally disbanded on July 18, 2002. Castaño and Mancuso promised to build a new national antirebel force (Reuters, July 19, 2002).

In an open letter dated September 7, 2002, the Dirección Política y Militar of the AUC (Dipom) announced the reestablishment of the AUC and its commitment to be part of the solution for national peace, enter a peace process, condemn narco-trafficking and terrorism (although it provided for a transition period to allow the AUC to adapt to losing the tribute from the coca growers in areas under its control), and respect human rights (Castaño and Mancuso 2002a). In a September 2002 interview with Reuters, Castaño announced that the AUC's drug ties had been severed: "We are committed to abandoning drug trafficking. I have never been a drug trafficker. If the United States seeks my extradition on drug-trafficking charges, I am prepared to turn myself in to the United States." In early February 2003, Castaño stated he would not surrender to the United States to face drug charges, since the

AUC is on the State Department's list of terrorist groups. In a Caracol Radio interview, he replied "I am not a terrorist, and I have no way to defend myself against that crime" (Associated Press, February 5, 2003).

The public statements and reorganization of the AUC were successful in positioning the AUC for peace talks. In a December 15, 2002, letter, the AUC declared a cease-fire with governmental forces (but not with FARC), beginning December 1, 2002. It also stated its openness to peace talks; requested to be recognized as a political actor; asked for the assistance of the Catholic Church, the United Nations, and the Organization of American States in a peace process; and expressed confidence in the Colombian government's ability to fulfill its obligations of governance (Castaño and Mancuso 2002b). Thus began a peace process that is currently ongoing. Individual paramilitary groups, such as the Alianza del Oriente and the Bloque Central Bolívar, have already disbanded. Nonetheless, strains among the different groups threaten the coherence of the paramilitaries as a negotiating group. As peace talks progressed, the organization appeared to fracture. In 2004, the disappearance and probable killing of Carlos Castaño, perhaps by rival paramilitary groups, and the killing of another politically motivated paramilitary leader opposed to coca cultivation, Rodrigo Franco, indicated the questionable cohesion of paramilitary forces and underlined the importance of examining differences among different fronts within the AUC. Despite the fractionalization of the AUC, leaders Salvatore Mancuso, Ramón Isaza, and Iván Roberto Duque, all considered drug traffickers by the United States, were invited to address the Colombian Congress in July 2004. A discussion of the progress and concerns of the ongoing paramilitary peace is contained in Chapter Eight.

CONCLUSION

Colombia provides an ideal case to test theories of civil war and nonstate violence because there are significant variations of violence, economic performance, and political factors within the country. In addition to separate guerrilla groups, there are active paramilitary groups. The purpose of this chapter has been to provide a brief historical overview of the origin of these groups in order to examine and identify potentially different drivers of nonstate violent groups.

FIVE

DIFFERENCES WITHIN COLOMBIA AND AVAILABLE SUBNATIONAL DATA

From the period of Spanish colonization through contemporary times, significant regional differences have persisted. Much of Colombia retains regionalisms, and the country remains poorly integrated. Moreover, as Guillermo O'Donnell points out, "current theories of the state often make an assumption which recurs in the current theories of democracy: that of a high degree of homogeneity in scope, both territorial and functional, of the state and of the social order it supports" (1999, 130). Colombia, like many developing nations, does not fulfill assumptions of homogeneity: "Since colonial times Colombia has been a collection of diverse regions with little communication and trade among them. Physical barriers are so great that many regions remained very isolated and self-sufficient" (Thoumi 2005, 14). In the Colombian case, clarity may be gained by examining differences among departments.[1] Significant differences in the amount of violence, level of development, and coca cultivation throughout the country merit a subnational analysis. This chapter provides an overview of the diversity within the country and a discussion of the data used in the book.

Colombia is divided into administrative departments (*departamentos*), which are analogous to states within the national unit. Since 1991, there have been thirty-three departments. In that year, nine "New Departments" (*Nuevos Departamentos*) were created. The departments are the subnational geographic units for which most demographic, economic, and political data are collected and maintained. Moreover, as part of President Gaviria's apertura, more power and responsibility have been devolved from the national government to the departments (Lemus 1998). The Colombian National Statistical Center (DANE, or Departamento Administrativo Nacional de Estadística) functions as the collection agency for census data and publishes much departmental-level data. Variation within the country, coupled with the availability of data at the department level, makes the department the appropriate level of analysis.

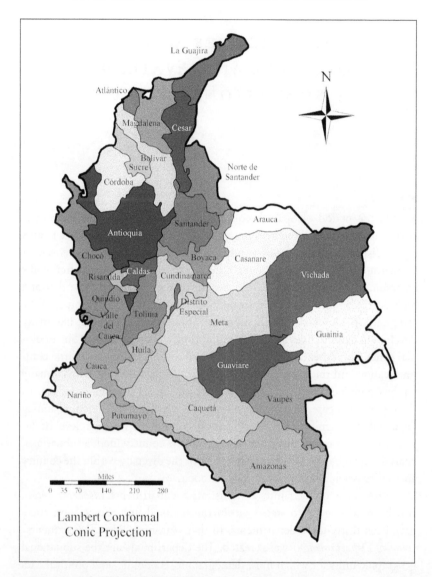

FIGURE 5.1 *Colombian Department Boundaries and Names*

In Colombia, the provision of public services—and the cost of those services to the citizens—is based on a classification system in which municipalities are assigned to an *estrato*. Using this stratification, the federal government determines the tariffs on goods, the taxes, and the prices of utilities it charges to the residents. The value of housing units within a geographic area is the basis for assigning an estrato level. The factors considered are the building

66

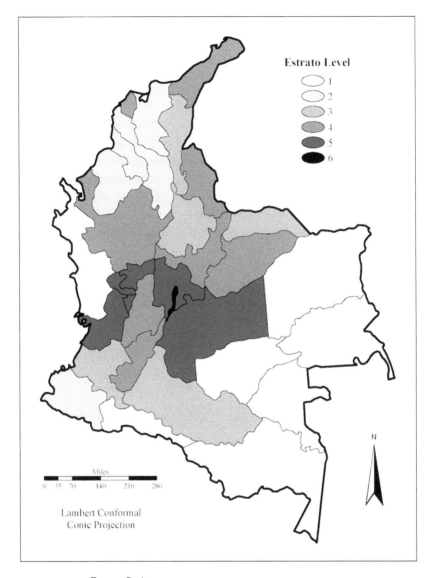

Estrato Level

○ 1
○ 2
○ 3
○ 4
● 5
● 6

Miles

0   35   70   140   210   280

Lambert Conformal
Conic Projection

N

FIGURE 5.2   *Estratos Regions*

materials used for the houses as well as environmental characteristics such as
road conditions, public lighting, sidewalks, pollution, and access to water and
electricity, as reported by DANE.

The estrato scale ranges from 1 to 6, 1 being the poorest and 6 the wealthi-
est. The map of regions by estrato (Figure 5.2) was constructed by aggregating
estrato levels of municipalities to the department level (Organización Pan-

americana de la Salud 1998). This classification illustrates significant differences in development within the country.

The least developed departments include Amazonas, Chocó, Guainía, Guaviare, Putumayo, Vaupés, and Vichada. Although there is a clustering of these relatively undeveloped areas on the periphery of the country, there is wide range of variation throughout the country.

Similarly, patterns of coca cultivation vary significantly within the country. The following figure provides a view of coca cultivation in 1999. Over time, both the relative distribution and amounts change. In this year, Putumayo, Caquetá, Guaviare, Meta, and Norte de Santander saw relatively large amounts of coca cultivated, even after eradication efforts were undertaken. Although there is some clustering of coca cultivation around Putumayo, coca cultivation is distributed throughout Colombia, although with varying density.

Patterns of violence also vary over time and across the country. Figure 5.4 provides an overview of FARC and paramilitary violence in 1991, 1995, and 1999. Few violations are reported in Amazonas, Vaupés, Vichada, Guainía, and Guaviare. Antioquia has a much higher level of reported violence. However, even in this department there is variation over time and by type. For example, Antioquia remains relatively violent throughout the time period, but paramilitary violations are low in 1991, peaking in 1999. Figure 5.4 suggests the utility of examining these issues over time as well as across departments.

The dataset used for this book is original, and was compiled from numerous Colombian sources. Variables are included to capture incidents of violence, political aspects, demographic characteristics, and economic statistics. The subnational analysis allows for a more rigorous examination of the interactions among political, economic, and violence-related factors within the country over time.

The main violence variables are compiled from the Centro de Investigación y Educación Popular (CINEP) in Bogotá, Colombia, and its Banco de Datos sobre Derechos Humanos y Violencia Política. Numerous violence statistics are available. The violence variables from CINEP range from threats to killings. Ranges for FARC human rights violations: 0–93 (1993–1998) and 0–138 (1999–2001); for paramilitary violations: 0–315 (1993–1998 and 1999–2001); and for ELN violations: 0–87 (1993–1998) and 0–147 (1999–2001). These measures of violence show the escalation or de-escalation of violence (Sambanis 2004a) across departments and through time.

Some commentators and U.S. embassy officials have challenged the validity of CINEP's data. For example, in an article in the *Wall Street Journal* (February 6, 2004), Mary Anastasia O'Grady repeats State Department alle-

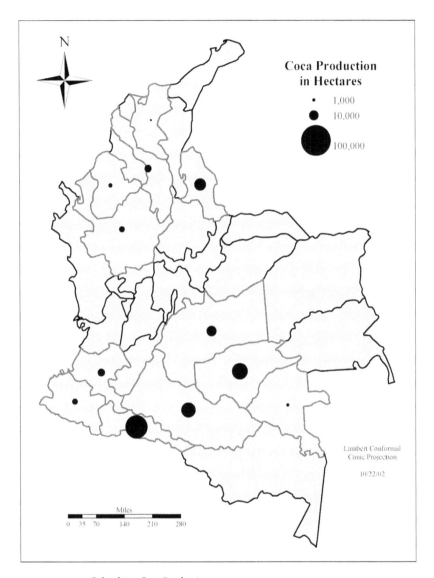

FIGURE 5.3   *Colombian Coca Production 1999*

gations that CINEP "methodology creates a heavy bias against the Colombian government while it grants a wide berth to guerrilla insurgents." O'Grady quotes an embassy report that claims CINEP "follows legal conventions that define 'human rights violations' as crimes that can only be committed by the state or state-sponsored actors, which it presumes paramilitaries to be." In reality, CINEP tallies human rights violations among both state and non-

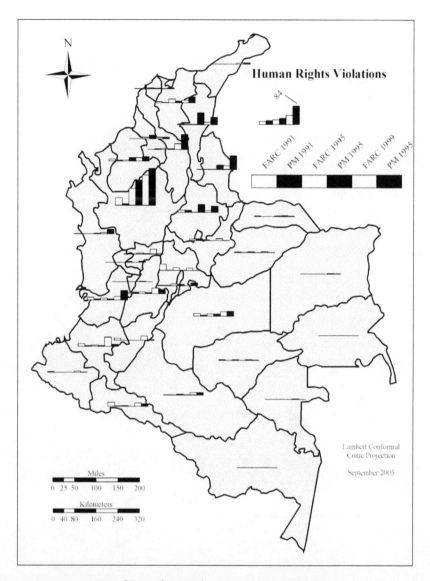

FIGURE 5.4 *FARC and Paramilitary Violence in 1991, 1995, and 1999.*
Source: Banco de Datos sobre Derechos Humanos y Violencia. Política Centro
de Investigación y Educación Popular (CINEP). Bogota, Colombia—2002.

state actors and differentiates between human rights violations committed by different actors, ranging from FARC to the police. At times, CINEP includes incidents in multiple categories (see CINEP 2001); however, this issue is not relevant to this analysis, since only one category is employed in this study. As with any dataset, the potential for bias exists. However, we believe that any bias is consistent throughout time in this study, since the included data were generated directly from CINEP's Banco de Datos by using consistent categories. Especially in politically sensitive areas such as violence statistics, it is prudent to compare nongovernmental and governmental numbers, since different groups may have incentives to overreport or underreport.

Because of this possibility and the controversy surrounding CINEP figures, we have compared official governmental data on terrorism with CINEP figures for this period. The correlations between CINEP figures for total leftist-guerrilla-group violations and governmental figures for terrorism are high (.8277 in the 1994–1998 period, and .7285 in the 1999–2001 period). The governmental figures for terrorism are also correlated with CINEP data for paramilitary violence, but not to the degree that CINEP figures for FARC violence are (.6793 in the 1994–1998 period, and .6696 in the 1999–2001 period). This is not surprising, given the changing legal status of paramilitaries, which creates a potential problem in governmental reporting of these incidents. This bias could be due to two factors: the hesitancy of persons to report paramilitary violations to the government, and potential governmental resistance to report them, given the charges of government-paramilitary cooperation. A comparison of terrorism incidents with human rights violations is not a direct comparison of the same phenomena, but the relatively high correlation provides confidence for CINEP's numbers. Moreover, the CINEP database differentiates attribution of responsibility, which is essential when analyzing the violence of distinct groups with different goals.

An important political factor, state strength, can be assessed by examining figures for spending on justice and security. Outlays for municipal justice and security (aggregated to the department level) are indicators of governmental police and military capabilities. These figures are provided by the Departamento Nacional de Planeación (DNP), in constant 1998 pesos per capita, with a range of 0 to 52 (1993–1998) and 0 to 81 (1999–2002). Additionally, the sectoral GDP for oil output is a proxy for government-provided security, since the pipelines and production facilities receive heavy security and military assistance.[2] As measured in millions of constant 1994 pesos, the sectoral GDP of oil ranges from 0 to 1,140,061 (1993–1998) and from 0 to 1,629,563 (1999–2001).

A diverse set of economic variables is included in these analyses. These data are provided at the department level by DANE. Gross domestic product per capita provides both an indication of the general level of development and a control for the overall level of economic development by department. In 1990, GDP per capita ranged from 18,585 to 12,957,160 pesos. Yearly estimates in 1994 pesos are provided at the department level, and range from 18,585 to 17,411,810 pesos (1993–1998) and from 25,425 to 16,932,040 (1999–2002). The sectoral GDP of animal products is used to capture the ranching sector of the economy. Ranges for the sectoral GDP of animal products are 0–463,619 (1993–1998) and 0–570,311 (1999–2001). The sectoral GDP of coffee ranges from 0 to 470,932 (1993–1998) and from 0 to 284,270 (1999–2001). Poverty, as measured by insufficient provision of basic needs, ranges from 15 percent to 92 percent (1993–1998), and from 13 percent to 91 percent (1999–2001). The percentage of youth population (under age fifteen) ranges from 0.1 to 32.1 (1993–1998) and from 0.1 to 34.3 (1999–2001). Gini coefficients range from .53 to .81 (1993–1998) and from .54 to .81 (1999–2001).[3]

Coca cultivation numbers, in hectares, are provided by the Colombian National Police for 1994–1998, ranging from 0–39,400, and by the United Nations Office on Drugs and Crime for 1999–2001, ranging from 0–66,022. The analyses are divided into two time periods, 1994–1998 and 1999–2001, because of a change in the estimation of coca production, a key variable. Since 1999, coca estimates have been based on satellite images from the United Nations Drug Control Program (UNDCP). Before 1999, they were based on estimates from the Colombian National Police. The Colombian National Police changed their own estimation procedures in 1998.[4]

This overview of some of the main variables used in the later analyses provides evidence of the wide range of variability among economic and political factors within Colombia, which makes a subnational analysis particularly appropriate. Chapter Six examines models of different types of violence. Chapter Seven examines the effects of drugs and violence on the economy. Both chapters are based on subnational analyses.

SIX

GUNS AND PROTECTION

Guerrillas and Paramilitaries

Although Colombia is one of Latin America's oldest democracies, with a history of unusually competent economic governance, it is also home to one of the most entrenched leftist insurgencies in the world and a brutal paramilitary movement. Many factors have been put forward to explain the insurgency, including geography and history, as discussed in Chapter Two, as well as the economy, government, and demography. Although historical and geographic legacies influence contemporary Colombia—and to some extent influence the characteristics of the conflict and any potential solutions—they do not change during the time period covered by this chapter (1990–2001), so they are not included in the statistical models. However, many other important factors do vary, both in intensity and geographic range. We will address first the political factors and then the economic factors theorized to be important. Colombia is an ideal case to test these factors, given the quality of the subnational-level data and the variability of violence, economic performance, and political factors within the country. Furthermore, although there are indigenous communities in Colombia, neither ethnic nor religious divisions fuel the conflict, so a clear examination of alternative explanations is possible.[1]

As discussed in Chapter Four, the main leftist guerrilla groups have long histories and an established presence in Colombia. These groups were partially motivated by the exclusionary nature of the Colombian political system during the National Front. Gonzalez (2002) states that the expansion of FARC is a result of a lack of opportunities for the population, a failure of the political system to be inclusive, and a lack of professionalism in public administration. The AUC is a more recent phenomenon, although paramilitary groups have also been active in Colombia for many years. Since these violent groups have very different origins and aims, it is important to examine different types of violence separately. Additionally, and especially in such a protracted conflict, it is crucial to acknowledge that factors encouraging the emergence of violent groups may not be the same as those explaining the persistence of conflict. Pécaut (1997) and Sánchez Torres, Diaz, and Formisano (2003) remind scholars, especially in the case of FARC, that factors contributing to its later growth can be independent of factors that encouraged its emergence. Pécaut (1997) states that the pervasive Colombian violence has created its own influences on society, regardless of the original causes of the violence. Understanding old and new dynamics is essential to crafting an appropriate and effective policy response to the challenge of insurgency.

Much of the discussion of insurgency has emphasized greed or grievance. As discussed in Chapter Four, guerrilla groups have historical grievances against the Colombian state, traditional parties, and political elites. The paramilitaries have been motivated by grievances against the guerrillas and by a desire to act where the state has not or cannot. Moreover, the field of the conflict is one whose geography makes establishing centralized control difficult, as discussed in Chapter Two. Duffield (2000) cites the following requirements for a successful insurgency: a home base, a resource base, access to a supply network, and access to international trade. The fractious history of Colombia, its open markets, its history of gem smuggling, and its rugged geography create numerous places that are favorable for the creation of home bases for insurgencies and access to underground networks. Bayart, Ellis, and Hibou (1999), in a study of African conflicts, cite remote border regions as ideal places for bases, especially if the governmental presence is already ineffective. Although Colombia has a history of internal strife in remote regions, the current conflict has evolved to envelop much of the country. Figure 6.1 provides an overview of changes in overall magnitudes of violence.

Figure 5.3 provided an overview of the changing geographic spread of the violence. Figure 6.1 provides an annual overview of national violence trends. Governmental human rights violations were fairly stable, peaking in 2001. Total leftist violence spiked in 1992 and 1994, then generally increased from 1998 until 2000, when it began to decrease. Paramilitary violence increased from 1995 to 1997 and again from 1998 until 2001. In general, violence trends tended to follow trends in coca cultivation. Figure 6.2 demonstrates the changes in both the geographic distribution and the magnitude of coca cultivation during the time periods studied. In 1995, three departments had substantial coca cultivation; by 2001, production had both disbursed throughout the country and increased.

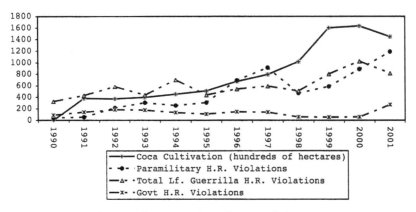

FIGURE 6.1   *Violence Trends 1990–2001 (HR = human rights)*

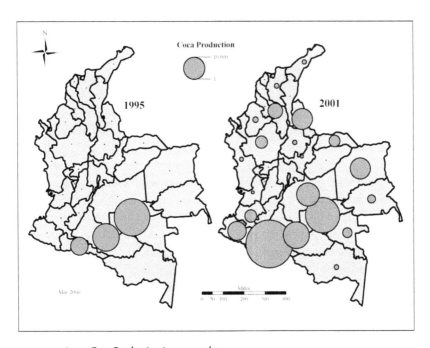

FIGURE 6.2   *Coca Production in 1995 and 2001*

THE THEORETICAL DEBATE
AND TESTABLE HYPOTHESES

Numerous literatures are relevant to this study, and definitional issues should be examined. Classic works regarding vigilante groups, revolutionary violence, civil war, terrorism, and theories of insurgency can be useful for understanding the types of violence found in Colombia. At one time or another, Colombia could be considered as suffering from all of the aforementioned types of violence. It is essential to differentiate among different types of violence, since some factors are theorized to influence different types in varying ways.

Definitions of different types of violence, especially terrorism, have been described as "essentially contested concepts" in the style of Gallie (1956) and Connolly (1993, 10). Other types of violence, such as civil war, have relatively clear definitions. For example, Small and Singer define a civil war as "any armed conflict that involves (a) military action internal to the metropole, (b) the active participation of the national government, and (c) effective resistance by both sides" (1982, 210). Traditionally, there is a threshold of 1,000 deaths annually; see also Sambanis (2004b) for a critique of this definition. Insurgency (or guerrilla warfare) has more generally agreed-upon definitions: "Insurgent activity—including guerrilla warfare, terrorism, and political mobilization . . . is designed to weaken governmental control and legitimacy while increasing insurgent control and legitimacy. The common denominator of most insurgent groups is their desire to control a particular area. This objective differentiates insurgent groups from purely terrorist organizations, whose objectives do not include the creation of an alternative government capable of controlling a given area or country" (CIA, n.d., 2).

Paramilitary or vigilante violence is somewhat clearly defined. According to Rosenbaum, vigilantism "consists of acts or threats of coercion in violation of the formal boundaries of an established sociopolitical order which, however, are intended by the violators to defend that order from some form of subversion" (1974, 542). He recognizes three types of vigilantism, including crime control, social-group control, and regime control. According to Huggins, it is helpful to analyze these movements according to three variables: spontaneity versus extensive planning, organization (internal cohesion versus fragmentation), and state involvement (overt, covert, or indirect) (1991, 8).

Terrorism, however, as a concept, is significantly more muddled and contested. For example, Crenshaw states: "Terrorism is an ambiguous variable not easily measured or quantified, in part because there are multiple forms of terrorism, and they are easily confused with other styles of violence" (1995, 6).

Weinberg, Pedahzur, and Hirsch-Hoefler identify a consensus definition of terrorism: "Terrorism is a politically motivated tactic involving the threat or use of force or violence in which the pursuit of publicity plays a significant role" (2004, 786). However, as they point out, terrorism as a concept suffers "from 'border' and 'membership' problems. Where does terrorism stop and other forms of political violence begin?" (778–779). Colombia, in particular, suffers from such problems, since different types of violence overlap and interact cyclically. To better analyze the Colombian conflict, we have divided up the relevant factors into political and economic drivers of the different types of conflicts.

POLITICAL FACTORS

As discussed in Chapter Two, Colombia has a long history of internal conflict and a weak central government, problems dating from before independence. As a result, the central government has lacked a coherent and consistent presence throughout the country. The country, in some respects, is a nominal nation, of which many parts have never been under effective central government control. Power vacuums are filled by leftist guerrilla groups or rightist paramilitary groups: "Bogotá has lacked significant representation in whole sections of the country. This has engendered effects that are ignored until times of national crisis. The central government has not provided the basic services for peripheral areas that it has offered to urban or even coastal Colombia. Infrastructure in the interior, to include roads, health care and education, is far more rudimentary than in other areas" (Watson 2000, 530).

The lack of state presence has been theorized to be a contributing factor to many of Colombia's conflicts throughout its history (Pécaut 2001, 33). Ortiz Sarmiento (1990–1991) generally finds that violence during *la violencia* was a product of an incremental chain of retaliation between Liberals and Conservatives, and that private justice has been common throughout Colombian history because of a relatively weak police and military presence. For example, in 1949 there were only 15,000 soldiers, compared to 4,500 guerrillas. Later, under Rojas Pinilla (1953–1957), the military increased to 42,000, still a relatively small number in a country of 11.5 million (Ortiz Sarmiento 1990–1991, 253–254). Contemporary analysts still consider the Colombian military to be relatively small. Byman et al. (2001) criticize contemporary Colombia for its low military spending—only 3.1 percent of GDP in 1998. The relatively low military spending and small military force for a country facing a decades-long insurgency reflect the historical weakness of the Colombian state.

Although problems of state presence may be initially more evident in rural areas, the reach of the state is not uniform even in heavily populated cities. Perhaps the most pressing urban issue in Colombia today is the forced eviction of poor inhabitants to the margins of urban areas (Everett 2001). Given the persistence of the classic Spanish colonial urban form, the peripheries of the cities are those areas with the least access to governmental services such as police and fire protection; the least likely to have access to basic utilities, such as water, sanitation, and electricity; and the least likely to provide educational services and economic opportunity. Rangel Suarez claims that "throughout the 1980s and 1990s, the guerrilla groups' parasitic relationship with regional economies has frequently developed in areas where the state's judicial norms and institutions have been abandoned in the face of sudden economic booms" (2000, 583). The comprehensive challenge of creating a consistent and coherent state has been recognized as a major problem for the control of nonstate violent groups. Marks claims that "drugs, to repeat, are not the central element of Colombia's problem. That is state fragmentation. We can talk of nothing until the government actually exercises its writ within national territory" (2003, 96).

For Colombia, two indicators of state presence are included in the analysis presented here. Actual justice and security spending at the department level is available. Additionally, we incorporate the sectoral GDP output of oil. Although many studies will use oil either alone or in conjunction with other primary exports to serve as an indicator of lootable exports, in this case, the inclusion of oil should be treated separately. It has long been known that Colombia has substantial reserves of petroleum. The first commercial concessions for the exploration and exploitation of oil resources were granted in 1905. By 1950, petroleum had become the second-largest export, behind coffee (Griess 1946). In recent years, the investment policies of the Colombian government regarding petroleum have been liberalized and the pace of exploration has increased. In Colombia, oil is a parastate asset, and the state gives it priority for protection. Because of this, we include it as an indicator of state presence.[2] In Colombia, the top oil-producing departments include Arauca, Casanare, Huila, and Santander.

The degree of state presence affects paramilitaries, but differently than it does the insurgency. Vigilantism "is fostered by what the state does not (or cannot) do, not so much by the state's direction of it" (Huggins 1991, 8). Vigilante groups typically emerge in response to an insurgency or a weak state. Colombia is a weak state facing a forty-year insurgency that the government has not been able to control. Rosenbaum theorizes that vigilante groups are more likely to form when there is a widespread belief that "a regime is ineffective in dealing with the challenges to the prevailing sociopolitical order" and that vigilante justice is therefore justifiable (1974, 545).

Regarding paramilitary violence, Hayes finds that widespread exposure to violence (in this case, guerrilla violence) results in support for paramilitary movements, and this support can lead to a "continuous and perpetual cycle" (2001, 902). Sprinzak further notes, "Vigilante movements rarely perceive themselves involved in conflict with the government and the prevailing concept of law. They are neither revolutionary nor interested in the destruction of authority" (1995, 29). Specifically in the Colombian case, based on 1985 and 1993 municipal-level data, Cubides finds strong correlations between a paramilitary presence and the periphery of the country, institutional weakness, and low state presence (1997, 24–25). For this reason, we incorporate leftist-guerrilla human rights violations to account for the level of insurgency.

As Rosenbaum (1974) recognizes, vigilantism poses a risk for the regime, since regime legitimacy may decline over time and vigilante groups may begin to usurp control. As for state involvement, even without officially blessing the operations, individuals within legitimate agencies may choose a vigilante route: "Unable to suppress terrorism through the ordinary legal system, police and military officers decided to take the law into their hands and to eliminate the leftist threat privately" (Sprinzak 1995, 30). Mason and Krane (1989) clarify how the organization of particular vigilante groups or death squads reflects the depth of state involvement.

Human rights groups and the Colombian government contest the extent of state involvement in Colombian paramilitary groups (Amnesty International 2000, 2002a, 2002b).

> They may consist of secret police, special counterinsurgency units, or regular units of the armed forces engaged in various forms of institutionalized violence. They may also consist of armed units structured along military lines but organizationally autonomous from state security forces, at least in a formal or legal sense. Among these are regional and local irregulars, mercenaries, private armies and vigilante units engaged in noninstitutionalized violence in the service of local elites who share the government's desire to preserve the economic and political status quo. (Mason and Krane 1989, 178; see also Stohl and Lopez 1984)

In other words, some in the government viewed the paramilitaries as a form of covert operations.

In general, governments may choose to hire mercenaries or to allow private military groups to operate as a way to supplement their regular forces.

According to Metz, "As nations seek ways to attain a surge capacity without the expense of sustaining a large, peacetime military, and as they face difficulties recruiting from their own populations, contracting will be an attractive option for filling their ranks" (2000, ix). Similarly, Eugene Smith argues that governments turned to private military corporations "when they lacked the requisite means to accomplish desired ends. Those organizations represented a convenient way to overcome strategic mismatches" (2002–2003, 111). Cynics counter with charges that resorting to mercenaries is a way to avoid oversight and accountability.

In addition to issues of state presence, it is important to include the proportion of youth population and levels of repression as explanatory variables for different levels of guerrilla violence. Rubio (2001) finds that youth (age of the population) and inequality are the only factors that explain the expansion of FARC. In general, scholars such as Schock (1996) find that higher levels of guerilla violence are more associated with semirepressive regimes than with more repressive or less repressive regimes. Holmes (2001) found that indiscriminate state violence undermined support for the government and could facilitate rebel recruitment and operation. For this reason, we also include paramilitary violence and governmental repression into the model to explain levels of guerrilla violence.

We test the following hypotheses to examine the relationship between political factors and violence:

In regard to guerrilla violence:

Hypothesis G1: Guerrilla violence is expected to emerge in the context of weak state presence. Low levels of per capita justice and security spending should be associated with higher levels of guerrilla violence. Additionally, it is expected that areas with higher oil production will have lower levels of guerrilla violence.

Hypothesis G2: Higher levels of governmental repression will be associated with higher levels of guerrilla violence.

Hypothesis G3: Guerrilla violence is expected to be higher in areas with proportionally high levels of youth population. Areas with high percentages of youth will have higher levels of guerrilla violence.

In regard to paramilitary violence:

Hypothesis P1: Paramilitary violence is expected to emerge in the context of an insurgency.

Hypothesis P2: Paramilitary violence is expected to be higher in areas of low state presence, as indicated by either low sectoral GDP of oil or low per capita justice and security spending.

ECONOMIC FACTORS

There are two main avenues by which economic factors may encourage insurgency in general. First, economic factors may serve as a grievance for conflict. Second, they can provide both a funding basis or a protective motivation for conflict. In short, it is important to examine economic factors to understand both recruitment and resource aspects of nonstate violence. We examine both types of economic drivers in this analysis.

Traditionally, guerrilla nonstate violence can be understood as partly motivated in response to economic grievance. Poor economic conditions, especially poverty, can inspire sedition. The endemic poverty in the squatter settlements on the fringes of urban cores has been seen to breed violence, as evidenced by the groups of young assassins from the deprived neighborhoods of Medellín (Von der Walde 2001). Bottía Noguera (2003) finds that FARC expands in areas of rural poverty, poor land quality, and natural parks. There is a difference of opinion among scholars about the relationship between inequality and violence. Some, after controlling for the level of economic development or poverty, find no relationship between inequality and violence (Hardy 1979; Weede and Tiefenbach 1981; Weede 1987; P. Collier 2000).[3] Whether or not inequality and poverty are direct causes of the Colombian conflict, they are well recognized as important contributing factors to it. Guerrero Baron and Mond find that "concerning the content of the conflict, there is consensus that great social inequality and instability give rise to a dynamic that confers legitimacy on revolutionary projects and violent alternatives" (2001, 13).

One direct connection between poverty and Colombian violence is that in many cases the guerrillas, regardless of ideology, offer relatively higher wages than other available agricultural jobs, and this facilitates recruitment (Sánchez 1998, 40).[4] Rural Colombia is plagued with poverty, low economic productivity, and underutilization of resources, including land (Heshusius Rodríguez 2005, 3). As discussed, the Colombian government has created a classification of estratos to determine the level of overall development. These municipal-level data are aggregated to the department level in Figure 5.2. Santafé de Bogotá, traditionally a department of low guerrilla violence, has the highest level of estrato wealth. Peripheral departments, such as Amazonas,

Vaupés, Guainía, and Chocó, have the lowest levels of estrato wealth. This is a visually separate pattern of the relative level of violence by department, as shown in Figure 5.4. For example, the highly conflicted department of Antioquia has a 4 out of possible 6 rating of estrato wealth. Likewise, Cauca, Norte de Santander, and Valle de Cauca, have middle ranges of estrato wealth, but relatively high levels of violence.

An alternative check is to examine GDP per capita and poverty (see Figure 6.3). Interestingly, although the poorest departments have both low GDP per capita and high rates of poverty, there is a wide range of poverty rates in departments with a lower-middle range of GDP incomes. Overall there is a wide range of poverty and wealth by department.

In the case of Colombia, long-standing structural challenges in the countryside have resulted in persistent land conflicts.[5] The concentration of land, especially agriculturally productive land, is a main underlying source of rural inequality. Land concentration is a source not only of rural inequality but also of rural violence: "If there is an epicenter, or flashpoint, that could have set the process leading to the war system . . . it would be the conflicts that have surrounded the distribution of land in Colombia ever since it became independent, in the 19th century. And in this century, the policies of the state toward the agrarian sector have done little, if anything, either to ameliorate that conflict and/or to protect the peasant settlers (colonos) on public lands from the incursion of big ranchers and large-scale agribusiness" (Richani 1997, 38). Generally speaking, the rapid increase in commercial agricultural activity over the past half century has changed patterns of landownership and influenced the evolution of the conflict: "Perhaps the most basic explanation for the high levels of violence in Colombia is the struggle for status, often over land, and economic advantage" (McLean 2002, 125).

Areas of severe inequality, as indicated by high Gini coefficients, include Nariño, Cauca, Chocó, Caldas, and Quindío. Although these departments experience violence, they are not historically the most violent departments, which calls into question any simple and direct causality between violence and inequality. Although inequality can cause grievances, there appear to be other factors directly affecting the levels of violence.

Gonzalez (2002) concludes that social problems in both urban and rural areas create an environment favorable to violence, and that the lack of effective agricultural reform and the criminalization of the peasant serve only to perpetuate the violence. Between 1955 and 1985, the land area under cultivation with modern commercial crops almost tripled, rising from 11.9 percent to 41 percent of total cultivated area. Although the growth rate of the agricultural sector has lagged behind the growth rate of the Colombian econ-

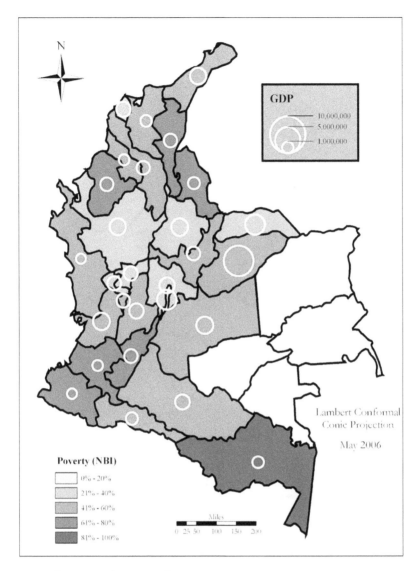

FIGURE 6.3   *NBI and GDP per capita*

omy as a whole, the production has been more efficient, given the ongoing and dramatic process of urbanization (T. Schultz 1971) and the concomitant reduction of the rural labor force (Pombo 1992). This transition of the rural agricultural economy aggravated the existing inequality and land conflict. According to Deininger, the lack of successful land reform also contributes to rural violence (1999, 655).

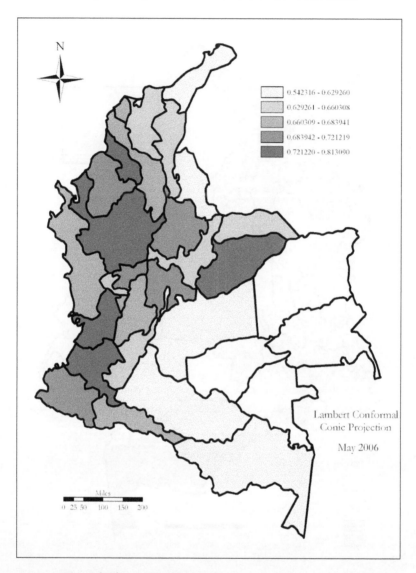

N

	0.542316 - 0.629260
	0.629261 - 0.660308
	0.660309 - 0.683941
	0.683942 - 0.721219
	0.721220 - 0.813090

Lambert Conformal
Conic Projection

May 2006

Miles
0 25 50   100   150   200

FIGURE 6.4   *Colombian Inequality (GINI)*

A specific transition of the rural economy concerns coffee. The coffee economy has changed dramatically in recent years, causing conditions of rural crisis. Because of declining world coffee prices, coffee production has not provided a sustainable income source for rural populations. Moreover, crop substitution plans have not been successful. As a result, rural economic conditions have deteriorated, creating dissatisfaction in the rural areas and conditions ripe for guerrilla recruitment (Richani 1997). Trujillo and Badel find that departments with the most violence are located in regions where coffee and coca are cultivated (1997, 273–275). Therefore, we separate out the sectoral GDP of coffee in our statistical models in order to examine the effect of the coffee economy on conflict.

Poverty and inequality have both been theorized to cause conflict. In the Colombian case, this is specifically manifested in long-standing land conflicts. According to Franco, "The fundamental aspect of the economic context is the structural inequality of Colombian society. Colombia is a good example of the fact that there is no unidirectional relationship between poverty and violence. It also is a good example of the fact that inequality and violence are strongly related" (2003, 2035). The Colombian government has recognized the threat to stability from rural poverty and inequality. However, land-reform efforts have largely failed, and in some cases have created conditions ripe for the emergence of paramilitary groups. This continuing conflict over land is the "underlying cause of many of the bloodiest incidents" (McLean 2002, 125). Many paramilitary groups originally formed to protect large landowners from peasant land conflicts.

In addition to hampering efforts at land reform, the violence also creates a negative cycle by increasing the costs of production and the risks to investment in rural areas while also preventing the formation of social capital and aggravating poverty (FIDA 2003). The loss of productive land reduces opportunities for rural employment, which is made worse by the high levels of urban unemployment. The Fondo International de Desarrollo Agrícola claims that this forces people to join either the illegal drug sector or the armed groups, intensifying violence and insecurity. Poor economic conditions precipitate violence, and violence has negative effects on the economy. The effects of this cycle are further examined in Chapter Seven.

Second, economic resources can serve as a financial basis for insurgent groups. In general, Paul Collier finds, "The factors which account for this difference between failure and success are to be found not in the 'causes' which these two rebel organizations claim to espouse, but in their radically different opportunities to raise revenue . . . the economic theory of conflict argues that the motivation of conflict is unimportant; what matters is whether the organization can sustain itself financially" (2000, 9). In particular, primary commodity exports are "lootable because their production relies heavily on assets which are long-lasting and immobile" (9). This prominent theory focuses on lootable primary exports and the onset of conflict; see P. Collier et al. (2003) for a more refined version of the theory, including probabilities for the onset of new conflicts relative to primary-commodity dependence. Scholars such as Arbelaez, Echavarria, and Gaviria (2002, 42–43) find the onset of violence is "related to the sudden development of primary products (gold, emeralds, oil, bananas, cocaine)" in particular areas, especially those with low state presence. Similarly, Baron, Pérez, and Rowland find that violence tends to be concentrated in regions of the country "where property rights are weak and where the concentration of lucrative commercial goods is high" (2004, 65). In general, new production (of coffee, coca, etc.) reignites old tensions. As new lands come under production and peasants are displaced, groups of bandits form to provide "protection" for the landowners from the recently displaced peasants. Beginning in the 1980s, with dramatic increases in drug agriculture, the aim has been to gain dominance in the form of land ownership (Meertens 1997).

It is theorized that products of enclave production are frequently targeted for looting: "It is evident that items produced in enclaves are more susceptible to predation. That makes them more attractive targets for both personal rulers and predatory rebels than are small agriculturalists because neither predation nor general state or market collapse will stop the revenue from flowing: even if their products are often looted, enclave producers will continue to generate goods because of extreme asset specificity, and because of general concentration, production will continue even in the face of general collapse" (Leonard and Straus 2003, 15). In Colombia, Sánchez documents that areas rich in primary export goods have become points of confrontation because of the importance of controlling these lucrative zones (1998, 39). Other scholars have taken the theory beyond onset to explain the magnitude and persistence of conflict: "Conflicts that begin in remote corners of failing states, which are sustained by marketable natural resources (diamonds, crude oil, coca) are difficult to bring to a conclusion. All too often, the perpetrators, both state actors and rebels, find the chaos of war conducive to the accumulation of personal wealth. Ongoing conflict provides opportunities for looting or the collection of protection money" (Silberfein 2003, n.p.).

In Colombia, the most important enclave product is coca. Our analysis, however, does not utilize the general category of primary exports, for two reasons. First, we refine Collier's analysis by examining illicit drugs separately, as a unique category of lootable exports. The coca question is particularly important for the paramilitaries, because of the mixed origin of paramilitary groups. Second, to understand paramilitary violence, instead of using a general category of primary exports, we choose the ranching sector of the economy, which has historically been associated with the emergence of private armies to protect landowners from land conflict with peasants. We also include the coffee sector to take into account the paramilitary presence in rural areas.

It is important to examine the key sources of financing for violent groups. In Colombia, as discussed earlier, oil should not be included as an easily looted enclave product, because it is prioritized for protection by the government. However, coca should be examined in this way. Many scholars and U.S. officials cite the importance of coca production in fueling the Colombian conflict (Rochlin 2003; Byman et al. 2001; Pécaut 1997; Bibes 2001; Bottía Noguera 2003; Rabasa and Chalk 2001; Thoumi 1995a). Sánchez, Diaz, and Formisano (2003) concur that increased participation by FARC in illegal-drug activities has helped perpetuate and fuel the conflict; additionally, areas with a high FARC presence are associated with higher rates of violence, and vice versa. In Colombia, guerrillas fight for control of areas that can provide financing (Bottía Noguera 2003, 44). Finally, Gonzalez (2002) finds more FARC fighting in areas of economic expansion, weak state presence, and agricultural production, including coca.

Scholars have discussed the financial basis of FARC, but there is disagreement regarding the extent to which it is funded through drug activity. Some claim that FARC is itself a cartel. For example, Villamarín Pulido cites military documents claiming that FARC is the third-largest cartel in Colombia (1996, 19). Despite suggestions that guerrilla groups such as FARC are nothing more than another drug cartel, the reality is much more complicated. In areas where the guerrillas are too strong to eliminate, the drug traffickers pay the guerrillas a "tax" on their proceeds. Some scholars have probed the pragmatism of the relationship (Steiner 1999). In testimony before the U.S. House of Representatives, Marc Chernick dismissed claims that guerrilla groups operate as cartels, calling them a distorted view of the true relationship between guerrillas and the drug trade. Instead, the groups tax the drug trade as any other source of income—illicit or licit (U.S. House 1996). FARC's financial basis rests upon both kidnapping and extortion of both licit and illicit businesses in areas under its control (Shifter 1999, 15; Sánchez, Diaz, and Formisano 2003, 12). Ortiz Sarmiento estimates that the group taxes production at rates of 10 percent and commerce at 8 percent (1990–1991, 269). Rochlin (2003) discusses the complicated relationship between FARC and coca producers. He cites an interview with the UNDCP in which officials explain that some FARC members are involved, but it is not uniform among the leaders or the rank and file. However, he claims that much of the department-by-department spread of FARC was due to drug cultivation in areas of its control (137, 99).

Some scholars cite particular times and circumstances in which there have been ties between narcos and guerrillas, and other instances in which the narcos worked with (or formed) paramilitaries to counter guerrillas. Edgar Torres Arias (1995) tells of a decision by the narcos in 1977 to locate processing facilities in guerrilla-controlled areas, beyond governmental purview. As the narcos purchased lands, their incentive to cooperate with guerrillas changed. Eventually, instead of having the guerrillas provide order (and impose their tax), the narcos funded their own paramilitary armies, often fighting the guerrillas for local control (Pécaut 1997, 908; Rochlin 2003, 100). Economic resources are important, independent of group motivation or ideology. Romero finds that both the guerrillas and the paramilitaries have financed their increased military capacities through drug-related income (2003, 33).

In addition to directly fueling the conflict, drug money can undermine the legal economy, creating conditions ripe for guerrilla conflict: "The trafficking of illegal drugs to the numerous consumers in the first world nations, which was commonly perceived in the mid-1970s as a path toward a more even distribution of wealth in Colombia, has worsened the concentration of rural property and other resources and has increased the levels of inequality, and thereby, the levels of violence" (Franco 2003, 2035). Similarly, Thoumi points out that the drug trade "has had pervasive effects on the Colombian economy, the most important of which has been its catalytic effect that promoted greater disregard for the law and social norms" (1995a, 249). Moreover, it has hampered local development efforts, thus creating economic discontent that may benefit guerrillas.

Another factor for understanding paramilitary violence is the presence of assets. Instead of examining enclave production, which may be associated with the onset of conflict, paramilitary violence should be understood as emerging to protect assets: "In the Latin American experience, most important among such actors have been large landowners, who have mobilized paramilitary forces to defend their properties not only against rebel attack, but against any imaginable agitation" (Jones 2004, 129). According to Cubides, "From being defenders of newly acquired and threatened agricultural property, they [the paramilitaries] have become controllers of territory. Through that process they have learned that violence, in addition to accomplishing retaliatory objectives to satisfy private aims, is an efficient mechanism of social control" (2001, 132). Restrepo, Spagat, and Vargas find a general association of higher levels of paramilitary violence with "zones of concentrated land tenure, previous guerrilla activities and presence of coca crops" (2003, 24). Especially in conjunction with low state presence, we expect higher levels of violence in areas of higher economic growth and higher economic development.

From the preceding discussion, the following hypotheses are developed for guerrilla violence.

Hypothesis G4: Guerrilla violence is expected to be more common in areas of economic crisis. This can be indicated by high levels of coffee production, poverty, and negative growth rates.

Hypothesis G5: Higher levels of insurgency will be associated with income inequality.

Hypothesis G6: Guerrilla violence is positively associated with coca cultivation because it provides an accessible source of funding and long-term sustainability for guerrilla groups. Coca cultivation should be associated with higher levels of guerrilla violence.

In regard to paramilitary violence, the following hypotheses are developed.

Hypothesis P3: Paramilitary violence is positively associated with coca cultivation because it provides an accessible source of funding and long-term sustainability for paramilitary groups. Coca cultivation should be associated with higher levels of paramilitary violence.

Hypothesis P4: Paramilitary violence should be associated with the protection of assets. Violence should be higher in areas with more ranch-animal production and in coffee growing regions. Additionally, more violence should occur with higher GDP growth.

Hypothesis P5: Paramilitary violence should be higher in areas of high inequality.

METHODOLOGY

The data used in this study present two challenges for proper model specification: appropriate distribution and an excess of zeros. Many studies of event data utilize a Poisson distribution. Considering our data and theory, the assumptions inherent in the Poisson model make it an inappropriate choice. First, the Poisson distribution assumes that the arrival rate of the dependent variable (violence) is constant. In other words, it assumes that incidents of violence are independent of one another. Second, this independence results in a rough equivalence between the mean and the distribution of the events. This assumption is violated both in theory and by the characteristics of all the different types of violence data used in this study. In theory, we would expect that once violence occurs, more would follow, creating a cycle of violence. An alternative expectation is that a hegemonic situation would result in which violence would decrease as enemies were eliminated. For example, Duncan finds lower levels of violence (at the municipal level) when either the guerrillas or the paramilitaries exercise hegemonic authority (2004, 9). In either case, the next violent event is not independent of the previous one, making the Poisson an inappropriate choice theoretically. Additionally, our data are overdispersed—the means and variances are not equal. The use of the Poisson distribution in this case would result in a loss of efficiency, a potential inconsistency, incorrect reported standard errors, and a poor fit. Since our dependent violence variables are overdispersed, a negative binomial distribution was chosen, since overdispersion and event dependence do not violate inherent assumptions of this distribution.

Additionally, our data have a large proportion of zeros (departments that do not experience particular types of violence). Because of this, we need to use a model that can take into account this distribution of the dependent variable. Formally, to test whether a zero-inflated model is appropriate, a Vuong test is utilized. All our models in the first period have a strongly significant Vuong statistic, indicating that the zero-inflated model is appropriate. Theoretically, the zero-inflated negative binomial model allows for different factors to account for the absence of violence (zeros) and the presence of violence (nonzeros). In the case of Colombia, the forces that contribute to an absence of violence may be different from those that explain the intensity of violence. The negative binomial is a better fit for the theory, since the underlying assumptions about why there is, or is not, violence are different. For example, a zero may exist because there are no resources to capture in a particular area or because there is a hegemonic situation. In the later period, a negative binomial model is used because the Vuong statistic is less significant.

After extensive testing of alternative specifications, the zero-inflated negative binomial regression was selected to model the different types of violence in Colombia. For our analyses of violence, we use a zero-inflated negative binomial regression model because the dependent variables (human rights violations committed by one group or another) are counts; there is an excess of zeros in the dependent variables (many departments do not have the relevant type of political violence at one time or another); and the data are overdispersed (the conditional standard deviation is much larger than the mean in the sample, reflecting the dependence of the incidents of violence in the dependent variables). For a discussion of model specification for count models, see Simpson and Horowitz (2005), Cameron and Trivedi (1998), and

Yau, Wang, and Lee (2003). Moreover, to further account for unobserved heterogeneity, the errors have been clustered by department.

This first model examines FARC violence (see Table 6.1).[6] GDP per capita in 1990 is included as a control variable for the overall level of economic development. The included variables are consistent across the two time periods, so comparisons are valid. For the political variables, it is expected that weak state presence, repression, and high youth population will be positively related to high levels of guerrilla violence. In the first time period, in areas that already had some guerrilla violence, FARC activity was increased as less money was spent on justice and security. In the second time period, the reverse occurred (see Table 6.2). This may reflect Plan Colombia's priorities to increase state presence and security spending in areas of guerrilla activity. Interestingly, in both time periods, oil production is associated with lower levels of FARC violence. As noted earlier, oil in Colombia is a parastate asset prioritized for protection by the Colombian military. In Colombia, repression can come from two sources: the government or the paramilitaries. Although the rhetoric of the paramilitaries is that they are effective at fighting guerrillas, FARC models consistently show the conflict escalating along with paramilitary violence, as opposed to paramilitary violence being effective at ending guerrilla violence. Governmental violence is positive in both periods, but significant only in the later period. It should be noted that these variables measure human rights violations—not traditional military conflict between warring parties. For youth population, in both time periods in areas experiencing guerrilla violence, a higher percentage of youth population was associated with higher levels of FARC violence. Economically, it is expected that areas of economic crisis, high inequality, and coca cultivation will have high levels of guerrilla violence. As for economic crisis, negative GDP growth in the first time period aggravated levels of FARC violence. High levels of both poverty and coffee production are associated with the emergence of FARC violence and the intensification of FARC violence. In the first model, high levels of inequality are associated with increased risks of new FARC violence. In the early time period, coca cultivation is associated with both the emergence and the intensity of FARC violence.

Guerrilla groups other than FARC that contribute to guerrilla violence tend to be more localized. This fact makes a statistical analysis of each group more difficult, since the sample sizes of these groups are smaller. Because of this, we do not conduct analyses of groups that do not have a wide geographic spread. However, by aggregating all the violent leftist groups together, we can check for commonalities among them. Table 6.3 examines all guerrilla violence,

6.1 ZERO-INFLATED NEGATIVE BINOMIAL REGRESSION OF HUMAN RIGHTS VIOLATIONS COMMITTED BY FARC, 1993–1998

Independent variable	Logit estimate	z	Negative binomial estimate	z
GDP per capita (1990)	2.1235	0.55	0.3857	1.19
GDP growth	0.1827	1.12	-0.0185†	-1.66
Government HR violations (lagged 1 year)	1.6752	1.46	0.0056	1.06
Paramilitary HR violations (lagged 1 year)	0.9991*	1.98	0.0154**	2.50
Coca cultivation (lagged 1 year)	0.0054***	3.75	0.00004*	2.09
Justice and security spending (per capita, lagged 1 year)	-0.2217	-0.84	-0.0286***	-3.28
Youth (%, lagged 1 year)	-0.0409	-0.20	0.0237**	2.43
Poverty (lagged 1 year)	-0.0718	-0.53	0.0230**	2.37
Gini*100 (lagged 1 year)	0.4536*	2.25	0.0056	0.23
Sectoral GDP of coffee (lagged 1 year)	-1.3797	-1.290	.4002***	4.05
Sectoral GDP of oil (lagged 1 year)	0.00002	1.05	-0.0000†	-1.61
Constant	0.9141	1.36	-0.0324	-0.02
Ln α			-0.9513	-1.35
α			0.3862	
N	134			
(FARC HR violations) > 0	109			
Mean FARC HR violations	8.87			
LR χ² (12)	749.78***			

***p < .001; **p < .01; *p < .05; †p < .10 (standard errors adjusted for clustering by department)

Note: Logit model of the probability that the number of FARC human rights violations is greater than 0.

combining leftist groups such as the ELN and FARC. In the first time period, the zero-inflated negative binomial is used. For the second time period, the zero-inflated negative binomial did not converge with the same variables. To facilitate interpretation, the model was run as a negative binomial with the same variables. For the political variables, it is expected that weak state presence, repression, and a high youth population will be associated with high levels of guerrilla violence. Justice and security spending was insignificant in these models. Oil was contradictory, with increased oil production being associated with the emergence of guerrilla violence, but in areas already experiencing violence, higher levels of oil production are associated with lower levels of violence. This contrary finding could be due to the combination of ELN and FARC violence. The ELN often recruits among disaffected oil workers. Both governmental and paramilitary human rights violations are associated

6.2 ZERO-INFLATED NEGATIVE BINOMIAL REGRESSION OF HUMAN RIGHTS VIOLATIONS COMMITTED BY FARC, 1999–2001

Independent variable	Logit estimate	z	Negative binomial estimate	z
GDP per capita (1990)	−2.1565	−0.090	−0.1586	−1.05
GDP growth	0.2411	1.53	−0.0003	−0.05
Government HR violations (lagged 1 year)	0.3577†	1.67	0.0790***	3.88
Paramilitary HR violations (lagged 1 year)	1.3348†	1.74	0.0031†	1.80
Coca cultivation (lagged 1 year)	0.00001	0.24	0.00001	1.17
Justice and security spending (per capita, lagged 1 year)	1.0582†	1.84	0.0746*	2.25
Youth (%, lagged 1 year)	−2.1333†	−1.71	0.1677***	3.82
Poverty (lagged 1 year)	0.2511**	2.71	0.0021**	2.75
Gini*100 (lagged 1 year)	1.742	1.13	0.1372	0.83
Sectoral GDP of coffee (lagged 1 year)	3.3891*	1.94	0.4874***	6.10
Sectoral GDP of oil (lagged 1 year)	0.0333†	1.88	−0.00084*	−2.82
Constant	−20.6699	−1.63	0.3477	0.24
Ln α			−1.3239	−1.29
α			0.2661	
N	82			
(FARC HR violations) > 0	69			
Mean FARC HR violations	14.32			
$LR\,\chi^2$ (12)	542.32***			

***p < .001; **p <.01; *p <. 05; †p <. 10 (standard errors adjusted for clustering by department)

Note: Logit model of the probability that the number of FARC human rights violations is greater than 0.

6.3 MODELS OF HUMAN RIGHTS VIOLATIONS COMMITTED BY LEFTIST GUERRILLAS, 1993–2001

| | 1993–1998 | | | | 1999–2001 | |
| | Zero-inflated negative binomial | | | | Negative binomial | |
Independent variable	Logit estimate	z	Negative binomial estimate	z	Negative binomial estimate	z
GDP per capita (1990)	−3.2281	−1.40	0.4995†	1.83	0.0408	0.17
GDP growth	0.1139	0.87	−0.0136	−1.06	0.0192	1.48
Government HR violations (lagged 1 year)	21.265***	6.24	0.0634***	7.28	0.0543	1.50
Paramilitary HR violations (lagged 1 year)	1.7930**	3.02	0.0069†	1.86	0.0124*	2.06
Coca cultivation (lagged 1 year)	0.0059***	13.49	−0.0000	−0.11	−0.0000	−0.20
Justice and security spending (per capita, lagged 1 year)	−1.7974	−1.22	−0.0140	−1.39	0.0077	0.15
Youth (%, lagged 1 year)	0.5309*	2.34	0.0130	1.10	−0.0030	−0.11
Poverty (lagged 1 year)	−0.4380**	−2.77	0.0331*	2.42	0.0193	1.17
Gini (lagged 1 year)	−8.6985	−0.36	0.3381	0.20	1.2628	0.61
Sectoral GDP of oil (lagged 1 year)	3.3765*	2.40	−0.2479**	−2.44	−0.0005	−0.98
Sectoral GDP of coffee (lagged 1 year)	−3.4215*	−2.24	0.1182	0.85	0.3436*	1.94
Constant	33.909	1.65	−0.3581	−0.31	0.7174	0.49
Ln α			−.7478	−1.57	−0.7236	−2.02
α			0.4764		0.4850	
N	134				82	
(LG HR violations) > 0	121				69	
Mean LG HR violations	20.09				27.54	
LR χ² (12)	675.63***				137.07***	

Note: "LG" = leftist guerilla; ***p < .001, **p < .01, *p < .05, †p < .10

with the emergence of violence and greater intensity of it. Youth population is significantly associated with the emergence of violence only in the early time period. For the economic variables, areas of economic crisis, high inequality, and coca cultivation are expected to have high levels of guerrilla violence. Poverty is related to higher incidences of guerrilla violence in the first period, as is coffee production in the later time period. However, some surprising and contradictory findings emerge in the combined model for the first time period: a negative relationship between coffee production and the emergence of guerrilla violence, and a negative relationship between poverty and the emergence of guerrilla violence.

To facilitate interpretation of these models, Tables 6.4 and 6.5 provide a summary of significant variables organized by group and time period. Table 6.4 examines the factors that increase the probability of departments experiencing violence, if they have not already. Table 6.5 examines the factors that are associated with increases in the intensity of violence.

Hypothesis G1 states that this violence is more likely to occur in the context of a low state presence. For the sectoral GDP of oil, in the combined guerrilla model in the early time period, as oil is found in previously peaceful areas, the department is more likely to experience guerrilla activity for the first time. This could reflect both the movement of leftist guerrillas to hit-and-run in areas with pipelines and the subsequent inflow of military protection. However, in areas where guerrilla activity is already established, more oil is associated with less-intense guerrilla violence. This is likely due to the prioritization of the pipelines for protection by the military. For justice and security spending in the early time period, greater justice and security spending meant less FARC violence. However, there is a positive and significant relationship between justice and security spending and FARC violence in the later period. This surprising result is most likely due to plans to increase state presence and to fight the guerrillas in their traditional territory.

Hypothesis G2 concerns repression. It is expected that repression creates a negative cycle with leftist guerrilla violence. This is strongly supported in both the FARC and combined models. In both time periods, the more paramilitary violence, the more likely FARC or guerrilla violence was to emerge in previously peaceful areas. In the combined model in the first time period, more governmental violence meant more guerrilla activity was likely to emerge. In the later model of FARC violence, both governmental and paramilitary human rights violations led to more guerrilla violence. In the combined guerrilla violence model for the later time period, paramilitary violence is associated with higher guerrilla violence. This finding strongly supports the idea that paramilitary violence, instead of being an effective counterinsur-

6.4 SUMMARY OF FACTORS INCREASING THE PROBABILITY OF EXPERIENCING VIOLENCE IN DEPARTMENTS WITHOUT PRIOR GUERRILLA VIOLENCE, 1993–2001 (LOGIT MODEL)

	1993–1998		1999–2001
Political factor	FARC	All leftist guerrillas	FARC
G1: Weak state			
Justice and security spending			+†
Oil production		+*	+†
G2: Repression (combined)			
Paramilitary	+*	+**	+†
Government		+***	+†
G3: Youth		+*	−†
Economic factor			
G4: Economic crisis			
Coffee production		−*	+*
Poverty		−*	+**
GDP growth			
G5: Inequality	+*		
G6: Coca cultivation	+***	+***	

Note: Logit model of the probability that violence will be greater than zero; ***p < .001, **p < .01, *p < .05, †p < .10.

gency strategy, creates higher levels of guerilla violence and facilitates rebel recruitment and operation.

Hypothesis G3 anticipates that high youth populations make an area relatively more susceptible to guerrilla violence. This theory is strongly supported in both time periods in areas where FARC violence already exists. It is also supported in the first time period in the combined model of guerrilla violence. When this finding is considered in concert with youth unemployment rates, it reinforces the need for a comprehensive development policy. Youth unemployment is high—higher than the overall rate for all age groups (27.1 percent in 1990, 18.5 percent in 1995, and 36.3 percent in 2000, according to International Labour Organization estimates).

Hypothesis G4 concerns economic crisis. Contrary to expectations, the more coffee that was produced, the less likely leftist-guerrilla violence was to emerge during the first time period. However, in the FARC models, where

FARC violence already exists, coffee production is associated with higher levels of FARC violence. In the second time period, greater coffee production in previously peaceful areas increased the likelihood of FARC violence emerging. This finding reflects an increasing volatility in rural coffee areas (discussed in Chapter Seven), which can facilitate guerrilla recruitment and operations. There is strong evidence of the destabilizing effects of poverty. In almost all models reflecting the intensity of both FARC and combined guerrilla violence, the higher the poverty, the more violence. (Although the combined model has a contrary finding in the early time period, showing lower poverty associated with a greater likelihood of guerrilla violence.) Additionally, in the second FARC time period, high poverty is associated with the emergence of FARC violence. GDP growth is weakly supported as a predictor of violence in the negative binominal model of FARC intensity in the early period, and insignificant in the rest.

6.5 SUMMARY OF SIGNIFICANT FACTORS EXPLAINING THE INTENSITY OF VIOLENCE IN DEPARTMENTS ALREADY EXPERIENCING GUERRILLA VIOLENCE, 1993–2002 (NEGATIVE BINOMIAL MODEL)

	1993–1998		1999–2002	
Political factor	FARC	*All leftist guerrillas*	FARC	*All leftist guerrillas*
G1: Weak state				
Justice and security spending	+***		+*	
Oil production	−†	−**	−*	
G2: Repression				
Paramilitary	+**	+†	+†	+*
Government		+***	+***	
G3: Youth	+**		+***	
Economic factor				
G4: Economic crisis				
Coffee production	+***		+***	+*
Poverty	+**	+**	+**	
GDP growth	−†			
G5: Inequality				
G6: Coca cultivation	+*			

Note: ***p < .001, **p < .01, *p < .05, †p < .10

Hypothesis G5 theorizes a relationship between inequality and guerrilla violence, which is supported in the model of the emergence of FARC violence in 1993–1998. The hypothesis of a connection between coca cultivation and guerrilla violence is strongly supported, but only in the first time period. In the early time period, the FARC models show a positive relationship for both the emergence and intensity of violence. The combined model shows a strong relationship between the emergence of leftist guerrilla violence and areas of coca cultivation. Table 6.6 presents the models of paramilitary violence.[7] Tables 6.7 and 6.8 present the summary results.

Hypothesis P1, which theorizes that paramilitary violence is more likely in the context of insurgency, is strongly supported. This hypothesis is tested using the number of FARC human rights violations. In a department not already experiencing paramilitary violence, the more leftist guerrilla violence, the more likely paramilitaries are to move in. In departments that already suffer from paramilitary violence, higher levels of leftist guerrilla violence are matched by higher levels of paramilitary violence.

Hypothesis P2 proposes that paramilitary violence is more likely when the state presence is low, and this is tested with justice and security spending and sectoral oil GDP. In areas without paramilitary violence, the more oil production, the less likely paramilitaries are to emerge. However, in the first period, when paramilitary violence is already in an area, oil production is associated with a higher level of paramilitary violence. In the second period, oil production is negatively associated with paramilitary violence. Interestingly, contrary to expectations, justice and security spending are associated with both the emergence of paramilitary violence and higher levels of paramilitary violence in all models and time periods. Direct or indirect cooperation between the military and the paramilitary groups could be an explanation. The contradictory significance of oil could be due to many factors, but it is possible that increasing pressure from human rights groups and predications of U.S. aid (beginning with the Leahy amendment to the Foreign Operations Act for fiscal year 1998) upon breaking ties between the Colombian government and paramilitary forces may have begun to have an effect in the later time period. Multinational corporations working in the oil industry are more susceptible to international pressure and have more transparency in their security practices. Moreover, in 2000, President Uribe made a commitment to protect the oil industry. As he sent in more troops to protect the pipelines, there may have been less temptation to rely upon paramilitaries to provide protection.

Hypothesis P3, which theorizes that paramilitary violence is positively associated with illicit exports, is also somewhat supported. In the first period,

6.6 ZERO-INFLATED NEGATIVE BINOMIAL REGRESSION OF HUMAN RIGHTS VIOLATIONS COMMITTED BY PARAMILITARY FORCES, 1993–2001

Independent variable	1993–1998				1999–2001	
	Zero-inflated negative binomial				Negative binomial	
	Logit estimate	z	Negative binomial estimate	z	Negative binomial estimate	z
GDP per capita (1990)	9.4131	1.81	−0.7966***	−3.66	−0.3216	−3.22
GDP growth	2.3607**	2.92	−0.0340**	−2.88	0.00788	0.69
Sectoral GDP of animals (lagged 1 year)	9.3926**	2.56	0.1929	0.96	−0.0000	−0.27
Sectoral GDP of oil (lagged 1 year)	−3.2786**	−2.97	0.3102*	2.24	−0.00897**	−2.66
Sectoral GDP of coffee (lagged 1 year)	−1.4888**	−2.83	−0.0561***	−3.34	−0.00089†	−1.71
Leftist HR violations (lagged 1 year)	2.0720**	2.72	0.0359***	5.33	0.0212*	2.39
Agricultural land in coca cultivation (%)	7.1608**	2.42	.2176***	3.41	−0.0617*	−2.17
Justice and security spending (per capita, lagged 1 year)	2.2281**	2.62	0.0022***	3.26	0.1714**	2.42
Gini (lagged 1 year)	2.7087**	2.90	0.0104	0.51	0.0487*	1.93
Constant	−5.2694**	−2.68	2.0511	1.52	−0.6233	−0.38
Ln α			−0.0333	−0.17	−0.0843	—
α					0.9192	
N	138				82	
(PM HR violations) > 0	109					
Mean PM HR violations	18.55				27.79	
Wald χ² (8)	466.37***				104.40***	

Note: "PM" = "paramilitary"; ***$p < .001$; **$p < .01$; *$p < .05$; †$p < .10$

6.7 SUMMARY OF FACTORS INCREASING
THE PROBABILITY OF EXPERIENCING
PARAMILITARY VIOLENCE IN PREVIOUSLY
PEACEFUL DEPARTMENTS, 1993–1998
(LOGIT MODEL)

	1993–1998
Political factor	*Paramilitary*
P1: Insurgency/guerrilla violence	+**
P2: State presence	
Oil	–**
Justice and security spending	+**
Economic factor	
P3: Coca cultivation	+**
P4: Assets	
Ranching/animals	+**
Coffee	–**
GDP growth rate	+***
P5: Inequality	+**

Note: Logit model of the probability that violence will
be greater than zero; ***p < .001; **p < .01; *p < .05;
†p < .10.

paramilitary violence is more likely to emerge in areas with coca cultivation
and becomes more intense as more coca is produced. However, the relationship is reversed in the second time period. This finding in the later time
period could be due to Carlos Castaño's efforts to reshape the movement and
remove the paramilitaries from the drug trade in preparation for peace talks
with the government.

Hypothesis P4 proposes that paramilitary violence is associated with the
protection of assets. To better approximate historical funding sources, we
have included sectoral GDP of animals to capture the influence of ranching, as
opposed to export figures, since the products of this sector are generally con-
sumed internally. We also expect to see more paramilitary violence in rural
areas, as represented by the coffee sector. Interestingly, the models show contrary findings—the more coffee production, the less paramilitary violence. In
the first time period, in areas without prior paramilitary violence, the higher
the sectoral GDP of animals, the more likely paramilitaries are to emerge.
In the first time period, GDP growth is associated only with the emergence of

paramilitary violence and is negatively associated with the intensity of paramilitary violence. This may suggest that it is not growth per se but inequality of assets that leads to paramilitary violence.

Hypothesis P5 expects higher levels of paramilitary violence in areas with high inequality. In the first time period, in areas that did not already have paramilitary violence, the higher the inequality, the more likely paramilitary violence was to emerge. In the second time period, the more inequality, the more intense was paramilitary violence.

CONCLUSION

These analyses both sharpen the larger debates on civil war and nonstate violence and provide insights into the particular Colombian case. Much of the debate focuses on greed versus grievance as a way to understand the sources and patterns of violence. In this study, we examined appropriate sources of support and motivation for each group, relative to its historical evolution. The analysis supports both greed and grievance, perhaps confirming the mixed

6.8 SUMMARY OF SIGNIFICANT FACTORS EXPLAINING THE INTENSITY OF VIOLENCE IN DEPARTMENTS ALREADY EXPERIENCING VIOLENCE, 1993–2002 (NEGATIVE BINOMIAL MODEL)

	1993–1998	*1999–2002*
Political factor	*Paramilitary*	*Paramilitary*
P1: Insurgency/guerrilla violence	+***	+*
P2: State Presence		
Oil	+*	–**
Justice and security spending	+***	+**
Economic factor		
P3: Coca cultivation	+***	–*
P4: Assets		
Ranching/animals		
Coffee	–***	–†
GDP growth rate	–**	
Inequality		+*

Note: ***$p < .001$; **$p < .01$; *$p < .05$; †$p < .10$

origin and nature of the paramilitaries and the evolving nature of the guerrillas. This analysis of the Colombian case also refines the general theory in
the following ways. First, different factors drive different nonstate violent
groups. Aggregating guerrilla groups with paramilitary or vigilante groups
masks underlying competing causalities. The divergent aims and origins of
violent groups influence their actions and support. Second, a more accurate
measure of state strength or capacity should be used. The Colombian subnational analysis provided a precise measure—actual security and justice spending and sectoral GDP of oil. Third, instead of focusing on primary exports
to predict lootable resources, specific indicators should be chosen that are
appropriate for the historical evolution of the group in question.

The results of this chapter highlight the complexity and interdependence
of factors fueling Colombian violence. There are reinforcing cycles of violence: as guerrilla, government, and paramilitary activities emerge in response
to one another and in turn provoke further violence. There is evidence of
paramilitary violence being used to protect assets, as measured by sectoral
animals, coca, and inequality. The link between the volatile coffee sector and
guerrilla violence highlights the need for effective rural economic reform
and development. Poverty also clearly needs to be addressed, considering its
strong links to guerrilla violence. Coca cultivation is associated with both
guerrilla and paramilitary violence, but previous studies (Holmes, Piñeres,
and Curtin 2006) also demonstrate the negative effect of eradication. These
models highlight the importance of state presence to reduce guerrilla violence. However, since paramilitary violence is associated with higher levels
of security and justice spending, police and military forces must be reformed
to prevent abuses, which inspire more violence. These results demonstrate the
need for a comprehensive strategy to address the necessary economic reforms,
reduce poverty and inequality, strengthen and professionalize the military
and police forces, and craft a response to the drug trade that is not counter-
productive. When examining the economic basis of conflict, it is important
to closely match variables to the type of violence studied.

SEVEN

THE EFFECTS OF ILLEGAL DRUGS AND VIOLENCE ON THE COLOMBIAN ECONOMY

According to many scholars, pundits, and diplomats, the illegal-drug industry harms the Colombian economy. Colombia suffers also from high rates of both political violence and violent criminal activity, which may also have corrosive economic effects. What are the effects of drugs and violence on the economy? Although these two issues are interrelated, we attempt to differentiate them. As background for a department-level analysis, a brief overview of the national-level relationships is provided. Substantively, we examine the effect of violence on the economy and the economic consequences of illegal drugs at both national and subnational levels. Because of data limitations, we focus on the time period of 1990–2001. We conclude with a quantitative subnational analysis. Analyzing relations at the department level allows for a more precise differentiation of the effects of violence on the economy.

NATIONAL ECONOMIC TRENDS: COCA, UNEMPLOYMENT, AND GDP

An examination of national trends of coca cultivation, unemployment, and economic growth for the period in question appears to show that increases in coca cultivation negatively affect long-run employment.[1] Through the mid-1990s, GDP growth and coca production were fairly stable. However, as coca production began to increase in the latter half of the decade, GDP growth slowed and unemployment increased (see Table 7.1). GDP growth declined during the 1990s, eventually resulting in contractions of per capita output. Some scholars, such as Cardenas, blame the drop in productivity on the shift of capital to unproductive activity because of the increase in drug-related crime (2007, 1). Furthermore, it is not surprising that labor moved from the legal to illegal sector, since the income from criminal sources is estimated

7.1 ECONOMIC PERFORMANCE, VIOLENCE TRENDS, AND COCA CULTIVATION, 1990–2004

Year	Inflation (consumer prices, %)	GDP growth (%)	Unemployment (% of total labor force)	Coca cultivation	Total LG violence	Total PM violence	Total UN violence
1990	29.14	6.04	10.20				
1991	30.39	2.28	9.80		32.41	31.71	−15.22
1992	27.03	5.03	9.20	−1.07	35.20	298.15	−25.23
1993	22.61	2.37	7.80	7.01	−25.34	41.40	65.46
1994	23.84	5.84	7.60	13.35	61.89	−16.12	−61.46
1995	20.96	5.20	8.70	13.11	−37.80	20.00	−15.45
1996	20.24	2.06	12.00	32.02	23.85	126.80	−49.79
1997	18.46	3.43	12.10	18.30	9.44	31.56	99.16
1998	18.67	0.57	15.00	28.05	−14.04	−48.74	12.18
1999	10.87	−4.20	20.10	57.29	58.27	24.79	63.48
2000	9.22	2.92	n/a	1.98	27.36	51.88	161.86
2001	7.97	1.47	n/a	−11.32	−20.31	34.27	128.70
2002	6.35	1.93	15.70	−29.51			
2003	7.13	4.02	n/a				
2004	5.90	3.96	15.70				

Sources: World Bank Indicators, CINEP, and UNDCP
Note: "LG" = "leftist guerilla"; "PM" = "paramilitary"; "UN" = "unattributed"; "n/a" = data not available; all drug and violence variables represent the annual percentage change.

to be twice the minimum wage (Richani 1997). Arbelaez, Echavarria, and Gaviria (2002) find that both volatile sociopolitical conditions and declining economic conditions negatively affect total factor productivity (TFP). In Chapter Three, we saw that it was not until President Uribe established confidence in the government's ability to combat the violence that economic indicators began to improve.

Economic Effects of the Drug Trade

While some scholars have argued that the illegal drug trade has benefited the economy, most agree that any benefits that may have occurred in the early 1980s are no longer there. The initial benefits included capital inflow during a period when lending was tight, and this helped stabilize the Colombian economy during the Latin American debt crisis. Estimates of the relative importance of illegal drugs range from a high of 7 percent of GDP and 70 percent of exports during the 1980s to 3 percent of GDP and 25 percent of exports in the mid-1990s (Steiner 1998, 1027–1028). Despite providing initial economic benefits, the drug trade has imposed high costs, such as the war on drugs and increased security costs.

The costs are both direct, such as governmental resources diverted to fight the problem, and indirect, such as the effects of violence and uncertainty on economic, political, and social institutions. For example, Cardenas acknowledges initial positive effects of drug income approximating 3 percent of GDP; however, he finds negative indirect effects on productivity to be much greater and widespread throughout the economy (2002, 13–19). Steiner finds additional negative effects, including increases in smuggling, concentration of land ownership, deterrents to both foreign and domestic investment, and changes in prices (1999, 1). Additionally, he sees a "Dutch disease" effect, in which huge capital inflows led to an appreciated peso, which, in turn, harmed exports, increased currency speculation, fueled inflation as demand for nontradables increased, and changed the economic power structure. Thoumi concludes that overall the drug industry was a principal driver of current economic problems, capital flight, and the contemporary social crisis (2002, 111).

The effect of drugs on political credibility and, consequently, the economy should not be underestimated. Despite an otherwise favorable investment climate, Colombia has become an increasingly dangerous place to do business, and multiple forms of violence have reduced the attractiveness of Colombian investments (Bibes 2001, 251). In Chapter Three, it was established that Colombia received the lowest amount of net inflows of foreign direct investment in its peer group. Moreover, these risks serve as a deterrent to foreign nationals, who are often a source of technical and managerial expertise. The costs of insecurity extend throughout the economy, often influencing peripheral decisions that can have long-term negative consequences. The effect extends beyond the industrial sector. For example, in the rural economy, both the internal conflict and the growing drug trade added to an already challenging economic environment.

Drivers of Drug Production

Does poverty drive farmers into illicit drug production, or is inequality the source? Or is the relationship more complex? As mentioned earlier, there has been research to support the idea that farmers in remote regions of Colombia move into coca production because they lack any other economically viable alternatives. Rocha (2000) finds a positive correlation between illegal drugs and sociopolitical instability, and negative correlations between education, health, poverty levels, and inequality in illegal drug-producing zones. Díaz and Sanchez (2004) blame the expansion of coca cultivation on poverty, inequality, poor economic conditions, and weak state support (18). However, Thoumi (2002) does not agree that there is a direct relationship between poverty and illicit-drug production. Yet the main departments producing illegal drugs, Caquetá, Guaviare, and Putumayo, have the highest indices of poverty. For instance, in 1988 the index of rural unsatisfied basic needs (composed of infrastructure, housing, education, and health measures) was 100 percent in Guaviare and Putumayo, and 72 percent in Caquetá (Moreno-Sanchez, Kraybill, and Thompson 2003, 376). These underdeveloped departments on the margins are characterized by entrenched poverty, lack of opportunity, and weak state presence (McGuire 2002, 3). Under these conditions, coca may appear as the only viable alternative for survival.

According to an article in the *Economist* (February 12, 2005), in 2005 one hectare (2.47 acres) of coca could produce a crop worth up to $7,500, compared to only $600 for coffee or $1,000 for cocoa. Furthermore, perennial coca crops can be harvested at least three times a year, and some varieties of coca can be harvested every seventy-five days. Additionally, each coca plant can remain viable for up to twenty-five years (Peterson 2002). Traditional crops like plantains have only two harvests a year, and alternative crops can take years to yield fruit, making them a less viable option for poor rural farmers with limited access to credit (McGuire 2002). Other advantages to coca production include a well-established logistical network, the crop's adaptability to bad soil conditions, and price stability. Many farmers use illegal-drug production to supplement their incomes, especially in the face of declining coffee prices and farm employment opportunities (Giovannucci et al. 2002). Moreover, transition costs are high. Farmers would need to find similarly hardy crops that can grow in such difficult terrain; transportation issues would have to be solved; and the relative lack of profitability of licit crops would have to be addressed. Aside from its legal status, coca is an attractive crop because it matures quickly, traffickers provide market access and transportation, and it generates approximately twice the profit of the most lucrative legal crop (Peterson 2002, 436). Even if the prices for illegal crops, such as coca and poppies, are lower than those for coffee or other primary goods, illegal crops are easier to plant, maintain, and transport; they have a longer storage life; and their producers have access to a more developed distribution system (UNDCP 1994).[2]

Conditions in the Rural Economy

Rural departments such as Guaviare, Putumayo, and Caquetá have favorable conditions for coca production. Fundamentally, poor soil in these areas makes agriculture more labor intensive and makes the harder-to-grow legal crops less viable (McGuire 2002, 13). Between 1995 and 1996, the production of coca increased by more than 22 percent nationally, the largest increases coming in Putumayo, Caquetá, and Guaviare (Castro, Wartenberg, and Celis 1999, 96). Rocha (2000) found more coca cultivation in peripheral areas with histories of mining and agriculture, which typically have higher levels of inequality and vulnerable populations. Chapter Three noted that in the 1990s mining shifted to more capital-intensive techniques, displacing workers. Morrison (1997) concurs that contributing factors include isolation, economic insecurity in rural areas, and a lack of law enforcement caused by corruption and insurgency. Additionally, Diaz and Sanchez (2004) blamed the collapse of legal exports, the scarcity of capital, the difficulty of attracting modernizing technology, and a weak commercial infrastructure for the economic crisis in the 1980s (19). Economic crisis may have pushed peasants and workers from the lower income sectors into the illegal-drug sector, since it often provided the only stable source of income.

Lack of opportunities or development in rural areas may potentially drive increased illegal activity. In particular, declining coffee prices, the negative effects of an appreciated peso, and global competition from other agricultural exports have worsened conditions in the rural economy. The percentage of total GDP attributable to agriculture has been consistently declining. In 1995, there was a sharp fall in overall agricultural value added to the economy (see Figure 7.1). Furthermore, the agricultural sector, in terms of value added, showed little or negative growth after 1995. These conditions do not represent a typical economy in transition. Normally, as different sectors of the economy develop, one would expect productivity in the agricultural sector to increase, even though its GDP share is falling. These negative economic conditions potentially make the production of coca more attractive (Vellinga 2000, 123).

Consequences of the Changing International Market

Price volatility and competition from Asian countries, especially in coffee, make legal-crop production a financially risky choice for poor farmers. For some Colombian farmers, the shift from coffee production to drug crops can be attributed to falling incomes and rising unemployment in the coffee

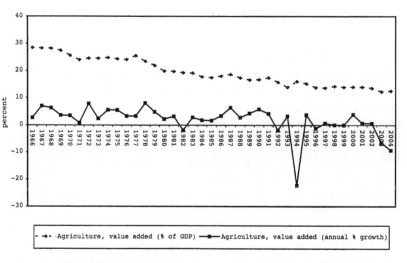

FIGURE 7.1 *Agricultural Productivity*

growing regions. Incomes from primary commodities have been falling since the 1980s (UNDCP 1994, 12), but production costs have been rising. Giovannucci and others (2002) estimate that real income in the coffee sector has fallen by more than 50 percent. This decline has had a significantly negative impact on coffee farmers. Vargas (2002) estimates the Andean coffee belt supports approximately 350,000 small farms and 2,000,000 workers (44). From 1986 to 1994, real income contracted by 56 percent and many jobs were lost, including 71,000 in 1992 and 1993 alone (44). Faced with competition from lower-cost foreign producers and falling coffee prices, farmers are supplementing their incomes by growing drug crops (Wilson 2001), since in absolute terms the farmer is still better off doing that than participating in the regular economy. Furthermore, coffee farms in Colombia generally lack the ability to switch production or diversify their crops. Therefore, they are more vulnerable to falling coffee prices.

Coffee is planted on small farms employing about one million people in Colombia, while the illegal drug trade is dominated by a few producers and employs a relatively small number of people (Steiner and Corchuelo 1999). It is estimated that the illegal drug sector employs almost 7 percent of agricultural workers, whereas the main legal crop, coffee, employs 12 percent. Although there may be short-term wage gains for individual peasants choosing to grow coca, in the long run there are negative consequences, since farmers have less incentive to work toward building a modern and competitive agricultural sector; declining productivity in the agricultural sector bears this out

(Steiner and Corchuelo 1999). The map illustrates a move from coffee to coca in certain departments.

Figure 7.2 demonstrates a shift in agricultural patterns: farmers are reallocating cropland so that they can grow illegal drugs. Drugs are easily stored and are hardier than many legal crops. Because of this, further investments in product distribution and land improvements are not made, making it even more difficult for legal crops to be produced and sold. The United Nations Drug Control Program (UNDCP) highlights the opportunity costs of the illegal-drug trade, including the loss of investment in legitimate enterprises as farmers funnel their savings into drug cultivation and production, a loss of investment in human resources as children participate in the drug trade, and a loss as other productive investments are crowded out (UNDCP 1994). From 1995 to 2000, coca cultivation increased by just less than 22 percent, while production of other agricultural commodities decreased by a slightly more than 1 percent, suggesting a displacement of legal crops by illegal commodities (Eduardo, Ballén, and Percipiano 2002). Additionally, illicit crop eradication also affects productivity, since the chemicals used to destroy illegal drug crops also make it difficult to grow and sustain legal crops.

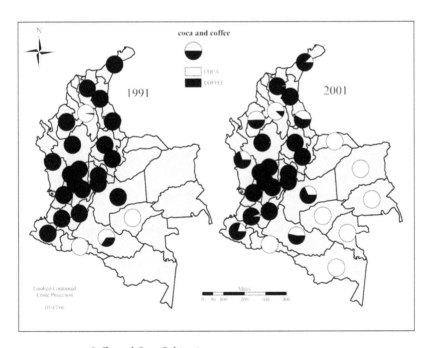

FIGURE 7.2   *Coffee and Coca Cultivation*

In short, difficult and multidimensional challenges of economic development would have to be solved in order to change the incentives for individual farmers. Lack of complementary infrastructure has made it difficult for farmers to leave illicit-crop production. Compared to coca, most proposed alternative crops require more labor, technical expertise, and time (McGuire 2002, 13). Furthermore, high and often prohibitive transportation costs make licit crops an unfeasible choice for farmers in remote areas of Colombia. As discussed in Chapter Two, Colombia continues to suffer from serious transportation and infrastructure problems. McGuire (2002) concludes that only when the non-coca farmer finds the same level of financial security as the coca farmer, and the coca farmer moves into legal activities, will Colombia make progress toward rural development.

Illegal Drug Money and Construction Booms and Busts

In rural areas, drug money affects real estate values as well as prices for legitimate agricultural crops. A survey of existing research demonstrates that in the short term, increased drug incomes boost the construction sector, creating jobs for the lower classes. However, in the long run, there is evidence of a collapse of asset and real estate values. Any gains made by the lower classes from the construction boom disappeared during subsequent busts. When construction, measured as a component of GDP in constant pesos, is used to proxy real estate activity for Antioquia, Atlántico, Cundinamarca, and Valle de Cauca, the data show a decline after 1997 (see Figure 7.3). Thoumi highlights a common money-laundering technique: funding real estate construction and recycling drug money into additional construction projects (2003, 186). A real estate boom, however, poses a threat to the economy, since property values rise at increasingly unsustainable rates, eventually resulting in a collapse of assets (*Economist* 1994, 25). This leads to a loss of wealth for all those who purchased and invested in the assets at the higher prices. Camacho Guizado and Restrepo assert that the 1990s recession resulted from a decline in money-laundering activities by imprisoned members of the Cali cartel (2000, 164). Similarly, Steiner blames the drug business for the real estate bubble, by inflating the value of luxury accommodations and displacing investment in low-income, working-class housing (Steiner 1999, 12). Construction booms may lead to short-term gains for local economies; however, in the long term their effects are negative. Figure 7.3 shows a peak in 1997, followed by a steep decline in construction.

Illegal Drugs, Money Laundering, and Contraband

The illegal drug trade has a secondary effect on the economy as a result of money laundering and attempts to control it. The most common method of laundering money is to traffic in contraband. Drug traffickers purchase goods abroad using dirty money, smuggle the goods into Colombia, and then sell them, often at a "loss." While sale of these items launders money for the traffickers, it undercuts legitimate businesses: drug traffickers are likely to sell for less than cost, since the dollars invested have already generated an initial profit from the drug sale. The main goal of money laundering is the conversion of dollars to pesos through the importation of goods. Successful money laundering depends on high volume and a quick turnover of product, further reducing the incentive to sell at market price. The industrial and business sectors most affected by smuggling are household appliances, clothing, textiles, footwear, liquor, and cigarettes (Gilbert 2004, 113). Moreover, the typically trafficked items displace products of the labor-intensive and nonspecialized economic sectors, in which Colombian products have a comparative advantage, further undermining employment (Steiner and Corchuelo 1999). Additionally, legal businesses often cannot compete with the loss-making money-laundering firms (*Economist* 1994, 25). This has occurred in both the manufacturing and the retail sectors, resulting in increased unemployment.

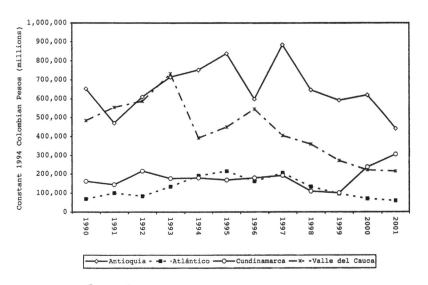

FIGURE 7.3 *Construction*

In the end, less efficient and less productive "dirty capital begins to replace clean capital" (UNDCP 1998, 28).

The second method by which illegal profits are repatriated and laundered is through direct cash transfers. The value of these was estimated to be approximately $260 million a year from 1985 to 1994 (Steiner 1999, 7). These cash transfers were a source of capital inflows that ultimately led to a real appreciation of the peso and to inflation. Finally, legal imports and exports are constrained by efforts to control contraband. Customs officials spend significant resources and time in the search of contraband, which results in delays and higher costs in processing trade shipments.

Land Ownership and Drugs

The drug trade has significantly affected land ownership. During the "land counterreform" of the 1980s, the narco-traffickers bought large parcels of land as legal investments, which increased land ownership concentration (Thoumi 2003, 181), and introduced labor-saving technology (Steiner and Corchuelo 1999). Moreno and Sarmiento (1989) estimate between 8 and 23 percent of the revenues repatriated by illegal drugs have been used to purchase approximately 5 percent of the arable land in Cauca, Antioquia, Meta, and the Caribbean coast. Most of this land is then used for cattle and horse ranches, which have low labor intensity and low productivity. For example, since the mid-1980s, drug money has funded the purchase of 4–6 million hectares (10–15 million acres) of land used to raise cattle (Richani 1997). Estimates of the drug cartels' land ownership vary from approximately one-third of the country's agricultural land (*Economist* 1994, 25) to upward of 42 percent of the best land in Colombia (Knoester 1998, 93). The repatriated profits that drug dealers used to purchase land also had a secondary effect of inflating land prices. For example in Puerto Boyacá, the price of a hectare of land increased from $100,000 in the early 1980s to $1,000,000 in 1989 (Cameron and Curtis-Evans 2000, 53).

The effect of coca production on land ownership exacerbates an already unequal distribution of income in Colombia. The International Monetary Fund (2001) reports that in 1995 the highest 20 percent of households earned 60 percent of the income, while the lowest 20 percent earned only 2 percent of the income. Gootenberg estimates that the drug trade had so negatively affected income equality in Medellín that inequality rose to levels higher than those seen in 1967 (1999, 172). The illegal drug trade, while providing short-term financial relief to peasants, in the long run further distorts the inequalities in Colombia. Farmers in the lowest quintile tend not to reap significant financial benefits from illegal drugs, since they "operate under conditions of competition so their profit margins are minimal" (UNDCP 1998, 25). In the late 1980s and early 1990s, approximately 30 percent of the country's wealth was in the hands of the cartels (UNDCP 1998).

Additionally, the situation is exacerbated by the lack of governmental control in these rural areas (Gilbert 2004, 113). As narcos bought land, acquiring property in approximately 40 percent of the municipalities, it is estimated that 800,000 campesinos were driven from the land (Knoester 1998, 94). Moreover, as land values increased, many of the narcos subsequently formed paramilitary groups to protect the land from displaced peasants and guerrillas (Thoumi 2003, 186). As a result, even more peasants were pushed into guerrilla groups or coca cultivation (UNDCP 1998, 20). Regardless of the difficulty of accurately estimating the size and profitability of the drug trade, it is clear that it has influenced the power dynamics in the country and countryside.

Drugs and the Environment

The environmental effects of drug cultivation and eradication are also substantial.[3] The environmental effect is widespread, including the destruction of primary tropical forest, contamination of water supplies, loss of biodiversity of plant and animal life in the tropics, and health hazards from aerial spraying (Thoumi 2003, 196–198; Camacho Guizado and Restrepo 2000, 160). Vargas (2002) attributes the environmental damage to the installation, control, and management of illicit crops and the chemical components used in the coca-paste-processing phase. It is estimated that for every hectare the government attempts to eradicate, two more hectares of forest are lost: one to pesticide drift, the other to clearing for displaced planting (Hansen 2000). The drift and overspray of chemicals also leads to loss of food crops and unintentional contamination (Hansen 2000).

Furthermore, farmers and traffickers have adapted to the spraying. They have changed their cultivation habits to create denser plots of coca in less visible areas, increased their conversion efficiencies, and planted glyphosate-resistant varieties (Lee and Thoumi 2005). Both McGuire (2002) and Moreno-Sanchez, Kraybill, and Thompson (2003) state concerns that eradication has forced farmers deeper into the Amazon, leading to further destruction of the rainforest. Eradication results in a balloon effect pattern of cultivation as new plants are cultivated elsewhere in response (LeoGrande and Sharpe, 2000).

COCA AND THE ECONOMY:
DEPARTMENTAL-LEVEL TRENDS

By examining the variation between GDP (measured in thousands of pesos) and coca production in the top coca producing departments, we are able to visualize the bilateral relationships at a subnational level. Before conducting an empirical analysis of the relationship between GDP and coca production, we use a graphical analysis to illustrate the relationship. To obtain a preliminary understanding, we examine four departments with high coca production. In Caquetá, Meta, Putumayo, and Guaviare, there are similar trends in both sub-value-added private GDP and coca cultivation. Sub-value-added private GDP is GDP minus public spending. This measure more clearly captures private economic activity. Coca, if included in estimates, would compose a large proportion of GDP for these regions.

In Caquetá, we see that coca cultivation and GDP move consistently together. In Meta, coca cultivation is virtually nonexistent until 1997, and then increases dramatically. Meta reflects a substitution of coca production for other activities. Yet GDP remains consistent throughout the time period. In Putumayo, we see that coca cultivation and GDP move consistently together. After 1996, coca cultivation grows at a faster rate than GDP and is larger in absolute terms. In Guaviare, coca cultivation is greater than GDP. After 1995, GDP declines dramatically. Coca cultivation and GDP have similar trends.

Using graphical analysis, we find that coca cultivation and reported GDP move together. Coca production leads to an influx of income. The cash inflow brings with it peripheral businesses, which have a positive impact on GDP. Only in Meta do we see coca production increase dramatically while GDP remains constant.

Similarly, an examination of the larger coca producing departments reveals a negative relationship between coffee and coca production. This is expected, given the difficulties of the coffee sector, which were theorized to encourage coca cultivation. The departments included in the sample are Bolívar, Caquetá, Guaviare, Meta, Nariño, Norte de Santander, and Putumayo. The correlation coefficient is -.3261 ($p < .004$) for the years 1991–2001. Looking at pairwise correlations by year, we find a consistent negative relationship between coffee and coca production for the top coca producing departments. The strong negative relationship is more apparent in the later years. When we look at the percentage of agricultural land used for coca, the coefficient remains consistent, but the level of significance increases over time. This indicates that in the coca producing departments there is movement out of coffee

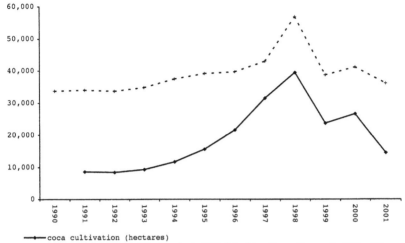

FIGURE 7.4   *Caquetá*

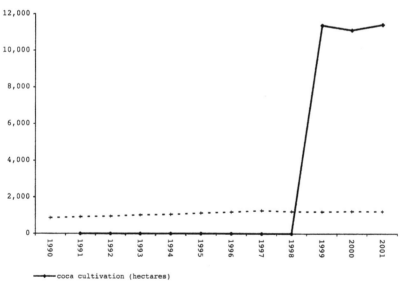

FIGURE 7.5   *Meta*

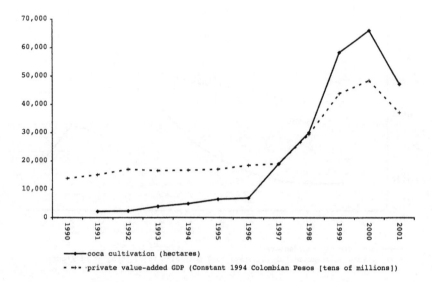

coca cultivation (hectares)

private value-added GDP (Constant 1994 Colombian Pesos [tens of millions])

FIGURE 7.6   *Putumayo*

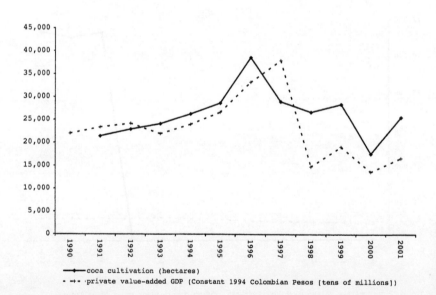

coca cultivation (hectares)

private value-added GDP (Constant 1994 Colombian Pesos [tens of millions])

FIGURE 7.7   *Guaviare*

into drugs. It is important to note that this relationship could result because the top coca producing regions are not well suited to growing coffee.

After reducing the sample of departments to the main coffee producing departments, we find that a simple correlation reveals a negative relationship between coffee and coca production. The departments included in the sample are Antioquia, Caquetá, Cauca, Meta, Nariño, Norte de Santander, and Santander. The correlation coefficient is $-.2455$ ($p < .035$) for the years 1991–2001. Looking at pairwise correlations by year, we find a consistent negative relationship between coffee and coca production for the top coffee producing departments. After 1999, we see a doubling of the correlation coefficient and a stronger negative relationship, although the level of significance declines. Additionally, we do see from the map that there is clear movement out of coffee and into coca.

Figures 7.8 and 7.9 provide a visualization of the relationship between poverty, GDP, and coca. Figure 7.8 shows coca cultivation in 2001 compared to the percent of the population living in poverty. Guaviare and Vichada grow large amounts of coca, but do not report poverty statistics. This is not unusual, since they are representative of the least developed departments. However, the relationship is not clear. Relatively less impoverished departments, such as Arauca and Antioquia, are reporting moderate amounts of coca cultivation. Major coca producing departments, such as Putumayo, are not the most impoverished. Figure 7.9 shows the pattern of coca cultivation in 1998 compared to GDP. Coca tends to be produced in areas with lower GDP, such as Putumayo, Caquetá, and Guaviare, although other less developed departments lack coca cultivation altogether. Furthermore, discerning clear relationships is difficult due to the changing geographic distribution of coca over time.

Based upon the previous literature review of the effects of illegal drugs on the economy, we test the following hypothesis to examine the relationship between illegal drugs and the economy. The model will be tested at a subnational level to disaggregate the effects better and to allow for a more precise determination of the impact of illegal drugs on the economy.

Hypothesis C1: Coca production has a negative impact on domestic gross domestic product. While the initial effect of illegal drug money may be positive, the negative externalities far outweigh any benefit accrued by net inflows of illegal dollars or capital.

7.2 PAIRWISE CORRELATIONS OF COFFEE AND COCA, 1991–2001

Year	Top coca-producing departments		Top coffee-producing departments	
	Absolute values	Agricultural land (%)	Absolute values	Agricultural land (%)
1991	-0.5498	-.4139	-0.2347	-.2347
	(.2010)	(.3559)	(.6125)	(.6125)
1992	-0.4541	-.3453	-0.2312	-.2312
	(.3061)	(.4481)	(.6178)	(.6178)
1993	-0.3514	-.3263	-0.2331	-.2331
	(.4396)	(.4750)	(.6150)	(.6150)
1994	-0.4739	-.3673	-0.2000	-.2000
	(.2827)	(.4176)	(.6672)	(.6672)
1995	-0.4882	-.3884	-0.2361	-.2361
	(.2664)	(.3892)	(.6102)	(.6102)
1996	-0.3896	-.3305	-0.2187	-.2187
	(.3876)	(.4691)	(.6376)	(.6376)
1997	-0.4555	-.3490	-0.2598	-.2598
	(.3043)	(.4430)	(.5737)	(.5737)
1998	-0.4367	-.2945	-0.3452	-.3452
	(.3273)	(.5214)	(.4483)	(.4483)
1999	-0.5005	-.2362	-0.6043	-.6043
	(.2526)	(.6101)	(.1507)	(.1507)
2000	-0.4456	-.2567	-0.5247	-.5247
	(.3163)	(.5785)	(.2266)	(.2266)
2001	-0.5294	-.2759	-0.6622	-.6622
	(.2217)	(.5492)	(.1051)	(.1051)

Note: Top coca producing departments: Bolívar, Caquetá, Guaviare, Meta, Nariño, Norte de Santander, and Putumayo; top coffee producing departments: Antioquia, Caquetá, Cauca, Meta, Nariño, Norte de Santander, and Santander

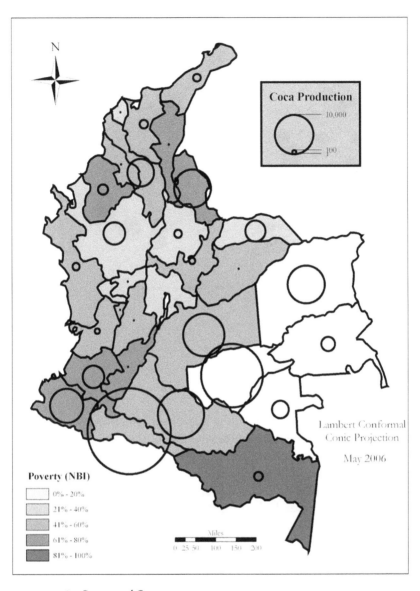

FIGURE 7.8 *Poverty and Coca*

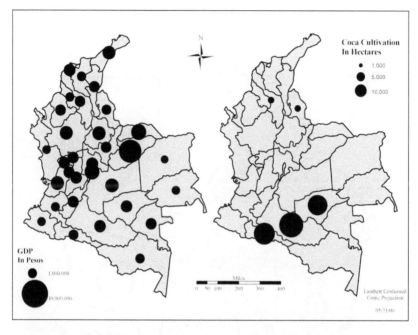

FIGURE 7.9 *GDP and Coca*

VIOLENCE AND THE COLOMBIAN ECONOMY

In addition to the effects of the drug trade, the Colombian economy faces special challenges because of pervasive violence. The strife is extensive. In 2002 alone, 373,020 people were displaced within Colombia, 2,986 were kidnapped, more than 500 people were "disappeared," and 4,000 civilians were killed (see Red de Solidaridad, n.d.; País Libre, n.d.; and Amnesty International 2003). Macario and others (2002) explain that in addition to the common liquidity and infrastructure constraints that Latin American exporters face, the Colombian situation is complicated by violence. Blomberg and Hess (2004, 2) find that terrorism reduces investment, but tends to increase governmental spending. Moreover, in rural Colombia, violence, like the drug trade, further harms the economy, which was ravaged by macroeconomic and trade reforms in the 1990s (Vélez et al. 2001, 64), and plagued with poverty, low productivity, and underutilization of resources, including land (Heshusius Rodríguez 2005, 3). The insecurity and violence caused by the civil conflict serve only to increase the costs of production and risks to investment in rural areas, while also preventing the formation of social capital and aggravating poverty (FIDA 2003).

The Fondo Internacional de Desarrollo Agrícola (FIDA) claims that the lack of economic opportunities forces people either to seek employment in the illegal drug sector or to enlist with different armed groups. This creates a negative cycle in which poor economic conditions precipitate violence, which in turn has additional negative effects on the economy. Some scholars, such as Trujillo and Badel (1997, 273–275), have found that the departments with the most violence are located in coffee and coca cultivating regions.

In Colombia generally, violence has the potential to affect the economy directly through resource misallocation and the shifting of governmental resources toward combating the internal conflict rather than promoting social and economic development. Castro, Wartenberg, and Celis (1999) report that excessive military spending, homicides, kidnapping, armed conflicts, and illegal drug activity are all direct costs associated with violence in Colombia. They divide the costs of the violence between direct costs (approximately 4.5 percent of GDP yearly) and indirect costs (an additional 1.5 percent of GDP); examples of the latter include increased risk to investment, abandoned lands, illegal cultivation displacing legal production, environmental damage, negative effects on the health and safety of the population, and costs associated with political instability (Castro, Wartenberg, and Celis 1999, 83–84). While excessive military expenditures have a negative effect on growth, there appears to be an initial threshold level at which the effects are positive if they create a more stable investment environment (Arias and Ardilla 2003).

Because of the extensive violence, infrastructure is destroyed rather than built. In addition to the direct effects of violence, there are significant indirect effects: the government diverts resources that could be used for social or economic development to suppress violence and the drug trade. The principal indirect costs are loss of productivity, decreased investment, redirection of resources to security from production, and increased transaction costs (Trujillo and Badel 1997, 277–279). Castro, Wartenberg, and Celis point out that Colombia spends approximately 1 percent more of its GDP on military expenditures than other Latin American countries, and approximately 60 percent of that can be attributed to the costs of the armed conflict (1999, 99). Ozak and Valencia (2002) estimates that the costs of the extra military expenditures reduce GDP by 0.2 percent to 0.9 percent. According to Arbelaez, Echavarria, and Gaviria (2002, 38), the conflict contracts growth rates by at least 2 percent, in addition to the effect of military spending. Caballero Argaez (2003) conducts a simulation to determine the effects of military spending on the economy, assuming a direct negative effect of the spending on the conflict. He finds that growth would increase to 4.6 percent from 3.5 percent, productivity would increase to 1.5 percent from 0.6 percent, investment would

7.3 COSTS OF VIOLENCE, 1991–1998

Year	Direct costs (% GDP)	Indirect costs (% GDP)	Total GDP % cost
1991	5.2	1.66	6.86
1992	4.2	1.34	5.54
1993	4.3	1.50	5.80
1994	4.0	1.12	5.12
1995	4.4	1.69	6.09
1996	4.6	1.81	6.41
1997	4.9	1.83	6.73
1998	4.7	1.61	6.31
Mean	**4.5**	**1.55**	**6.05**

Sources: Badel 1999; Castro, Wartenberg, and Celis 1999, 89
Note: Direct costs include spending on urban violence and armed conflict. Indirect costs include those associated with extra military spending, health, infrastructure attacks, extortion, and other estimates.

increase by 11.3 percent as opposed to 8.8 percent, and the rate of investment to GDP would be 17.4 percent instead of 16.1 percent. Finally, by 2010 the economy would be growing by 6 percent annually and investment could reach 20 percent (Caballero Argaez 2003, 31). It is clear that while the short-term benefits of military spending for increased security may be positive, the long-term costs of both the violence and the failure of military spending to control the violence are negative.

Resources diverted away from productive uses to fight violence can have a long-term negative effect on the economy. Arbelaez, Echavarria, and Gaviria (2002, 39) suggest that civil wars negatively affect growth rates by promoting negative macroeconomic effects such as corruption and inflation. More often than not, a country must use deficit spending to finance wartime expenditures. The printing of money has a direct negative effect on inflation and the purchasing power of its domestic currency. Second, in the case of Colombia, the use of illegal funds to finance the war against suspected guerrillas and paramilitaries has led to increased corruption (Waldmann 1997). The conflict has negative economic effects throughout the economy.

Furthermore, an examination reveals that all types of violence increased throughout the 1990s until 2001, when leftist guerrilla violence began to decline (however, paramilitary violence continued to increase). According to Arbelaez, Echavarria, and Gaviria, although the particular causal mechanisms are unclear, the conflict retards growth (2002, 41). Trujillo and Badel (1997) state that in addition to the economic costs it imposes, violence is similar to a regressive tax whose high costs in lives and human capital are borne disproportionately by the poor. Moreover, uncertainty about security increases the importance of the short term, decreasing the attractiveness of long-term investments. Macario and others (2002) conclude that while Colombia was once in the forefront of promoting nontraditional exports, until it resolves its internal conflict the country will be unable to take advantage of its supplies of human capital and its hospitable institutional environment and return to a position of regional leadership in manufactured and nontraditional exports. Similarly, violence and the accompanying risk reduce efficiency, increase uncertainty, and create negative incentives to investment (Steiner 1999, 14). Yet it remains to be seen if these trends are seen when different types of violence are treated separately at the subnational level.

Figure 7.10 provides an overview of the scope and range of different types of violence. This graph delineates the trends of leftist guerrilla, paramilitary, and unattributed violence. Unattributed violence is violence that has been classified as political violence, but the agent responsible has not been identified. Although trends of the different types of violence move together at the national level, paramilitary and guerrilla violence are motivated by different factors and serve different aims. Moreover, there are different geographic

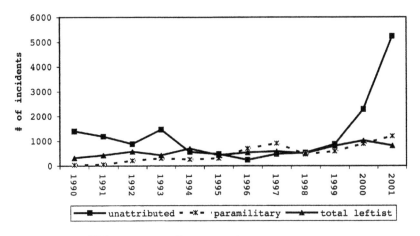

FIGURE 7.10   *Violence 1990–2001 (Source: CINEP)*

patterns of violence emergence and intensity within Colombia, as illustrated in Chapter Six.

There are controversies about where FARC activity is more likely occur. Some scholars theorize that FARC is more likely to operate in areas characterized by higher rural GDP, the cultivation of illegal drugs, the presence of coal and oil—that is, where there are resources to control. Others focus on areas of relative disadvantage—where it may be easier to recruit. Bottía Noguera (2003) finds that FARC expands in areas of rural poverty, poor land quality, and natural parks. Interestingly enough, she does not find that inequality or state presence is significant with respect to FARC. She concludes that the most important factors for FARC expansion are sources of financing and recruitment. Sánchez, Díaz, and Formisano (2003) concur that increased participation by FARC in illegal drug activities has helped perpetuate and fuel the conflict. They also find that areas with a large FARC presence are associated with higher rates of violence, and vice versa.

Gonzalez (2002) states that the expansion of FARC has to do with lack of opportunities for the population, failure of the political system to be inclusive, and lack of professionalism in public administration. He concludes that illegal drugs escalated the war and that FARC fighting is more likely in areas of economic expansion, weak state presence, and agricultural production. However, when FARC locates in areas of higher potential GDP, the negative effect is greater and the economic cost to the violence higher. Rangel Suárez (2000, 578) notes how the guerrillas have siphoned off resources from otherwise productive sectors of the economy. Moreover, he finds that many of these areas were previously home to successful economic activity that earned foreign currency. In Chapter Six, we find that there is a negative association between GDP growth and the intensity of FARC violence. A subnational analysis allows a closer examination of the effect of violence on the economy.

Figure 7.11 compares economic trends with the violence of the main leftist guerrilla group, FARC. In general, unemployment appears to fuel both types of violence. Paramilitaries have traditionally existed to protect assets: they originated as self-defense forces for large landowners in areas of low state presence. Restrepo, Spagat, and Vargas (2003, 24) find paramilitary violence in areas of concentrated landownership, guerrilla activity, and coca. Holmes and Piñeres (2006) find that paramilitary violence is negatively related to GDP and positively related to exports, while FARC violence is negatively related to exports. These divergent types of violence suggest the need to separate out the types of violence and their effects on the economy.

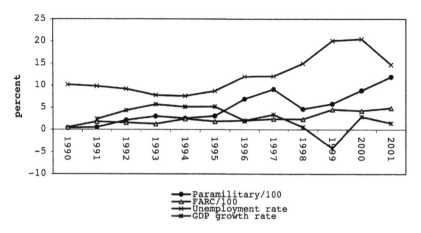

FIGURE 7.11 *Colombian Violence and Economic Performance (Source: CINEP, DANE)*

High-Violence Departments and the Economy

A brief overview of high-violence departments suggests a minimal relationship between violence and GDP. The different types of violence move together, yet GDP remains consistent. After 2000, violence decreased and GDP increased slightly. In Antioquia, paramilitary and leftist violence moved together, while GDP remained consistent throughout the time period. After 2000, when violence began to decline, GDP also showed signs of improvement. In Bolívar, the different types of violence moved together, while GDP remained consistent, showing signs of improvement in 1998. In Cauca, as violence increased in 1997 and 1998, so did GDP (slightly). Additionally, GDP remained constant, even in the face of dramatic increases in violence in 1998. In Santander, there appears to be little relationship between violence and GDP, since GDP consistently rose, but violence decreased and then increased. Examining the departments with high levels of violence reveals little or no relationship between violence and GDP. In fact, GDP appears immune to increases in violence in these departments. A more thorough empirical analysis follows.

We test the following hypotheses to examine the relationship between violence and the economy:

Hypothesis V1: There is a negative relationship between insecurity and economic growth.
Hypothesis V2: FARC violence harms GDP.
Hypothesis V3: Paramilitary violence is associated with higher GDP.

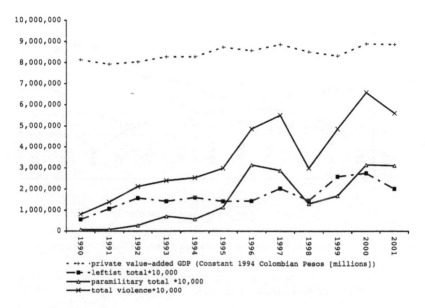

FIGURE 7.12 *Antioquia*

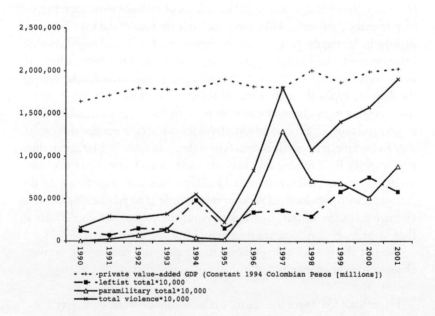

FIGURE 7.13 *Bolívar*

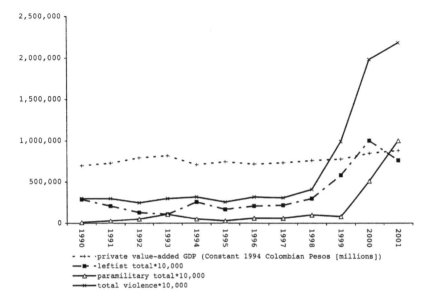

FIGURE 7.14 *Cauca*

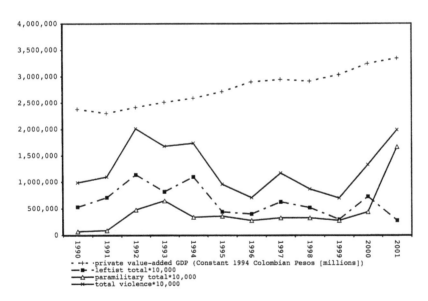

FIGURE 7.15 *Santander*

We propose that insecurity influences investment decisions and reduces future economic growth. While our limited data set precludes a long-term analysis, we use lagged justice and security spending to capture the short-term impact on economic growth. FARC violence is purported to reduce GDP, since FARC tends to be extractive, as we saw in Chapter Six. Paramilitary violence is expected to have a positive impact on GDP, since the paramilitaries tend to exist to protect resources.

SUBNATIONAL DATA AND ANALYSIS

We use data disaggregated at the departmental level to capture the internal dynamics of the economy. An ordinary least squares fixed-effects model allows the variables to vary across departments. Departmental GDP data are reported in constant 1994 pesos by DANE. We calculate private net domestic product (NDP) as the sum of productive activities minus public spending on schools, health, services, and others, as stated by DANE. Public services were removed to better capture private sector activities. Additionally, we use public health as a proxy for level of development, since more governmental funds are spent in poorer departments for health. The data range from 1990 to 2001. The model includes one-period-lagged private NDP, population, coca cultivation, total leftist violence, total paramilitary violence, current and one-period-lagged justice and security spending, one-period-lagged exports, current-period public health spending, and a constant. Two models are presented. The first is from 1990 to 1998 and the second from 1999 to 2001.[4] Violence data are from CINEP. Coca cultivation figures in the early period are from the Colombian National Police and from the UNDCP in the later period. The model was robust to various specifications and estimation techniques.

We test the following hypotheses:

Hypothesis C1: Coca production has a negative impact on GDP.
Hypothesis V1: There is a negative relationship between insecurity and economic growth.
Hypothesis V2: FARC violence harms GDP.
Hypothesis V3: Paramilitary violence is associated with higher GDP.

Consistent across both time periods, control variables of past private NDP and population are positive, even though the level of significance for population declines in the second time period. The positive sign on population

Independent variable	1990–1998		1999–2001	
Lagged private GDP	0.4930***	0.4943***	0.5520**	0.5436**
	(0.1004)	(0.1009)	(0.2280)	(0.2266)
Population	0.7521**	0.7881**	2.2173	2.2116
	(0.3870)	(0.3879)	(1.4668)	(1.4702)
Coca cultivation (hectares)	4.3165		4.3977	
	(3.1524)		(14.7819)	
Agricultural land in coca cultivation (%)		1532886		92203.63
		(1801317)		(1133726)
Total leftist violence	−722.3607	−655.904	2638.487	2779.831*
	(−950.5316)	(−953.8085)	(1624.41)	(1553.736)
Total paramilitary violence	199.0366	197.8513	1197.337	1142.598
	(412.31)	(414.5222)	(754.1851)	(732.4686)
Justice and security spending	0.0010	0.0012	−0.0148	−0.0151*
	(0.0053)	(0.0053)	(.0089)	(.0089)
Lagged justice and security spending	−0.0028***	−0.0029***	−0.0090*	−0.0088*
	(−0.0009)	(−0.0009)	(0.0047)	(0.0047)
Lagged exports	0.0041	0.0037	−0.0001	−0.0001
	(0.0167)	(0.0167)	(0.0005)	(0.0005)
Public health	−0.8525	−0.9283	−11.6863*	−11.1817*
	(−1.0146)	(−1.0180)	(6.2371)	(6.0048)
Constant	1440.979	−34081.48	−1551348	−1543688
	(408214.7)	(409338.2)	(1921212)	(1925390)
N	158	158	59	59
R^2	0.9778	0.9767	0.9588	0.9592
	$F_{(9, 117)} = 33.70$	$F_{(9, 117)} = 33.25$	$F_{(9, 18)} = 45.38$	$F_{(9, 18)} = 45.16$

*** $p < .001$; ** $p < .01$; * $p < .05$

is consistent with past studies: the more populated an area, the higher the output. Additionally, people tend to migrate to regions of higher output. The positive sign on lagged private GDP is also consistent with past studies: regions with higher past GDP have higher future GDP. Finally, public health spending, a proxy for development, is negative and significant in the later period. This implies that areas receiving more public health spending have lower private GDP. In Colombia, areas receiving more spending are relatively poorer.

The first coca hypothesis states that coca production should have a negative impact on GDP. Contrary to expectations, coca cultivation is not significant in either time period. The positive coefficient is likely a result of coca being cultivated in regions where there are no other viable alternatives. The negative effect of coca production on the economy appears to be indirect and likely occurs through its positive effect on violence, as we saw in Chapter Six. Our results support the idea that coca cultivation in and of itself does not have a negative effect on the economy, but rather its indirect effects are detrimental to the economy. Coca production leads to violence when groups fight to gain territorial control. The repatriated illegal profits have inflationary effects in addition to displacing clean capital and legitimate businesses.

The first violence hypothesis theorizes that there is a negative relationship between insecurity and economic activity. Lagged justice and security spending is significant and negative in both periods. Current justice and security spending is negative and significant in the later time period; this could reflect the tendency of regions with less violence to have fewer security costs and to be better able to focus on production. Alternatively, it could be a result of productive resources seeking out stable regions in which to operate. These results indicate that both current and short-term investments are reduced by insecurity. This result is consistent with other studies discussed earlier that conclude that insecurity has a negative effect on GDP and investment. Our limited data precludes an analysis of the long-term effect of insecurity on GDP, but it is unlikely that the effect would be anything but negative. Stability appears to be an important factor for increasing output.

The second violence hypothesis presents the expectation that FARC violence harms GDP. Total leftist violence is negative and insignificant in the first time period. In the later time period, it becomes positive and significant in the model using percentage of coca production on agricultural land. Our model does not support the hypothesis that FARC violence has a direct negative effect on the economy.

The third violence hypothesis associates paramilitary violence with areas of relatively high GDP. While total paramilitary violence is not significant by traditional measures, the probability that the coefficient is not equal to zero does fall from 63 percent to 13 percent. The sign on paramilitary violence is positive, which is also consistent with the theory that paramilitary groups protect resources.

CONCLUSION

The most surprising results of this analysis are that many of the direct theorized effects of violence and illegal drug production are not evident. However, the importance of security to private GDP is clear. The result of the previous year's justice and security spending can be interpreted in two ways. First, regions that are more stable tend to attract more investment, so increased justice and security spending in the previous year indicates (and signals to investors) higher levels of instability. Increased justice and security spending this year indicates a region in turmoil and would have a negative effect on current GDP. Higher justice and security spending in the previous period implies a region that was in turmoil, and the negative impact on current GDP could be a result of lower levels of previous-period investment or an inability to recover from the previous period's loss in GDP attributable to violence. Therefore, we can interpret the results to indicate that justice and security spending has both a negative current-period impact on GDP and negative effects on future GDP in the short term.

This analysis highlights the complexity of the relationships among violence, coca cultivation, and the economy. While we do not find a direct effect of drugs or violence on the economy, our results, when coupled with those in Chapter Six, do suggest a negative indirect effect on the economy. To conclude that a negative effect is not present because the models do not show a strong direct negative impact of drugs and violence on the economy would be to oversimplify the problems in Colombia. Examining the results of the models with the other types of analyses presented allows certain broad conclusions to emerge. The negative relationship between coffee and coca underscores the need for improvement in the rural sector to replace lost opportunities in the rural economy. Guerrilla violence needs to be controlled so that resources spent on security and war costs can be reallocated to infrastructure and other domestic programs. Stability that does not create new types of violence is necessary for sustained economic growth. This analysis reveals that stability and the resulting ability of companies and citizens to make long-term economic decisions are fundamental to sustainable long-term economic growth in Colombia.

EIGHT

ACKNOWLEDGING CONSTRAINTS TO FINDING COMPREHENSIVE PEACE

The Four Cornerstones of Pacification

> Colombianos: Las armas os han dado independencia.
> Las leyes os darán la libertad.
> *Colombians: Weapons have given us independence.*
> *The law will make us free.*
>
> FRANCISCO DE PAULA SANTANDER (1792–1840)

A sustained commitment and a coordinated strategy are required to successfully calm the decades-long conflict in Colombia. After a brief discussion of recent peace attempts, we will discuss four crucial cornerstones for success. Throughout, we use the empirical findings of this project to inform policy choices and identify constraints. There are four cornerstones of a successful pacification strategy: military dominance, increased state capacity, a strong political community, and economic reform. Each of the four is necessary, but there are multiple feedbacks and overlaps among them. Moreover, it is important to have both a long- and a short-term perspective of the conflict so that an immediate goal does not hinder progress toward a long-term goal. Unfortunately for Colombia, progress is not entirely in its control—other factors present constraints to success. For example, as discussed in Chapter Two, there are geographic and historical hindrances to a strong, unified central government. Moreover, the history of unsuccessful demobilization (of the Unión Patriótica) has created problems of trust among potentially demobilized guerrillas. After almost a half century of conflict, the Colombian political community is fractious and full of distrust. Finally, international factors, such as the international economic environment and U.S. foreign policy, constrain available options for Colombian policy makers.

PEACE PROCESSES, GOVERNMENTAL POLICIES

Since the late 1970s the Colombian government has tried to craft political and military solutions for the rebel and drug conflicts, but few of these efforts have enjoyed lasting success. President Julio César Turbay Ayala (1978–1982) relied on military and paramilitary units to control guerrilla violence. President Belisario Betancur (1982–1986) initiated talks that resulted in a 1982 peace process and amnesty, and ceasefire agreements were reached with four out of five guerrilla organizations in 1984. A national dialogue convened in 1984 and 1985. However, paramilitary groups killed more than six thousand Unión Patriótica members, and the 1984 cease-fire agreement failed. At the same time, the Colombian army dealt severe blows to the military operations of the largest guerrilla groups. Rural and urban violence escalated under President Virgilio Barco Vargas (1986–1990). President César Gaviria Trujillo (1990–1994) attempted to restart talks with guerrilla insurgents, holding extensive negotiations in 1991 and 1992, but these discussions did not produce an agreement.[1]

Shortly after election in 1998, President Andrés Pastrana initiated talks with FARC and the ELN for the first time in six years. In exchange for participating in peace talks, both guerrilla groups were offered safe havens that would be free from governmental interference. Concurrently, President Pastrana released his three-year program called Plan Colombia in 1999. This plan promoted alternative development, the strengthening of Colombia's political and judicial institutions, and military successes in the guerrilla conflict. Pastrana estimated that it would cost more than $7 billion to achieve these goals, with the Colombian government committing $4 billion and the remainder coming from the international community, including the European Union and the United States.[2] However, these peace talks were widely viewed as failures (see the discussion in Kline 2007). The next section provides an overview of peace efforts by violent groups. Two groups, M-19 and the Unión Patriótica, demobilized in the late 1980s and early 1990s. FARC and the ELN had frustrated peace processes in the 1990s. Under President Uribe, the AUC began a process of demobilization, followed by a new round of talks with the ELN.

Unión Patriótica (UP)

During the 1980s, the Partido Comunista de Colombia (PPC) and a small part of FARC took advantage of an amnesty and formed a political party, the Unión Patriótica (UP), in an attempt to reach their goals through nonviolent means. The new party participated in the 1986 elections and won fourteen congressional seats. The paramilitaries, however, sought to preclude the participation of members from the UP and killed more than six thousand members. From the perspective of the left, the government did little to protect the newly incorporated party or to pursue the paramilitary groups that targeted them: "With each new assassination, the erosion of the state's capacity to uphold public order and render justice was confirmed and the democratic participation was made less possible" (Chernick 1989, 76). Consequently, the 1984 cease-fire agreement between the government and FARC failed. Moreover, relatives of UP victims filed a case in 2006 with the Interamerican Commission on Human Rights charging the Colombian government with failure to protect UP members. The suit claimed that the government encouraged the prosecution of members, that threats against the UP have continued, and that the government was not acting in good faith in negotiations with the families. The wounds from this failed experiment have yet to heal.

M-19

The seizure of the Palace of Justice by M-19 in 1985 polarized the Colombian people. The issue of public order became paramount for voters in 1986. Tired of the peace initiatives of the Betancur administration, Colombian voters gave a vote of no confidence to Betancur and his policies. The backlash from the siege led to Virgilio Barco Vargas winning the presidency and to a heightened awareness among the Colombian public about the level of insecurity and lack of public order. Before the siege, M-19 had enjoyed a level of tolerance among the Colombian public that the ELN and FARC lacked. After the debacle, the remaining M-19 leaders signed an agreement in 1989 to abandon their armed struggle and become a political party, today known as the Democratic Alliance/M-19. The incorporation of M-19 and other smaller guerrilla groups into the peace process led to the Constitutional Assembly of 1991. The new Constitutional Assembly was charged with rewriting the Colombian constitution to guarantee human rights and to make politics more democratic and participatory. Today, the group remains part of the legal left in Colombia.

FARC

Shortly after Pastrana was elected in 1998, FARC negotiated for a demilitarized zone as a precondition of participating in peace talks. The FARC *despeje* zone of forty-two thousand square kilometers was located in the center of Colombia.

The area was equivalent in size to Switzerland, and was located in the heart of the coca producing region of the country. This safe haven failed to lead to meaningful peace talks but allowed FARC to fully develop its coca infrastructure. On February 20, 2002, the day after FARC hijacked an airplane, peace talks between the government and FARC failed. In this attack, FARC took a fifth member of Congress hostage; it was already holding four. In response, the military retook the *despeje* zone. Many believed that FARC was not truly interested in peace, instead using the zone as a base from which to consolidate and prepare for attacks. Before FARC's safe haven was granted in November 1998, there were 239 FARC human violations reported by CINEP for all of 1998. However, for the three following years, CINEP reported over 430 FARC human rights violations annually. FARC claimed that the government blockaded the zone and did not stop paramilitary incursions or attacks.

ELN

The ELN began peace talks in 1991 and 1992 along with the other guerrilla groups, but did not continue. In 1998 and 1999, the ELN met with business and civic leaders and agreed to begin discussions about possible peace talks. The ELN reached an agreement with the government in Maguncia in July 1998. This agreement was procedural rather than substantive: it sought to create a framework for a series of peace conventions the following year. On April 25, 2000, the Colombian government announced the creation of a zone for the ELN.[3] However, this initiative was resisted from the beginning by elements within the government, by the population at large, and by the paramilitaries. A top negotiator resigned in protest. In January 2001, the process was restarted in accordance with many proposed rules, but was suspended again in August. However, this accord, which granted the ELN a demilitarized area called the *zona de encuentro*, was not consecrated, because of nationwide roadblocks, resistance by local officials, and general paramilitary resistance to the plan. As the military moved out, the paramilitaries moved in to resist the implementation of the zone (*Semana* 2001).

As peace talks and the implementation of the zone failed, the ELN conducted some high-profile incidents. In April 1999, the ELN hijacked an Avianca airplane and kidnapped the majority of the passengers. In May 1999, the ELN attempted another mass kidnapping in an attempt to show its strength. The *pesca milagrosa* of a church in Cali led to the kidnapping of 143 parishioners. In August, peace talks began again, but no real progress was made. The peace process under Pastrana continued, with numerous interruptions and suspensions, through May 2002 (Kline 2007). The ELN continued to kidnap and to damage oil infrastructure, although the conflict was at a lower level of intensity than previously. However, the number of governmental attacks against the ELN increased from 213 in 2001 to 328 in 2004 (Espejo and Garzón 2005, 43).

President Uribe's commitment to protect the oil pipeline, including the so-called Rehabilitation and Consolidation Zone, which the pipeline crosses, required a major military offensive in traditional ELN strongholds. Furthermore, Uribe is now able to use U.S. aid to protect the pipeline and fight the ELN. The U.S. aid package in 2003 included $98 million in counterterrorism aid, U.S. Army Special Forces to provide counterinsurgency training to Colombian soldiers, and additional training and helicopters. The ELN increased its attacks in response to the government's counterinsurgency efforts; at the peak, in 2001, there were 170 bombings of the Caño Limón pipeline. However, only 41 bombings were recorded in 2002 (Energy Information Administration 2003).

By March 2002, the ELN announced that it would consider the possibility of a cease-fire; in December 2005, exploratory peace talks began. Previously, the ELN's negotiations with the government had been facilitated by the Mexican ambassador, Andrés Valencia, but, according to a story in *El Nuevo Herald* (June 9, 2005), talks broke down in April 2005 because of Mexico's vote against Cuba in the UN Human Rights Commission. After the breakdown, Uribe proposed a bilateral cease-fire conditioned on the ELN's participation in peace talks, renunciation of kidnapping, and the selection of a mediator. However, even without official peace talks, at least one ELN front, the Héroes de Anorí, demobilized in June 2005. Uribe invited other ELN fronts to participate in the demobilization program. By March 2007, there had been five rounds of preliminary talks between governmental and ELN representatives in Havana, Cuba.

AUC

The last group examined is the umbrella paramilitary group, the AUC. In a December 15, 2002, letter, the AUC declared a cease-fire with governmental forces (but not with FARC), beginning December 1, 2002. The AUC also stated its openness to peace talks; requested to be recognized as a political actor; asked for the assistance of the Catholic Church, the United Nations, and the Organization of American States (OAS) in a peace process; and expressed confidence in the Colombian government's ability to fulfill its obligations of governance.[4] Thus began a peace process that is currently ongoing. Uribe initiated peace talks with the AUC, granting them a zone free from governmental interference. The possibility of negotiation was also included, but with strict compliance of cease-fires. With reference to the fate of the UP, this plan guaranteed that the legal opposition would be afforded all the rights and protections of friends and partisans of the government (Ministerio de Defensa Nacional 2003).

Uribe's approach to peace was very different from that of the previous presidents. Previously, from 1992 to 1997, there was no available legal framework for negotiating with the paramilitaries, except for *sometimiento a la justicia* (submission to justice), which is not a political process. In 2002, Uribe changed this with Law 782. This law allowed groups that have "a recognized command structure, a capacity to undertake sustained military operations, and a significant territorial control or presence" to have the status of a party to an internal conflict so that it could enter into a dialogue with the government, independent of its political motivations or platform (Pardo 2005, 17). Uribe focused on demobilizing the paramilitary groups, with the aim of completing demobilization by December 31, 2005. Individual paramilitary groups, such as the Alianza del Oriente and the Bloque Central Bolívar, have already disbanded. Despite the fractionalization of the AUC, the peace process continues.

The official dialogue with the paramilitaries began in July 2003 in Santa Fé de Rialto, Córdoba. The demobilization process began before the legal status of demobilized paramilitaries had been settled. In August 2003, the government proposed the Proyecto de Ley de Alternatividad (Alternative Penalties Law), which would subject individual paramilitaries to penalties but would not include prison time. This proposal was criticized as being too lenient. The first block to demobilize was the Medellín-based Bloque Cacique Nutibara (BCN) in November 2003, followed by the Autodefensas Campesinas de Ortega in December. While the Colombian government tried to finalize the legal details of the demobilization, in January 2004, the OAS committed to monitor the paramilitary peace process. The Fátima Agreement, signed in Santa Fé de Rialto on May 13, 2004, created the *zona de ubicación* for AUC leaders. The agreement also created a tripartite entity—made up of the Colombian government, the OAS, and the paramilitaries—to monitor the cease-fire and investigate any complaints. Individual paramilitaries would not be arrested or extradited as long as they stayed in the zone.

In July 2004, the government announced a new law, Verdad, Justicia y Reparación (Truth, Justice, and Reparation), which would require any paramilitary or guerrilla group member who entered into peace talks to undergo an investigation by the newly proposed Attorney General's Office. In August

2004, the 6,000-member AUC of the eastern plains agreed to demobilize. Under the proposal, prison terms for all of them would range from five to ten years, depending on the seriousness of the crime. In August 2004, Decree 2767 was announced, allowing demobilized persons to receive governmental support in return for cooperating with security forces. In June 2005, the government's proposal was altered to include prison sentences of between four and eight years; it was signed into law in June 2005. The investigation of each individual would be completed within sixty days, and reparations to victims would be considered by the investigating court (Pardo 2005).

In December 2004, a decision had been made not to extradite paramilitary leader Salvatore Mancuso if he complied with the peace process, although the government did not rule out extradition in general. This decision had serious implications, since many in the AUC leadership have been indicted in the United States. Nonetheless, AUC leaders intimate that they will not be extradited. The final law included the possibility that paramilitary leaders could avoid extradition. In 2006, the United States agreed to financially support demobilization efforts with over fifteen million dollars.

By the end of 2006, more than 30,000 paramilitaries had been demobilized in exchange for promised leniency for their crimes. However, in May 2006, the Colombian Supreme Court issued a ruling that altered the relevant law by correcting items that seemed overly biased in favor of the paramilitaries. Sentences handed out before the peace process had to be served in their original terms. Reparations would be paid from both legal and illicit assets of paramilitary leaders. The ruling required paramilitaries to fully disclose their illegal activities in order to benefit from the peace process; if they did not, they would lose all benefits and could be prosecuted fully and without leniency. Whereas the law as passed included a set time period for investigations to begin and end—as soon as a paramilitary demobilized—the court ruled that the authorities would have six months to investigate. The time to investigate would begin when the authorities were ready, not when the paramilitary demobilized. Finally, the court ruled that time spent during negotiations would not be counted toward the maximum eight-year sentence for crimes covered under the peace process. AUC commander Ernesto Báez described the ruling as a blow to the peace process (*Semana* 2006b). In spring 2007 he was threatened with losing the benefits of the peace process because he was not cooperating with the terms of the law.

As discussed in Chapter 4, the AUC has been involved in efforts to influence politicians and policymakers. The issue is whether this was done legally, or whether it reflected indifference on the part of certain officials or politicians to human rights abuses by paramilitaries. Because of this, some members of the opposition have insisted on the release of the names of officials and politicians who maintained ties with paramilitaries outside of the peace process.

Serious questions about the integrity of the official process remain. First, more people have been demobilized than were supposedly members of the paramilitary organizations (approximately 17,000). This leaves open the possibility that nonparamilitaries were being "demobilized" and that many real paramilitaries were not participating. Second, efforts to make paramilitary leaders surrender their wealth have stalled. Third, violence continues. Concerns are amplified because of continued paramilitary killings and disappearances since the December 2002 cease-fire—more than 2,750, according to Amnesty International (2006). These concerns corroborated earlier charges of collaboration between governmental officials and paramilitaries in zones that had increased state presence. Despite governmental claims that paramilitary violence had declined during the demobilization process, a laptop computer belonging to paramilitary leader "Jorge 40" documented hundreds of murders in one department during the demobilization period of 2002–2005, providing chilling evidence that paramilitary violence had not ended during the demobilization.

Moreover, the OAS organization in charge of mobilizing the peace process has noted some troubling developments. The sixth and seventh quarterly reports, released in 2006, show that some paramilitaries have not demobilized, that previously demobilized paramilitaries are re-forming violent and illegal groups, and that a new generation of paramilitaries is emerging. The OAS reports that this last problem has been particularly acute in areas where neither the guerrillas nor the government have a strong presence: "In these areas, the problem arises when middle-level demobilized combatants step into the vacuum. They assume control of the criminal activities that were traditionally the preserve of the units or groups based there (extortion, levies on drug production, social cleansing, alliances with local administrations) and organize themselves" (OAS 2006, 8).

The problem continues to be noted in the next report. The OAS repeats its concerns and concludes that these "units, as noted in the Sixth Report, are expanding and taking control of illegal economic activities" (OAS 2006a, 4). Also undermining confidence in the process is the discovery of arms caches from allegedly demobilized paramilitaries, raising concern about the sincerity of the demobilization (OAS 2006a, 6). Moreover, the commission laments gaps in the coverage provided by the reintegration process, which undermines the success of those sincerely trying to reintegrate: "These gaps are particularly apparent in the fields of health, psychosocial support, and education, and many former combatants have no possibility of finding work or pursuing productive projects" (OAS 2006a, 4). As noted in earlier chapters, economic growth and a sustainable peace policy require that the Colombian government create economic opportunities for youth and the demobilized, and provide social services to rural areas.

THE POLICY OF PRESIDENT
ALVARO URIBE (2002–)

President Alvaro Uribe introduced the "Política de Defensa y Seguridad Democrática" (Democratic Security and Defense Strategy) shortly after being elected in 2002. There are four strategic objectives: the consolidation of state control over territory, the elimination of drug trafficking and cultivation, the maintenance of state strength, and improvement in efficiency and transparency. In general, the aim is to restore the rule of law and a climate of security through a coordinated effort between the security forces and the judiciary. The plan rests upon three principles: the protection of the rights of all Colombian citizens; the protection of democratic institutions, pluralism, and values; and the cooperation and solidarity of all Colombian citizens in defense of democratic values. To achieve this, the plan calls for the consolidation of state control throughout the country, a permanent presence in all the municipal capitals, improvement in the functioning of the judicial system, and the coordination of efforts led by the Consejo de Seguridad y Defensa Nacional (National Council for Public Safety). Reform efforts to increase interagency integration within the intelligence agencies were especially stressed. Agencies specifically named include the intelligence agencies of the armed forces, the national police, and the DAS (Departamento Administrativo de Seguridad, or Administrative Department for Security) and the CTI (Cuerpo Técnico de Investigación, or Technical Investigation Unit) of the Fiscalía General de la Nación (attorney general). Additionally, Uribe declared a "state of internal commotion"—essentially a state of emergency—which gave him emergency powers to deal with the immediate security situation, to implement a 1.2 percent war tax on assets, and to propose antiterrorism legislation.[5]

In general, Uribe has pursued a hard line against drug and guerrilla violence. Part of the democratic security plan includes the Plan Patriota, which involves Operation Jorge Mora. This operation put 18,000 soldiers in the departments of Caquetá, Meta, and Guaviare to uproot FARC from its stronghold and infrastructure.[6] Plan Patriota is unique both because of the size of the forces involved in the singular mission and because of the role of the United States. In particular, the Colombian military used a "clean and hold" technique to gain control of territory. In March 2004, the government reintroduced the Search Bloc police unit to hunt drug traffickers in the south. It targeted specifically the Norte de Valle drug cartel in much the same way the governmental forces had earlier attacked the Medellín cartel.

Uribe was reelected in 2006. In December 2006, the government announced Plan Victoria, which is an extension of Plan Colombia and Plan Patriota. At the same time, President Uribe began circulating a new six-year plan, entitled "Strategy of Strengthening Democracy and Social Development (2007–2013)," which proposes a much heavier emphasis on social and economic programs, as compared to military and police aid. The proposed spending for 2007–2013 includes $43.8 billion spread over the following areas: aid to the displaced (3 percent), social development (48 percent), promoting justice and human rights (6 percent), opening markets (27 percent), demobilization, disarmament, and reintegration (2 percent), and the war on terrorism and drug trafficking (14 percent). The Colombian government must follow through with the social and economic spending if Colombia's success under Uribe is to continue.

THE FOUR CORNERSTONES OF PACIFICATION AND THE PROSPECTS FOR SUCCESS OF URIBE'S POLÍTICA DE DEFENSA Y SEGURIDAD DEMOCRÁTICA (DEMOCRATIC SECURITY AND DEFENSE STRATEGY)

The four cornerstones of a successful pacification strategy overlap significantly and depend on one another for successful implementation. Militarily, the government must be strong enough to produce at least what is known as a "hurting stalemate" in order to make opponents serious about negotiating for peace. Second, the state must be strong enough to both maintain a security presence and also offer governmental services to its citizens. Third, the integrity of the political community must be maintained. In countries suffering internal conflict, this is especially challenging, since members of the legal opposition can be viewed with suspicion. Finally, the economy must be reformed and strengthened in order to pay for improvements in security and infrastructure and to alleviate poverty and inequality, which facilitate guerilla recruitment. This section discusses the main challenges of each and assesses the current efforts of President Uribe to end the conflict.

The Quest for Military Dominance

There are three main concerns regarding military dominance: overwhelming force, hearts and minds, and the resources necessary to successfully implement a counterinsurgency strategy: "Counterinsurgency is expensive business; it cannot be done on the cheap and requires the full mobilization of a nation's resources over a relatively long period of time" (Marcella 2003, 46). Historically, there have been concerns that the Colombian military and police forces were neither large enough nor professional enough to control the country, limitations that hampered implementation and discouraged successful peace talks. Even in contemporary times, Colombian military spending is considered relatively low, given the long-standing conflict. Rabasa and Chalk (2001) estimated that Colombia spends only 3.56 percent of GDP on military spending—a figure unchanged since the early 1990s. Governments can easily win short-term battles, but in the long-term it is more difficult to achieve victory: "The essence of guerrilla tactics is to trade space for time" (O'Sullivan and Miller 1983, 115). Although much of the territory is under the control of either the government or the paramilitaries, the guerrillas have been able to survive concentrated counterinsurgency efforts. Even with military progress, small groups of guerrillas have been historically able to rebound. Moreover, the intransigent paramilitaries can regroup. After military success, the state needs to move in and provide a sufficient presence to maintain any progress gained in the battlefield; otherwise, new groups may move in to fill any remaining power vacuums.

Efforts to strengthen military capacity are ongoing. For example, in mid-2002, only 60,000–80,000 soldiers in Colombia were combat ready. The rest were in training or support roles (Marcella 2003, 10). Under Uribe, the size of the military has increased by approximately 100,000 soldiers, and the army was reorganized to become a more efficient, offensively oriented military.[7] Police presence increased from 1,670 per million in 1993 to 4,300 per million by the end of 2003 (Marcella 2003, 18). Military expenditure as a percent of GDP increased from 2.2 percent in 1990 to 4.4 percent in 2003 (UHDR). Additionally, Uribe imposed "rehabilitation and consolidation zones" in areas with endemic violence. These zones included increased military and police presence, house searches, curfews, and restrictions of individual rights.

In his second term, Uribe has continued to take a hard line against the guerrillas. In an interview with *El Nuevo Herald* (March 2007), he stated his "government is always ready for dialogue. But what we have in mind is to militarily defeat the FARC. When they don't want dialogue, our objective will be to militarily defeat terrorism."[8] To this end, Uribe continues to build the military and police forces in the country. According to a story in *El Mercurio* (February 2007), the government announced plans to invest over 3.7 million dollars in additional airplanes, helicopters, and weapons as well as an additional 38,000 troops, 20,000 of which will be police.

Aid to the Colombian government from the United States has also increased. Beginning with Plan Colombia under President Pastrana and continuing with aid to President Uribe, U.S. military aid has averaged over a half billion dollars a year. This supplementary foreign funding has helped build and professionalize the Colombian police and military forces.

According to official governmental statistics, the effort has paid off militarily. Comparing the first trimesters of 2006 and 2005, government-initiated battles with FARC increased from 288 in 2005 to 446 in 2006. The government still attacked paramilitary forces, but only 21 attacks took place in the first part of 2006, down from 56 in 2005 (Fundación Seguridad y Democracia 2006, 41). FARC attacks on governmental forces decreased 7 percent from 2005 to 2006, unknown attacks decreased 19 percent, ELN attacks decreased 80 percent, and paramilitaries had one attack in each year (52). Comparing January through March 2006 with the same period of 2005, total kidnappings decreased 64 percent, with decreases of 86 percent for paramilitary kidnappings, 47 percent for ELN kidnappings, and 76 percent for FARC kidnappings (71). Similarly, homicides decreased in same period, comparing first trimester statistics to an average of 9.89 percent (77).

The Colombian conflict is fought in numerous small battles throughout the country, where the geography is rough and state presence is limited. Moreover, at one time or another, groups have had safe havens and support from the local population, creating a difficult strategic situation for official governmental forces. To hold an area that has been won, not only do the citizens need to be separated from the guerrillas or paramilitaries, but they also need to be safe. Without security, a hearts-and-minds approach will not work: "The winning of hearts and minds . . . must, however, offer genuine improvement in the quality of life. . . . Indeed, for insurgency to develop at all is frequently an indication that the government of a country has failed to accommodate the basic aspirations of its population" (Beckett and Pimlott 1985, 10–11). A strong state, with accountability and sufficient resources to implement policies, is essential.

8.1 U.S. AID TO COLOMBIA (MILLIONS OF DOLLARS)

Aid type	1997	1998	1999	2000	2001	2002	2003	2004	2005	2006	2007	2008
Military & police	88.6	112.5	308.8	765.4	242.8	401.9	621.0	555.1	634.3	632.2	615.9	603.4
Economic & social	0	0.5	8.8	214.3	5.7	120.3	136.7	135.0	131.3	132.2	132.2	139.5

Note: Military and police aid includes the following programs: International Narcotics Control (INC, also known as the Andean Counterdrug Initiative), Foreign Military Financing, International Military Education and Training, Section 1004, Section 1003, Emergency Drawdowns, Antiterrorism Assistance (NADR/ATA), Small Arms/Light Weapons, Counter-Terror Fellowship Program, Center for Hemispheric Defense Studies, Excess Defense Articles, Discretionary Funds from the Office of National Drug Control Policy. Economic and social aid includes the following programs: Economic Support Funds, PL 480 "Food for Peace," International Narcotics Control (INC, also known as the Andean Counterdrug Initiative).

Source: Center for International Policy (CIP), www.ciponline.org

State Presence and Institutional Capacity

Chernick asked "whether national reconciliation through negotiated settlement, at any stage in the conflict, is possible without a relatively strong state, specifically in the areas of preserving public order, administering justice, and executive control over the military" (1988, 56). The state needs to be strong enough to guarantee the safety of the demobilized, maintain a functioning judicial system, discourage the emergence of violence, vigorously defend the country, and maintain citizen support: "That is the essential condition for countering terrorism, without which the most efficiently organized, trained and led security forces could not succeed" (Mark 1986, 161). A strong state with sufficient institutional capacity is essential to maintain progress in the other areas. Without a state able to do what no previous Colombian national government has done—eliminate internal rivals through conquering, cajoling, co-opting, etc—Colombia will continue to be made up of a pattern of numerous and competing "political archipelagoes, in many of which the national government is not the strongest actor" (Kline 2007, 1).

Building state capacity also demands attention to transportation and basic infrastructure issues. Since the lack of transportation infrastructure has hindered economic expansion and state cohesion, as state control is expanded into previously remote and inaccessible areas, basic infrastructure should be a top priority. Better transportation would facilitate military and police movement, improve market access for rural areas, and improve consolidation of state building in these areas. At the beginning of the twenty-first century, Colombia had 3,304 kilometers (2,050 miles) of rails and 110,000 kilometers (68,200 miles) of roadways, figures that show improvement but still require more progress (CIA 2006). Progress in building a comprehensive state presence remains incremental, but is essential for advancement in other areas.

In general, Uribe has been successful in establishing a government, military, or security presence even in towns that previously had none, yet the provision of other rudimentary governmental services continue to be sparse or nonexistent, despite a comprehensive definition of security in his policy.[9] Since 2002, Uribe has achieved remarkable results in his effort to expand state presence throughout Colombia. According to the World Bank, "It took only 22 months for the Uribe administration to secure state presence in all the country's 1,098 municipalities, a target achieved in February 2004 with the establishment of a police garrison in Murindó, Antioquia" (World Bank 2007, 8). Progress is notable, but not complete.

Moreover, Uribe's government has also been willing to extradite citizens to the United States for prosecution, a step that can serve as a surrogate for

Colombian judicial competence and threaten both guerrilla and paramilitary leaders with compliance that is more difficult to undermine. With the concurrence of the Colombian Supreme Court, former Cali cartel leader Victor Patiño Fómenque was extradited in November 2002 to face drug charges in Florida. Furthermore, in April 2002, a FARC member was extradited to the United States for the first time to face charges of murder in the deaths of three Indian-rights activists in 1999. Compared to President Pastrana, President Uribe has extradited many more Colombians for prosecution in the United States. By December 2004, Uribe had already extradited about 200 persons, compared to only 64 during Pastrana's term (Dudley 2004). Extradition continues to be a controversial topic in Colombia. It was not legal from 1991 to 1997. Since 1997, extradition has been allowed with the permission of the president.

However, the process of how one eliminates internal rivals is also important. General studies have pointed to the importance of a "firm and consistent application of judicial control" (Wilkinson 1986, 179) to counter domestic terrorism. Colombia suffers from a well-recognized weak judicial system. According to Pécaut (1997), this is both a cause and consequence of the violence. Gutiérrez Sanín (2001) describes the Colombian judicial system as arbitrary, inefficient, and politicized. Corruption in the police and judiciary is doubly dangerous: in addition to hampering successful crime prevention and control, it helps further terrorists' goals. Democratic accountability, impartiality, and strong public support are necessary to facilitate the work of counterterrorism forces.

Consequently, the measure of state capacity needs to take into account the quality and the character of order. One of the strongest and most consistent findings in this book is that both paramilitary and governmental human rights violations are associated with higher levels of guerrilla violence. Other scholars have noted the explosive effect of repression. Goodwin concludes that "the persistence or defeat of large-scale revolutionary movements hinges crucially upon the variable capacity of armed forces to respect the rights of noncombatants and broadly tolerate peaceful political dissent while democratic regimes are consolidated" (2001, 247). Seligson highlights the combustive nature of repression: "It may well be that massive repression launched by the state to root out what are initially small groups of guerrillas . . . initiates a cycle of violence that eventually brings others into the fray" (1996, 154). Using paramilitary or governmental violence to solve a long-standing conflict may instead simply prolong it by creating a fresh cycle of vengeance and violence.

In Colombia, the inability to control violence has encouraged the creation of paramilitaries. At the same time, governmental repression has facilitated guerrilla recruitment and operations: "Over-reaction would not only poison our way of life, it would also play into the terrorists hands, by building more public sympathy for them, and by increasing what is now only a tiny trickle of recruits to their ranks. On the other hand, if a government fails to protect its citizens, those citizens may take the law into their own hands by forming, first, vigilante groups and then, as law and order breaks down, their own private armies" (Clutterbuck 1975, 149). The result is a cycle of violence. A long-standing charge is that despite a general decline of overt human rights violations by the military and police forces, paramilitary forces serve in an unofficial capacity of the state, as discussed in Chapter Four. In fact, Chapter Six uncovers a strong association between paramilitary violence and higher levels of security and justice spending. This could support charges of collaboration between the police and military forces and paramilitaries. These charges have been made regularly over the years and have become sharply salient and convincing as the "paragate" scandal unfolded in late 2006 and continues today.

Although both Pastrana's Plan Colombia and Uribe's Política de Defensa y Seguridad Democrática strategy promised to respect human rights and reject illicit ties to paramilitaries, many foreign governments, nongovernmental organizations, and international leaders have accused the Colombian state of committing human rights violations and contributing to the violence. Most of the recent controversy rests upon whether the Colombian armed forces maintained ties to and cooperated with paramilitary groups, despite their illegal status and violence. Human Rights Watch, in its 2000 *World Report,* documented specific ties between the Colombian Army's Fourth Brigade and the AUC, alleging that Castaño's men exchanged civilian corpses for weapons from the army. The army would then claim that the dead civilians were guerrillas killed in combat. Previous human rights reports from the U.S. State Department also document a range of military complicity. For example, in its *1999 Country Reports on Human Rights,* the State Department documents collaboration, intelligence sharing, and the provision of military supplies (U.S. Department of State 2000). According to a report by the United States Institute of Peace, "A large state presence in this zone of conflict has failed to guarantee public order. Although five military battalions are located in Barrancabermeja, local residents pointed out that paramilitaries are able to move freely about the zone without fear of persecution" (USIP 2004, 5). These charges have been brought up consistently since the paramilitaries were made illegal. In July 2005, the police allegedly withdrew before an attack in Buena-ventura, Valle del Cauca, by the supposedly demobilized paramilitary group, Bloque Calima (Amnesty International 2006b).

There have been attempts to reform the armed forces, reduce human rights violations, and prosecute complicit officials. As discussed in Chapter 4, many human rights organizations have charged that officials and officers complicit in human rights violations remain in their jobs (Amnesty International 2001). However, some have recently been held accountable. In 2002, a former army colonel was given a forty-year prison term for his involvement in the 1997 massacre in Mapiripán committed by paramilitaries. Two others from the army were sentenced to thirty-two and twenty-two years for the same incident (U.S. Department of State 2004). Nonetheless, charges of new and ongoing state violations of human rights continue. For example, CINEP documented ninety-six extrajudicial killings committed by state forces in the first half of 2005. In 2006, CINEP tallied 187 paramilitary disappearances or killings and 247 by governmental forces (CINEP 2007). Attempts at reform are ongoing, but the state is still plagued by accusations that it both cooperates with paramilitaries, and thereby is complicit in the violence they commit, and continues to violate human rights directly.

Moreover, while paramilitary demobilizations were ongoing, new evidence emerged of ties between high-ranking Colombian officials and paramilitaries—as long alleged by human rights groups—in an unfolding scandal dubbed "paragate" by the media. By March 2007, top officials or politicians charged and held for collaboration with paramilitaries included two top intelligence directors, one governor, six senators, two representatives, one former representative, and a colonel. Additionally, another former governor, a former representative, and a current representative are fugitives. Other top officials being investigated by the Colombian Supreme Court or attorney general include the general in charge of the army, six senators, five representatives, one governor, a former senator, and two former representatives. Additionally, powerful members of the Colombian business community and numerous foreign companies have been named as having funded paramilitaries or cooperated with them. Investigations are being carried out by the Supreme Court, the Fiscalía General, and members of the media.

Interviews with paramilitary leaders provided damning statements of ties between the government and paramilitary leaders. In May 2007, Salvatore Mancuso stated: "Paramilitarism was state policy . . . I am proof positive of state paramilitarism in Colombia." Moreover, paramilitary spokesman Iván Duque stated that the paramilitaries operated with the knowledge and co-operation of the leaders: "Could these three groups—I am talking about political people, economic people, the institutional people, meaning the military—operate without having contact with the chief of chiefs? That's impossible." He promised that paramilitary leaders would name more names so that governmental officials, military members, and members of the economic elite would be punished, not just the paramilitaries, for breaking the law (Forero 2007).

One of the most prominent politicians charged with aiding paramilitaries is Senator Álvaro Araújo. He stated in March 2007, "If they come for me, they come for 'Conchi' [his sister, Uribe's Foreign Minister], and for the President" (*Semana* 2007a).[10] Shortly afterward, his sister, Foreign Minister María Consuelo Araújo, resigned. Opposition senator Gustavo Petro of the Polo Democrático Alternativo has warned that the scandal is just beginning. Petro has accused Uribe of personally meeting with paramilitary leaders. This was the latest of a series of similar accusations. In 2006, *Semana* reported that President Uribe met with AUC leader Salvatore Mancuso twice. Petro also warned, "If the arising threats against sectors of the State, fearful of the truth, are quelled, El Polo Democrático will move this to International Courts so they can act against those who have committed crimes against humanity in Colombia" (Petro 2007).[11]

Although some believe the uncovering of these ties demonstrates both Uribe's resolve to eradicate paramilitary links and the growing independence of the Fiscalía and Supreme Court, and their willingness to punish high level politicians and officials, others worry about the depth of the scandal and Uribe's sincerity in prosecuting so many members of his governing coalition. Regardless of how extensive the complicity of the Colombian state is with paramilitary violence, the counterproductive effect of paramilitary and governmental violence is clear. Instead of effectively countering insurgency, it creates cycles of violence and vengeance. Governmental forces must be reformed to prevent abuses, which inspire more violence.

Popular Support and a Healthy Political Community

The maintenance of an inclusive political community is as necessary as stability for a state seeking to counter internal conflict. To this end, political support, tolerance of the loyal opposition, and maintenance of human rights must be made priorities. There is a delicate balance between maintaining security and promoting a healthy political community. Wilkinson describes it as a "tightrope of under- and over-reaction" (1986, 177–178). The Colombian political community has been negatively affected by legacies of violence. Whereas in general, "a civilization which can accommodate dissent has a better prospect of prolonged survival" (Clutterbuck 1975, 149), Colombia has fallen into a situation of private justice, which poisons the political community and further undermines stability.

At the same time, the weak political community undermines efforts to combat the conflict: "Most terrorist groups realize that public support for democratic values and institutions is a major obstacle to their schemes. Hence the democratic process is a key target. . . . The trick is to harmonize strategy on both the security and political fronts: this is the only basis for a winning strategy" (Wilkinson 1986, 177). Credible accusations of corruption, governmental denunciation of critics or opposition members, and a clumsy, indiscriminate response to internal violence potentially undermine the democratic community that Colombia has begun to build.

According to Amnesty International (2006), "All the parties to the conflict continue to show grave disregard for human rights." Moreover, the notion of human rights is generally politicized (Restrepo 2001). This situation continues into the presidency of Uribe, who in 2003 criticized many human rights activists as being selective in their application of human rights principles. Moreover, he charged them with facilitating terrorism.[12] Additionally, in June 2004, President Uribe said that by "not having the courage to denounce Amnesty International, we have allowed it to legitimize terrorism internationally" (Amnesty International 2005). In response to criticism from domestic and international human rights groups, Uribe entered into dialogue with Amnesty International in August 2004. However, mutual suspicion remains between the government and human rights activists. As Amnesty International forcibly stated in 2006: "Amnesty International considers that there is a coordinated strategy by the security forces and paramilitary groups to undermine human rights defenders by discrediting the legitimacy of their work and through intimidation and attacks" (Amnesty International 2006b).

Uribe's Política de Defensa y Seguridad Democrática strategy promotes a notion of democratic security that would guarantee the legal opposition all the rights and protections of friends and partisans of the government (Ministerio de Defensa Nacional 2003, 5). Moreover, it embraces the notion of human rights (15). However, strains with the media and human rights organizations have raised the possibility of collusion with illegal paramilitary activities and corruption within the security and intelligence agencies. Both the appearance and reality of this type of corruption and collusion are harmful in the short and long term: "To foster corruption is always a prime terrorist aim, because if the police corruptly connive at their activities they have greater scope, while if the police are corrupt in other ways they can be discredited" (Clutterbuck 1975, 148). These charges undermine the authority of the government, the police, the military, and the intelligence agencies, and this lack of trust hampers the government's ability to gain the cooperation of citizens and obtain intelligence from diverse sources—and may play into guerrilla accusations.

Before the presidential elections in 2006, Uribe attacked critical media outlets and prominent members of the media, particularly Alejandro Santos of *Semana* and Ramiro Bejarano (who also is a former head of the DAS [Departamento Administrativo de Seguridad] and a columnist of *El Espectador*). Santos published accusations and investigations of corruption and paramilitary ties to the DAS. Bejarano raised the possibility of official favoritism toward the paramilitaries and called for an exhaustive investigation.[13] The DAS, responsible for intelligence, reports directly to the president. According to Bejarano's report, a former information systems director, Rafael García, admitted to laundering money, tampering with records, and cooperating and sharing intelligence with paramilitary groups. Specifically, it is alleged that paramilitary Jorge 40's Northern Block cooperated with the DAS to assassinate union leaders and academics, commit electoral fraud, and draft plans to assassinate Venezuelan leaders. Although the DAS denies the accusations, former DAS director Noguera did admit to meeting Jorge 40 for talks relevant to the peace process. Jorge 40, with 4,000 of his men, demobilized in March 2006 (*Semana* 2006; see also Human Rights Watch 2006).

The perceptions surrounding Noguera's meeting with Jorge 40 are problematic, since the DAS is responsible for a persons-at-risk program, which includes the protection of people threatened by paramilitary forces. Human Rights Watch (2007) cites "reports of paramilitary infiltration of the Intelligence Service; increasing threats against academics, union leaders, human rights defenders, and journalists; and the formation of new paramilitary groups." Evidence of "demobilized" paramilitaries regrouping, continued paramilitary violence, and possibly collaboration with the DAS raises apprehension about paramilitary impunity.

Moreover, Colombia suffers from a culture of distrust in which suspicion is the norm, protest is unpatriotic, and groups are believed to be infiltrated by opponents, spies, etc. rather than legitimately mobilized. According to the United Nations Development Programme,

> Instead of being seen as citizens exercising a right and whose complaints are usually well-founded, public opinion has an image of them as "professional agitators," with a secret agenda and very unsavory connections. . . . Also, among army officers and other members of government one

could say there is a certain propensity to interpret popular demon-
strations as a problem of "public order." . . . And those who lead these
protests often lend fuel to these stereotypes by indulging in rhetorical
harangues and using counter-productive tactics. This culture of distrust
is not easily overcome. However, public opinion has to be re-educated
to accept the validity, legitimacy, usefulness and necessity of movements
in which citizens can mobilize themselves and act in peaceful defence
of their interests and rights (United Nations Development Programme
2003, 6).

Moreover, there is a long history of the suspension of individual rights and
liberties: martial law before 1991, "states of exception" and a "state of internal
commotion" afterward. According to the Comisión Colombiana de Juristas
(2003), these suspensions disproportionately affected human rights workers
and other activists.

Part of Uribe's response involved creating informant networks to counter
guerrilla activity. There were early concerns that this would further put civilians in danger and "could contribute, within the context of generalized violence and the conflict's degradation, to the civilian population's involvement
in military operations or exposed to situations of great risk" (Robinson 2002).
According to a story in *El Tiempo* (February 24, 2004), within two years,
although some useful intelligence was gathered, so many innocent citizens
had been detained based on informant leads that the program was severely
criticized by the procurador general of Colombia.

In spring 2007, troubling evidence of the extensive illegal wiretapping of
approximately 8,000 people, including journalists, members of congress, law-
yers, governmental officials, diplomats, ministers, and even the Alto Comisionado para la Paz (High Commissioner for Peace), came to light. However,
Uribe responded quickly, requesting the resignations of the head of the police
Jorge Daniel Castro and police intelligence chief Guillermo Chávez. This
incident reinforced the suspicions of the opposition as well as previous concerns about governmental overreach, but also demonstrated Uribe's resolve
to hold officials accountable.

The violence from all sides, the denunciation of critical members of the
media, and the charges of corruption and complicity in intelligence agencies
make it difficult to build the social ties of trust and political inclusion necessary for long-term success. The fragile nature of the political community was
evident on the evening of Uribe's election to a second term. Carlos Gaviria,
the 2006 presidential candidate of the Polo Democrático Alternativo (PDI),
stated in his concession speech: "Most importantly, we need to respect the

lives of our leaders. We proclaim that we are not communist guerrillas, we are the most important political opposition force in Colombia."[14] At the end of the speech, many in the crowd shouted, "Fascist Uribe, you are the terrorist" (Hoyos 2006).[15]

Despite severe polarization in parts of society, in general there is a lack of concern for the paramilitary violence. The polling firm Napoleón Franco was commissioned by *Semana* in May 2007 to measure attitudes about paramilitary violence and the ongoing paragate scandal. The results showed that the general population had a high level of tolerance for paramilitary violence, although there was less support the more explicit the cooperation became. Of those questioned, 58 percent agreed (40 percent disagreed) with the statement "In the regions in which the government does not protect the citizens, it is justifiable that the ranchers and landowners have defended themselves, including an armed response."[16] Similarly, 51 percent agreed (46 percent disagreed) with the statement "For many years, the guerrillas were very strong and the Armed Forces could not defeat them. It was logical that the Armed Forces worked with the paramilitaries."[17] When asked whether paramilitarism was justifiable, 25 percent replied "under some circumstances," 20 percent did not know or refused to respond, and 55 percent said it was not. However, when asked specifically about whether it was forgivable for politicians to make agreements with paramilitaries, only 14 percent thought it was, while 78 percent thought it was unforgivable (*Semana* 2007d).

When asked whether the government should confront the paramilitaries or leave them to fight guerrillas, less than half of those asked (42 percent) thought that the government should confront the paramilitaries. Only 32 percent favored action against them, and 26 percent did not know or did not respond. This tepid response toward confrontation with the paramilitaries continues despite a wide acknowledgement of paramilitary crimes. Among respondents, 82 percent know that paramilitaries kidnap to support their activities, 70 percent know that the paramilitaries have dismembered their victims, and 63 percent agree that the paramilitaries have been responsible for between 10,000 and 30,000 deaths. Additionally, the Colombian public is well aware of the unfolding scandal: 85 percent are familiar with paragate.

Nonetheless, Uribe retains a high level of public confidence. Before Uribe's first term started, in 2002, 89 percent believed the country was on the wrong track. In 2007, despite the scandal, only 42 percent believed this. On the contrary, whereas in 2002 only 9 percent believed the country to be on the right track, 53 percent did in 2007. Moreover, Uribe's approval rating remains in a band from 68 percent to 80 percent. Despite allegations to the contrary, only 38 percent believe that Uribe has made agreements with the paramilitaries at one time or another. Moreover, respondents predominantly blame the guerrillas for the violence (47 percent), followed by blaming the government (23 percent), narcos (13 percent), common crime (13 percent), and paramilitaries only (5 percent).[18] For Colombia to continue on the right track, it is imperative that the paramilitary scandal be handled transparently and that all responsible parties be held accountable.

Economic Reform

While violence, poverty, and inequality in Colombia are intricately related, since increased violence reduces economic growth and poverty tends to lead to more violence, it is important to look toward the future and ask what can be done to achieve accelerated sustainable growth and development. While Colombia lagged behind its Latin American cohort in the past, recently it has shown signs of rapid economic growth. Many investors believe Colombia is tackling its problems of insecurity and violence. Economic growth has reached its highest level in years. *Business Week* promoted Uribe as a success story: "President Alvaro Uribe, who took office in 2002, nearly five decades into a civil war that has pitted Marxist guerrillas against right-wing death squads, has made *confianza* his overarching goal" (Farzad 2007). Confidence among investors has risen to new levels as Colombia has become the investment choice among emerging markets. However, what needs to be done to make the hype a sustainable reality?

In Chapter Seven, the analysis revealed that increased insecurity, as evidenced by higher justice and security spending, has a negative effect on GDP. The World Development Country Brief (2007) estimated that "if Colombia had achieved peace 20 years ago, it is estimated that the income of an average Colombian today would be 50 percent higher and 2.5 million children would be living above the poverty line today (US $2 per day)." The statistical models in Chapter Six highlighted the importance of state presence to reduce guerrilla violence. Additionally, in Chapter Three our analysis of the data after 2002 showed that foreign direct investment has increased dramatically as President Uribe has restored confidence in the economy and addressed security issues. International confidence in the Colombian economy has risen sharply in the past three years, as evidenced by the recent article in *Business Week*: "The stats all scream 'Go! Go! Go!' Colombia's stock market has soared fourteen fold since October, 2001. Foreign direct investment and capital inflows have more than doubled, while real estate prices have tripled in many areas" (Farzad 2007).

For Colombia to continue to capture investment and reach its growth potential, four fundamentals must be addressed. Chapter Two outlined the infrastructure and geographic challenges Colombia faces. First, despite the increase in international interest, Colombia's transportation systems and basic infrastructure are inadequate. A Bear Stearns report discussed in *Business Week* warned that "growth could halt if tens of billions worth of infrastructure isn't soon built. . . . If the buildout stalls, it will undermine Uribe's reforms" (Farzad 2007). Additionally, the new infrastructure investment targeted in certain sectors can be utilized by other industries, leading to increasing returns in economic growth (Amin Gutiérrez de Piñeres 1999). New investment has positive spillover effects. For example, infrastructure built for the flower industry has been utilized by the fresh-fruit and vegetable industries to expand their export markets. Furthermore, modern technology works to Colombia's advantage, since terrain is much less an obstacle today thanks to air travel and cellular communication. In the past, remote farms and ranches in Colombia were difficult to reach, and owners could conduct business only by physically traveling there. Now business can be conducted via cell phone, minimizing the need for long, dangerous journeys.

Second, Colombia must tackle unemployment, education, and poverty if it is to develop the human capital necessary to sustain economic growth and peace. Chapter Six revealed the importance of addressing poverty, given its strong links to guerrilla violence. Chapter Three illustrated Colombia's relative position among its cohort of Latin American countries and its need to divert more resources into education and employment opportunities. With one of the highest labor-force participation rates, Colombia can hope to reduce future unemployment only by creating jobs and encouraging the youth to pursue higher education. The World Development Report (2007) states that "because labor is the main asset of the poor, making it more productive is the best way to reduce poverty. This requires enhancing the opportunities to earn money and developing the human capital to take advantage of those opportunities. Broad-based economic growth is important. So is providing basic education and health care, especially for children—to provide the foundation of basic skills and well-being" (World Bank Report 2007, 2). Marquez (1999) finds that training programs are one of the most effective methods for combating youth unemployment. In fact, the Pan American Development Foundation (PADF) is focusing efforts among the displaced in Colombia, providing them with skills-based training in the hope of integrating them into the labor market. The foundation has also supported microcredit efforts. Additionally, the PADF and the Organizacion de los Estados Americanos—Misión de Apoyo al Proceso de Paz (MAPP/OEA) are currently planning to offer similar programs to demobilized combatants (OAS 2006, 3). Colombia must find ways to incorporate its youth (and the newly unemployed former combatants) into its economic development plan for the current progress to continue.

Third, Colombia must create a rural development plan that offers more than simple land reform. Chapter Six revealed the link between the volatile coffee sector and guerrilla violence and highlighted the need for effective rural economic reform and development. What is needed is a long-term sustainable rural development plan that includes jobs and sustainable land reform. Large commercial farms can improve rural conditions if labor is treated fairly and paid equitably.

Many scholars confuse economic opportunity with land reform. Moloney (2004) recommends that any solution to the civil war involve a program that addresses the country's distribution of land and inequality. Kay (2001, 770) deems "resolving the land question so landless and poor peasants can gain access to sufficient land and economic resources to ensure a sustainable standard of living and proper participation in society" necessary to reduce rural conflict. Land redistribution alone, without increased opportunity, will not provide a sustainable income source for the rural poor. Land reform, which often provides access only to subsistence living, is considered a policy option only when other economic opportunities do not exist. Instead, opportunities to move up the socioeconomic ladder are more effective, as evidenced by the fact that developed countries are not plagued with rural unrest, nor do policies in these countries seek to redistribute land equally among the rural population to alleviate either inequality or poverty.

Land reform is plagued with problems: "where will the land come from," "the cost to the economy would be enormous and the prospects for recovering investment, dim . . . the political will to carry out such a reform is absent" (Seligson 1996 145). Colombia has experience with land reform attempts. The government established a large bureaucratic agency for land reform, INCORA, in 1961, but policy implementation was not successful (Deininger 1999, 655). Heshusius Rodríguez (2005) finds in her study that agrarian reform can have a positive impact on income and quality of life if certain conditions are met: access to credit, training, and secondary education. Unfortunately, the Colombian experiment was hampered by the lack of available financing for the 30 percent of the purchase price not subsidized by the government as well as by the bureaucracy and the lack of a market for purchasing the output (Heshusius Rodríguez 2005, 14–15, 27). In short, in addition to a poorly designed program and inefficient bureaucracy, there was insufficient infrastructure to support rural advancement. Without investment in education and training and without sufficient access to capital and markets, agrarian land reform is doomed, as is rural development in Colombia.

Even in cases in which land redistribution occurs, it can increase violence, since new land disputes are created. The "recognition of the land rights of sharecroppers and tenants increased land disputes and provoked landowners to evict them" (Ballantyne 2000, 703).[19] Moreover, persistent violence in rural areas further hampered INCORA efforts at land redistribution. As others gained land rights, there were more land disputes and more evictions. Contemporary attempts at land reform in Colombia may have aggravated land conflict instead of ameliorating it.

Finally, Colombia can take advantage of a factor, which, in the past, hindered development—regionalism. Colombia's high ratio of rural population density reflects numerous smaller cities that have the potential to support rural employment. In the past, regionalism hampered Colombia's economic growth. Now, punctuated rural centers across the various regions provide an opportunity for rural development and growth. A development strategy that identifies rural centers and potential investment opportunities will have positive externalities that extend beyond just economic growth. Rural centers have the advantage of being sufficiently dense for the government to provide them with services, precluding the need for rural migration to cities. For these rural centers to succeed, however, the government must invest in education, health care services, infrastructure, and its own state presence.

Economic development efforts, regardless of the strength of the plan or the thoroughness of implementation, are greatly influenced by international factors, which are outside Colombia's control. First, the economy is constrained by international economic conditions. Since Gaviria's reforms, the country has been increasingly liberalized. Two challenges arise because of openness. The economy is increasingly dependent on international market prices for important crops. For example, by 2002, coffee prices had reached a hundred-year inflation-adjusted low, with reports that production costs were higher than market value, resulting in the abandonment of coffee trees and the reduced use of fertilizer, which has contributed to reduced yield (USDA 2002). Moreover, rural development projects have also failed because of protective agricultural policies in the United States and the European Union, which undermine legal agricultural exports. Additionally, in an open global economy, competition forces efficiency and lower prices, making a wider range of goods and services more broadly available. However, unemployment can increase as inefficient businesses close. A closed economy has costs besides high prices and poor quality. In a closed economy, the owners of protected industries control the economy with the assistance of the politicians who restrict trade, potentially creating incentives for politicians and local business leaders to seek to exclude competition in both the economic and political arenas. This exclusivity can also potentially incite violence.

Second, in addition to creating hardship in rural coffee growing areas, the collapse in international coffee prices encouraged Colombian farmers to intermix coca and poppy with coffee to hedge their incomes (Wilson 2001). In a story in the *Economist* (September 29, 2001), Mr. Osorio, executive director of the National Federation of Coffee-Growers' Committee in Tolima, points out that poppies are four times as profitable as coffee and that "the coffee grower does not want to get into illegal businesses, with a lot of risk . . . but he accepts the risk because there is nothing else to do." Alternative crop production is risky and uncertain. A rural development program initiated in Colombia and other drug-producing nations will have a viable chance of succeeding only once the profitability of illegal drugs declines and approaches that of alternative crops.

Many agricultural crops, such as specialty fruits and vegetables, generate high profits, but their cultivation requires a much higher investment as well as political and economic stability. Currently, the policy of the Colombian government is to eradicate coca. However, there are unintended consequences to eradication: "Between 1995–1996, aerial eradication led to protest marches by peasants as fumigation destroyed their only source of income. More importantly, the spraying campaign exacerbates the government's problems of political control in coca growing areas, alienating large rural populations who stand to lose their main source of income" (Lee 2002, 550). When the state loses peasants' support, they may turn to illegal groups to protect their livelihood. One recent study has argued that U.S. counternarcotics policies actually strengthened FARC in the 1990s by pushing "coca cultivation into the areas of Colombia where the FARC had long had a significant presence. This shift in production provided the FARC with unprecedented opportunities to tax the drug trade" (Peceny and Durnan 2006, 97). This happened because of the fumigation and eradication policies that reduced governmental support, the dismantling of the large cartels, and the interdiction between Colombia and Peru. Our findings in Chapter Six confirm that coca cultivation is associated with both guerrilla and paramilitary violence, but previous studies (Holmes, Amin Gutiérrez de Piñeres, and Curtin 2006) also demonstrate the negative effect of eradication.

Colombia has made tremendous progress in the last five years. The World Bank Country Brief (2007) states that "in recent years, Colombia has achieved stable Gross Domestic Product (GDP) growth, with a GDP above 5 percent from 2005 to present in 2006, an indication that Colombia possesses a strong economic foundation. Unemployment, which stood at 12.1 percent as of April 2006, is the lowest since 2001, and poverty decreased from 58 percent in 2002 to 49 percent. All these indicators, added to a reduced insecurity, have fostered greater confidence among domestic and foreign investors." If Colombia is to further develop and start closing the gap with other leading Latin American economies, it needs a comprehensive strategy that builds (and protects) infrastructure, promotes social development, and invests in the rural economy. For these improvements to sustain long-term development and growth, a significant strengthening of the state and national cohesion would be necessary; yet none of this is likely without security. As recent reports by the World Bank and popular press reveal, increasing confidence will be met with increased domestic and international investment, but nothing is sustainable if confidence in the state's ability to manage the violence falters. Sustainable development and continued economic growth are within reach, but Colombia must stay focused on reducing violence, increasing state presence, addressing the complex illegal drug industry, and investing in physical and human capital.

CONCLUSION

Colombia must institute a comprehensive solution that addresses the multiple forms and sources of violence. The conflict is not intractable. Success is attainable with a broad, long-term strategy. Military and police strength need to be increased, and the institutions must be committed to sincere human rights protections. The state needs to be bolstered by improving transportation, increasing institutional efficacy, and improving transparency and accountability. Stability needs to be achieved, but not through the accommodation of paramilitary violence or governmental human rights violence, which exacerbate existing cycles of violence. The political community needs to transcend its current culture of distrust, which is complicated by continued accusations of governmental complicity with human rights abuses, corruption scandals, and inflammatory remarks from both the government and opposition members. Demobilized combatants (both paramilitary and guerrilla) need to be reintegrated into the political community, protected from their former enemies, and worked into the productive economy. Economic reform must provide broad opportunity, improve human capital, reduce rural poverty, fund the expanded state presence, and attract more investment. These four components are interrelated and dependent on one another.

For example, the problem of paramilitary violence has the potential to scare away much needed international investment.

Often progress is not pretty. In intensely personal conflicts, in which most people either know a victim or have been one themselves, it is essential to move beyond vengeance and toward a future that disavows violence, regardless of the source or aim. The greatest threat to progress is impatience, which increases the temptation to emphasize one aspect of a strategy in the short term. Lopsided efforts will not bring long-term success and may undermine the chances of achieving a comprehensive peace. Advancement in one area does not eclipse the need to progress in others.

NOTES

CHAPTER THREE

1. Useful and detailed surveys of Colombian economic development at various times are provided by Garcia Garcia and Montes Llamas (1988), Hallberg (1991), and Cohen and Gunter (1992).

CHAPTER FOUR

1. Other, smaller groups, such as the Quintín Lame (demobilized in 1991), the MOEC, etc. are not discussed in this book.

2. ANAPO, the "half conservative, half populist" challenge to the National Front led by Gustavo Rojas Pinilla, began running candidates in 1962. It reached the peak of its support in the presidential election of April 19, 1970, when ANAPO candidate José Jaramillo Giraldo ran against National Front candidate Misael Pastrana Borrero. Despite José Jaramillo Giraldo's early lead, Pastrana "won" (Pécaut 1992, 226; see also Bergquist, Peñaranda, and Sánchez 1992).

3. For a comprehensive discussion of the ELN, see Medina Gallego 1996.

4. For a discussion of differences between the FARC and ELN zones, see Romero (2003, 97).

5. Other Colombian groups, such as the MOEC, FAL, ELN, and PCML, can be considered more *focista*. For a discussion of how to characterize FARC, whether as a people's war, *focismo,* or "Bolivarian populism," see Marks (2007, 42).

6. For example, contemporary FARC leader Manuel Marulanda was a Liberal guerrilla in the 1940s. For a discussion, from FARC's perspective, of the peasant movements of the 1940's, see "Programa agario de los guerrilleros de las FARC-EP-EP."

7. "*Marquetalia fue el comienzo de una chispa que prendió en determinado momento histórico y que ya no es posible apagarla con ninguna candela.*" Unless otherwise noted, all translations are by the author.

8. For a discussion of the conditions of Marquetalia, see *Revista Semana,* "Informe Especial: Marquetalia 35 años después," May 31–June 7, 1999.

9. *"El Bloque Sur significaba precisamente el comienzo y la extensión de la lucha guerrillera."*

10. *"Ya los nuestros no van a luchar por un pedazo de tierra, no van a luchar por reconquistar sus fincas sino se convierten en combatientes revolucionarios, que van desde ahora hasta el triunfo de la revolución."*

11. *"Colombia está gravemente enferma porque los gobernantes liberales y conservadores han utilizado sus cargos para favorecer a los ricos y para su propio beneficio personal; porque sus gobiernos solo han servido para defender la insaciable voracidad de los dueños del gran capital, de los latifundistas y de los diferentes carteles del narcotráfico; y porque han entregado nuestra soberanía a los Estados Unidos de Norteamérica, en contravía de las más patrióticas tradiciones, de la economía y de la dignidad de todo el país"* (FARC 2000c).

12. Special thanks to Thomas A. Marks for an assessment of FARC in 2005.

13. Care should be taken in interpreting AUC documents, which have an explicit public relations aim. AUC documents show a public face and an "eagerness to pardon themselves . . . If readers lack basic information, they might regard the group as . . . [an] organization that only by pure accident shares its name with other violent groups"; there is an "artificial and cunning character of the communications and documents that can be attributed to the paramilitaries and their recently formed organization for national coordination" (Cubides 2001, 143). Nonetheless, they can be useful to document some of the tensions and aims of the organization. The same caution applies to the interpretation of guerrilla documents.

14. *"La etapa militar asumida históricamente por las Autodefensas ha sido un factor necesario y determinante que permitió a Colombia sostener hasta aquí su amenazada y frágil democracia y desarrollar sus incipientes capacidades económicas frente a las indecisiones e incongruencias del sistema político"* (Mancuso and Castaño 2003a).

15. *"Un proyecto político de índole democrática que busca ejercer una actividad política totalmente legal, uno de cuyos vectores está dirigido a colaborar en la eliminación de la debilidad e insuficiencias del Estado, en todos los órdenes, carencias estructurales que lo hacen vulnerable"* (Mancuso and Castaño 2003b).

16. *"Nuestra Organización, las Autodefensas Unidas de Colombia, nació de la unión de disímiles grupos con intereses igualmente diversos, pero siempre orientados a la legítima defensa de la vida y los bienes de los ciudadanos ante la evidente insuficiencia y falta de voluntad política del Estado colombiano para combatir a los grupos de guerrillas marxistas."*

17. *"Recuerdo que hace muchos años, cuando iniciaba mi lucha antisubversiva, solo pensaba en ejecutar guerrilleros, y a decir verdad, poco o nada me preocupaba de otra cosa. No tenía nada más en que pensar, ese era mi mundo, desconocía el otro, mi ignorancia era absoluta."*

18. *"Con respecto al narcotráfico, nuestra Organización ha sido clara y realista desde su fundación: aquellos de sus miembros que incurran en dicha conducta delictiva tendrán que responder ante los tribunales colombianos o extranjeros, y su actividad personal en ningún momento puede involucrar a la Organización, la cual no participa, de ninguna manera, en dicho negocio. En ese sentido, nuestros estatutos prevén los máximos castigos para quienes intenten utilizar la organización con fines de enriquecimiento personal, así como para quienes intenten ponerla al servicio de intereses particulares."*

19. *"Nuestras declaraciones en el sentido de que las* AUC *les han cobrado 'impuestos' a los cocaleros no deben ser interpretadas como evidencia de tráfico o exportación de drogas a los Estados Unidos. Los impuestos sobre los cultivos son necesarios para mantener la lucha contra las* FARC, *pero no evidencian lucro personal. No en mi caso. Puedo jurarlo."*

20. *"El treinta y cinco por ciento del congreso se eligió en nuestras zonas de influencia, pero eso no quiere decir que tengamos base política 'legal', si con ello se quiere señalar directamente a esos congresistas como aliados nuestros. Sería un error tasarlo así, como sería un error tildar de guerrilleros a los congresistas elegidos en zonas guerrilleras, o narcos a los elegidos en zonas narcas."* Also available at www.colombialibre.com.

21. *"El narcotráfico ha pretendido, de mil maneras, apropiarse paulatinamente de los diferentes grupos que integran las* AUC, *y las* ACCU *hemos sido su mayor obstáculo. Ahora deben estar celebrando la posible desintegración de las* AUC, *y sería indeseable verlos cerrando pactos con estos grupos atomizados. Por esto hago un llamado a todos los grupos que conforman las* AUC, *aunque se declaren en disidencia, a no caer en manos del narcotráfico que los llevará a actuar como mercenarios suyos y les cerrará cualquier puerta hacia el futuro."*

CHAPTER FIVE

1. For a discussion of the role of subnational comparisons in comparative research, see Lijphart (1971). For more recent studies, see Snyder (2001) or Peters (1998, 44).

2. See Ministerio de Defensa Nacional (2003), which specifically calls for the protection of critical assets.

3. Gini coefficients measure inequality. Values range from 0 (most equal) to 1 (most unequal).

4. Chow tests were performed to see if the 1994–1997 data could be combined with those from 1998 and 1999–2001. On the basis of these tests, 1998 was combined with 1994–1997. As suspected, the satellite-based estimates are significantly different from the estimates of the Colombian National Police. Therefore, we did not combine the 1994–1998 data with the 1999–2001 data.

CHAPTER SIX

1. For a discussion of the distinct causality of ethnic civil wars, see Sambanis (2001).

2. It should be noted that as the production of oil has increased in importance, the infrastructure that supports this economic activity has more frequently become the target of extortion via bombing campaigns by rebel forces within the country, especially the ELN. Because of this, and this tradition of ELN recruitment among disaffected oil workers, we run the guerrilla models combined, in addition to the ELN and FARC individually.

3. For the debate about violence and inequality, see Sigelman and Simpson (1977), Muller (1985), Muller and Seligson (1987), Boswell and Dixon (1990), and Schock (1996).

For a relevant discussion of the debate as it pertains to Colombia, see Gutiérrez Sanín (1999).

4. For a discussion of these factors and homicide rates, see Sarmiento and Becerra (1998), Sarmiento Gómez (1999), and Echandía (1999). A classic Colombian work attributing violence to poverty is *Comisión de Estudios sobre la Violencia* (1987).

5. See Ortiz Sarmiento (1990–1991) and Medina Gallego (1990).

6. In this model, 1990 GDP per capita is in millions of 1994 pesos, and justice and security spending is in 1998 pesos. This model was also run without clustering the error terms in order to check whether the zero-inflated models were appropriate. The Vuong statistic was positive and significant in both time periods (3.82 and 3.71 respectively). Moreover, the log of α was significant (−4.67 and −5.87), suggesting that unobservable heterogeneity is related to the dispersion.

7. In this model, 1990 GDP per capita is in millions of 1994 pesos, and justice and security spending is in 1998 pesos. The Gini index has been multiplied by 100. This model was also run without clustering the error terms in order to check whether the zero-inflated models were appropriate. The Vuong statistic was positive and significant in the first time period (3.88). Interestingly, the log of α was insignificant. However, compared to the models of guerrilla violence, this is not surprising, given the different nature of paramilitary violence. Guerrilla violence is more unpredictable because of the hit-and-run tactics. Paramilitary violence is less unpredictable, since the perpetrators, unlike guerillas, do not have to hide from authorities.

CHAPTER SEVEN

1. Gootenberg (1999) provides a detailed analysis of short-run employment gains as a result of the illegal-drug trade. For more on the effect of the drug trade on Medellín, see Gootenberg (1999); for the effect on Cali, see *Economist* (1993).

2. For more on coca production relative to legitimate crops, see Franko (1999), Chapter Ten.

3. For more information on issues regarding the environmental costs, see Bernal Conteras (2002) and UNDCP (1998).

4. The data reveal a structural break between 1998 and 1999. We performed Chow tests to determine if the data could be combined. Total leftist violence, total paramilitary violence, and coca production all failed the Chow test, making it impossible to run one model for the entire time period.

CHAPTER EIGHT

1. For an excellent discussion of peace talks in the 1980s, see Chernick (1988), Rochlin (2003), and Kline (1999).

2. A copy of Plan Colombia is available online at http://www.usip.org/library/pa/colombia/adddoc/plan_colombia_101999.html#pre.

3. See Romero (2003, 97) for a discussion of differences between the FARC and ELN zones.

4. Letter to President Uribe, Cardinal Rubiano Sáenz, and Peace Commissioner Restrepo, December 15, 2002.

5. For a critique of this decree, see CINEP's "Boletines de seguimiento a Conmoción," www.nocheyniebla.org.

6. By May 2006, 107 soldiers had been killed, 435 had been wounded, 10,000 were suffering from malaria or leishmaniasis, 1,285 FARC *campamentos* had been discovered, 7,135 mines had been located and destroyed, and 1,701 FARC weapons had been seized (*El Tiempo,* May 6, 2006).

7. For an excellent discussion of the recent military reorganization and reform, see Marks (2002).

8. "*Está siempre listo para el diálogo. Pero lo que tenemos en mente es derrotar militarmente a las FARC. En cuanto ellas no quieran el diálogo, nuestro objectivo será derrotar militarmente al terrorismo.*"

9. "*La seguridad no es principalmente coerción: es la presencia permanente y efectiva de la autoridad democrática en el territorio, producto de un esfuerzo colectivo de toda la sociedad*" (Ministerio de Defensa Nacional 2003, 14).

10. "*Si vienen por mí, vienen por la 'Conchi' y por el presidente Uribe.*"

11. "*Si la amenaza proveniente de sectores del Estado, temerosos de la verdad, los callan, entonces nosotros, El Polo Democrático, quedamos en libertad de mover la Corte Penal Internacional para que actúe contra los que cometieron crímenes contra la humanidad en Colombia.*"

12. "'*Mientras para el Gobierno y la Fuerza Pública los derechos humanos son un compromiso de todos los días, para otros sectores los derechos humanos son una bandera política de ciertas ocasiones,' indicó refiriéndose a los críticos que según él, 'son escritores y politiqueros que finalmente le sirven al terrorismo y que se escudan cobardemente en la bandera de los derechos humanos'*" (*Semana* 2003; see also *Semana* 2003b).

13. "*Es imposible callar la preocupación nacional por la suerte del DAS. De ser ciertas las sindicaciones sobre desapariciones de sindicalistas y la conformación de listas de opositores, se fracturaría irremediablemente la credibilidad del Gobierno y su política de seguridad democrática. Lo mismo puede decirse sobre las graves crisis que han estallado en los otros entes estatales, las cuales tienen en común un aparente favoritismo oficial a agentes del paramilitarismo o a sus bienes, situaciones escalofriantes que enrarecen la suerte de nuestra democracia*" (*El Espectador* 2006).

14. "*Y lo más importante, haremos respetar las vidas de nuestros líderes. Le decimos que nosotros no somos comunistas guerrilleros, somos la fuerza política de oposición más importante de Colombia*" (Hoyos 2006).

15. "*Uribe, fascista, usted es el terrorista*" (Hoyos 2006).

16. "*En las regiones en que el gobierno no los protegió, es justificable que los ganaderos y terratenientes se hayan defendido incluso con el uso de las armas.*"

17. "*Por muchos años, la guerrilla fue muy fuerte y las Fuerzas Militares no podían vencerla. Era lógico que las Fuerzas Militares actuaran con los paramilitares.*"

18. "*¿Quién tiene más responsabilidad en la violencia en Colombia?*"

19. It should be noted that Ballantyne has a distinctly different view of sharecropping: "Sharecropping, on the other hand, has succeeded in relieving the tension caused by the fear of expropriation. It also provided campesinos with access to land, increased productivity, and promoted land improvements" (Ballantyne 2000, 703).

BIBLIOGRAPHY

Alape, Arturo. 1985. *La paz, la violencia: Testigos de excepción*. Bogotá: Editorial Planeta.

———. 1994. *Tirofijo: Los sueños y las montañas*. Bogotá: Edición Planeta.

Amin Gutiérrez de Piñeres, Sheila. 1999. Externalities in the Agricultural Export Sector and Economic Growth: A Developing Country Perspective. *Agricultural Economics* 21:257–267.

Amin Gutiérrez de Piñeres, Sheila, and Ferrantino, M. 2000. *Export Dynamics and Economic Growth in Latin America: A Comparative Perspective*. London: Ashgate.

Amnesty International. 1998. *Annual Report Colombia*.

———. 2000. Colombia: Human Rights and USA Military Aid to Colombia II.

———. 2001. *Annual Report Colombia*.

———. 2002a. Colombia: Human Rights and USA Military Aid to Colombia III.

———. 2002b. Colombia: Human Rights and USA military aid to Colombia IV.

———. 2003. Annual Report: Colombia.

———. 2006. Open letter to presidential candidates. May 3, via AI, http://web.amnesty.org/library/index/ENGAMR230132006.

Arbelaez, Maria Angelica, Juan Jose Echavarria, and Alejandro Gaviria. 2002. Colombian Long Run Growth and the Crisis of the 1990s. Report submitted to Global Development Network/Interamerican Development Bank Project "Economic Growth in Latin America and the Carribbean."

Arias, Andres, and Laura Ardilla. 2003. Military Expenditure and Economic Activity: The Colombian Case. Documento 2003–20. Bogotá: CEDE, Universidad de los Andes.

Aranguren Molina, Mauricio. 2005. *Mi Confesión: Rebelaciones de un Criminal de Guerra* [an as-told-to autobiography by Carlos Castaño]. Madrid: Sepha.

Ashenfelter, Orley, Phillip Levine, and David Zimmerman. 2003. *Statistics and Econometrics: Methods and Applications*. New York: Wiley.

Associated Press. 2003. Colombia Gives Peasants Seized Land. April 4.

Baena, Javier. 2006. "Deal with Paramilitaries Dealt Harsh Blow by Court." *Miami Herald*. May 20.

Baffes, John, and Bruce Gardner. 2003. The Transmission of World Commodity Prices to Domestic Markets under Policy Reforms in Developing Countries. *Policy Reform* 6 (3): 159–180.

Bagley, Bruce Michael. 1984. Colombia: National Front and Economic Development. In *Politics, Policies and Economic Development in Latin America,* ed. Robert Wesson, 124–160. Stanford, Calif.: Hoover Institution Press.

———. 2001. Drug Trafficking, Political Violence and U.S. Policy in Colombia in the 1990s. http://www.mamacoca.org/bagley_drugs_and_violence_en.htm.

Bagley, B. M., and W. O. Walker, eds. 1995. *Drug Trafficking in the Americas.* Coral Gables, Fla.: Univ. of Miami Press.

Bahmani-Oskooee, M., and J. Alse. 1993. Export Growth and Economic Growth: An Application of Cointegration and Error-Correction Modelling. *Journal of Developing Areas* 27:533–542.

Bahmani-Oskooee, M., M. Hamid, and S. Ghiath. 1991. Exports, Growth and Causality in LDCs: A Re-examination. *Journal of Development Economics* 36 (2): 405–415.

Balassa, B. 1978. Exports and Economic Growth: Further Evidence. *Journal of Development Economics* 5 (2): 181–189.

Ballantyne, Brian, Michael Bristow, Buster Davison, Sean Harrington, and Khaleel Khan. 2000. How Can Land Tenure and Cadastral Reform Succeed? An Inter-Regional Comparison of Rural Reforms. *Canadian Journal of Development Studies* 21 (3): 693–723.

Baron, Juan David, Gerson Javier Pérez Valbuena, and Peter Rowland. 2004. A Regional Economic Policy for Colombia. http://www.banrep.gov.co/docum/ftp/borra314.pdf.

Bayart, Jean-Francois, Stephen Ellis, and Beatrice Hibou. 1999. *Criminalization of the State in Africa.* Bloomington: Indiana Univ. Press.

Beckett, Ian F. W., and John Pimlott, eds. 1985. *Armed Forces and Modern Counterinsurgency.* New York: St. Martin's.

Behar Olga. 1985. *Las guerras de la paz.* Bogotá: Editorial Planeta.

Bergquist, C. W. 1978. *Coffee and Conflict in Colombia, 1886–1910.* Durham, N.C.: Duke Univ. Press.

Bergquist, Charles, Ricardo Peñaranda, and Gonzalo Sánchez, eds. 1992. *Violence in Colombia: The Contemporary Crisis in Historical Perspective.* Wilmington, Del.: Scholarly Resources.

———. 2001. *Violence in Colombia, 1990–2000: Waging War and Negotiating Peace.* Wilmington, Del.: Scholarly Resources.

Bernal Conteras, H. H. 2002. Impacto Ambiental Ocasionado por las sustancias quimcas, los cultivos ilicitos y las actividades conexas. In *Problemática de las drogas en Colombia: Memorias del Seminario,* ed. Gabriel Merchán Benavides. Bogotá: Direccion Nacional de Estupefacientes.

Berry, Albert. 2004. Participation, Violence and Development in Four Andean Countries. *Latin American Research Review* 39 (3): 185–204.

Berry, R. A. 1992. Agriculture during the Eighties' Recession in Colombia: Potential versus Achievement. In Cohen and Gunter 1992, 185–215.

Betancourt, I. 2002. *Until Death Do Us Part: My Struggle to Reclaim Colombia.* New York: HarperCollins.

Bibes, Patricia. 2001. Transnational Organized Crime and Terrorism: Colombia, a Case Study. *Journal of Contemporary Criminal Justice* 17 (3): 243–258.

Blank, Stephen. 2001. Narcoterrorism as a Threat to International Security. *World and I* 16 (12): 265–281.

Blomberg, S. Brock, and Gregory D. Hess. 2004. How Much Does Violence Tax Trade? CESifo Working Paper No. 1222, Category 7: Trade Policy.

Boswell, Terry, and William Dixon. 1990. Dependency and Rebellion: A Cross-National Analysis. *American Sociological Review* 55 (4): 540–559.

Bottía Noguera, Martha. 2003. La presencia y expansión municipal de las FARC: es avaricia y contagio, más que ausencia estatal? Documento 2003–03. Bogotá: CEDE, Universidad de los Andes.

Bushnell, David. 1992. Politics and Violence in Nineteenth-Century Colombia. In Bergquist, Peñaranda, and Sánchez 1992, 11–30.

———. 1993. *The Making of Modern Colombia: A Nation in Spite of Itself.* Berkeley and Los Angeles: Univ. of California Press.

Byman, Daniel, Peter Chalk, Bruce Hoffman, William Rosenau, and David Brannan. 2001. *Trends in Outside Support for Insurgent Movements.* Santa Monica, Calif.: Rand Corporation.

Caballero Argaez, Carlos. 2003. La Estrategia de Seguridad Democratica y La Economia Colombiana: Un Ensayo sobre la Macroeconomia de la Seguridad. Working paper, series no. 234, Banco de la Republica, Bogotá.

Camacho Guizado, Álvaro. 1992. Public and Private Dimensions of Urban Violence in Cali. In Bergquist, Peñaranda, and Sánchez 1992, 241–260.

———. 2004. Paramilitarismo y mafia. *El Espectador* (Bogotá). October 3.

Camacho Guizado, Álvaro, and Restrepo, A. L. 2000. Perspectives on Narcotics Trafficking in Colombia. *International Journal of Polities, Culture, and Society* 14 (1): 151–182.

Cameron, A. C., and P. K. Trivedi. 1998. *Regression Analysis of Count Data.* Cambridge: Cambridge Univ. Press.

Cameron, Sara, and Marina Curtis-Evans. 2000. Reclaimed Territory: Civil Society against the Colombian War. *Development* 43 (3): 52–57.

Cardenas, Mauricio. 2007. Economic Growth in Colombia: Reversal of Fortune? Working paper no. 36, Fedesarrollo, Bogotá.

Cardenas, Mauricio, Roberto Junguito, and Monica Pachon. 2005. Political Institutions and Policy Outcomes in Colombia: The Effects of the 1991 Constitution. Fedesarrollo working paper, http://www.fedesarrollo.org/contenido/articulo.asp?chapter=90&article=373.

Castaño, Carlos. 2001a. Letter to Anne Patterson, U. S. Ambassador to Colombia. October 26. http://www.colombialibre.org.

———. 2001b. Quien sabe para dónde vamos. Letter of November 12. http://www.colombialibre.org.

———. 2001c. Las AUC de hoy. Letter of August 29. http://www.colombialibre.com.

———. 2002a. ¿Así nos ve el mundo? Letter of July 6. http://www.colombialibre.org.

———. 2002b. Notificación pública a secuestradores. Letter of July 17. http://www.colombialibre.org.

Castaño, Carlos, and Salvatore Mancuso. 2002a. Open letter to Marta Lucía Ramírez, Ministra de la Defensa Nacional (DIPOM). June 21.

———. 2002b. Letter to President Uribe, Cardinal Rubiano Sáenz, and Peace Commissioner Restrepo. December 15. http://www.colombialibre.org.

Castillo, Fabio. 1996. *Los nuevos jinetes de la cocaína*. Bogotá: Oveja Negra.

Castro Caycedo, Germán. 2001. *Con las manos en alto: Episodios de la Guerra en Colombia*. Bogotá: Planeta.

Castro de Posada, B. 2001. La crisis económica y social de Colombia. Working paper, Latin American Studies Association.

Castro, Manuel Fernando, Jorge Arabia Wartenberg, and Andres Eduardo Celis. 1999. El Conflicto Armado: La estrategia económica de los principales actors y su incidencia en los costos de la violencia, 1990–1998. *Planeación y Desarrollo* 30 (3): 81–107.

Castro Zuleta, A. 2001. El conflicto armado y la crisis de la economía colombiana. Working paper, Latin American Studies Association.

Caycedo, Carlos. 1996. *En Secreto*. Bogotá: Editorial Planeta.

Centeno, Miguel Angel. 1997. Blood and Debt: War and Taxation in Nineteenth-Century Latin America. *American Journal of Sociology* 102 (6): 1565–1605.

———. 2002. *Blood and Debt: War and the Nation-State in Latin America*. University Park: Pennsylvania State Univ. Press.

Chernick, Marc. 1988. Negotiated Settlement to Armed Conflict: Lessons from the Colombian Peace Process. *Journal of Interamerican Studies and World Affairs* 30 (4): 53–88.

CIA [Central Intelligence Agency]. 1997. *Guide to the Analysis of Insurgency*. Washington, D.C.: Government Printing Office.

———. n.d. *Guide to the Analysis of Insurgency*. Washington, D.C.: Government Printing Office.

CINEP [Centro de Investigación y Educación Popular]. 2000. Descripción general del sistema de información CINEP.

———. 2001. Síntesis del Marco Conceptual. *Noche y Niebla* 22:4–33.

———. 2007.

Clausewitz, Carl von. 1976 [1833]. *On War*. Trans. Michael Howard and Peter Paret. Princeton, N.J.: Princeton Univ. Press.

Clutterbuck, Richard. 1975. *Living with Terrorism*. New Rochelle, N.Y.: Arlington House.

CODHES [Consultoria para los derechos humanos y el desplazamiento]. For figures, see www.codhes.org.

Coffin, Phillip, and Jeremy Bigwood. 2001. Coca Eradication. *Foreign Policy in Focus* 6 (7): 1–4.

Cohen, A., and F. Gunter, eds. 1992. *The Colombian Economy: Issues of Trade and Development*. Boulder, Colo.: Westview.

Collier, David. 1998a. Comparative Method in the 1990s. *APSA Comparative Politics Newsletter* 9 (1): 1–5.

———. 1998b. Comparative-Historical Analysis: Where Do We Stand? *APSA Comparative Politics Newsletter* 9 (2): 1–5.

Collier, Paul. 2000. Economic Causes of Civil Conflict and their Implications for Policy. Washington, D.C.: World Bank Working Paper 9.

Collier, Paul, et al. 2003. Breaking the Conflict Trap: Civil War and Development Policy. Washington, D.C.: World Bank Group.

Comisión de Estudios sobre la Violencia. 1987. *Colombia: Violencia y Democracia.* Bogotá: Universidad Nacional de Colombia.

Committee to Protect Journalists. 2003. Attacks on the Press in 2002. http://www.cpj .org/attacks02/americas02/colombia.html.

Connolly, William. 1993. *The Terms of Political Discourse.* 3rd ed. Princeton, N.J.: Princeton Univ. Press.

Conteras Bernal, Hector. 2002. Impacto ambiental ocasionado por las sustancias químicas, los cultivos ilícitos y las actividades conexas. In *Problemática de las drogas en Colombia: Memorias del seminario,* ed. G. M. Benavides, 1–42. Bogotá: Dirección Nacional de Estupefacientes.

Crenshaw, Martha, ed. 1995. *Terrorism in Context.* University Park: Pennsylvania State Univ. Press.

Cubides, Fernando. 1997. Los paramilitares y su estrategia. Documento de Trabajo de Paz Publica no. 8. Bogotá: CEDE, Universidad de los Andes.

———. 1998. Los bemoles del despeje. *Coyuntura Política* 11.

———. 2001. From Private to Public Violence: The Paramilitaries. In Bergquist, Peñaranda, and Sánchez 2001, 127–150.

Dambaugh, L. N. 1957. Colombia's Foreign Trade Mirrors Her Economy. *Journal of Geography* 56: 437–441.

———. 1959. Colombia's Population Resource. *Journal of Geography* 58: 174–180.

DANE [Departamento Nacional de Estadística]. Bogotá.

Deas, Malcom. 1973. Algunas notas sobre la historia del caciquismo en Colombia. *Revista de Occidente* 127:269–298.

Deaton, Angus. 2006. Measuring Poverty. In *Understanding Poverty,* ed. Abhijit Banerjee, Roland Bénabou, and Dilip Mookerjee. New York: Oxford Univ. Press.

Deininger, Klaus. 1999. Making Negotiated Land Reform Work: Initial Experience from Colombia, Brazil, and South Africa. *World Development* 27 (4): 651–672.

De la Torre, Cristina. 1980. Nacimiento del ELN: Revelaciones de Ricardo Lara Parada. *Trópicos* (Bogotá) nos. 3–4.

Della Porta, Donatella. 2003. Violence and the New Left. In *International Handbook of Violence Research,* ed. W. Heitmeyer and J. Hagen, 382–398. Dordrecht: Kluwer Academic Publishers.

Del Río, Daniel A. 1965. *Simon Bolívar.* Clinton, Mass.: Bolivarian Society of the United States.

Diaz, Ana Maria, and Fabio Sanchez. 2004. A Geography of Illicit Crops (Coca Leaf) and Armed Conflict in Colombia. Documento 2004–19. Bogotá: CEDE, Universidad de los Andes.

Dinar, Ariel, and Andrew Keck. 1995. Determinantes de la inversion privada en riego en Colombia: Efectos de la violencia, la politica macroeconomica y las variables ambientales. *Planeación y Desarrollo* 26 (1): 203–222.

Dollar, David, and Aart Kraay. 2002. Growth Is Good for the Poor. *Journal of Economic Growth* 7 (3): 195–225.

Dudley, Stephen. 2004. Leader Won't Be Sent to America. *Miami Herald*. December 17.

Duffield, M. 2000. Globalization, Transborder Trade, and War Economics. In *Greed and Grievance: Economic Agendas in Civil Wars,* ed. M. Berdaland and D. Malone. Boulder, Colo.: Rienner.

Duncan, Gustavo. 2004. Violencia y Conflicto en Colombia como una Disputa por el Control del Estado en lo Local. Documento 2004-11. Bogotá: CEDE, Universidad de los Andes.

Echandía Castilla, Camilio. 1998. Indagación sobre el grado de concentración de la actividad armada. Documento de Trabajo de Paz Publica no. 12. Bogotá: CEDE, Universidad de los Andes.

———. 1999. Geografia del conflicto armado y de las manifestaciones de violencia en Colombia. Working paper. Bogotá: CEDE, Universidad de los Andes.

———. 2000. *El Conflicto Armado y las Manifestaciones de Violencia en las Regiones de Colombia*. Bogotá: Oficina del Alto Comisionado para la Paz.

ECLAC [Economic Commission for Latin America and the Caribbean]. 2002. *Meeting the Millennium: Poverty Reduction Targets in Latin America and the Caribbean*. New York: United Nations.

Economist. 1993. Cali High: Colombia. December 1993–January 1994.

———. 1994. The Wages of Prohibition. December 24, 1994–January 6, 1995.

Eder, P. J. 1913. *Colombia*. London: Unwin.

Eduardo, Alvarado R. Luis, Andrés Vergara Ballén, and Yilberto Lahuerta Percipiano. 2001. *Comportamiento e Impacto del Gasto en La Lucha contra las Drogas, 1995–1999*. Bogotá: Dirección Nacional de Estupefacientes, Departamento Nacional de Planeacion.

———. 2002. *Aproximación metodologica y cuantitativa de los costos generados por el problema de las drogas ilicitas en Colombia, 1995–2002*. Documento 185. Bogotá: Dirección Nacional de Estupefacientes, Departamento Nacional de Planeacion.

Edwards, Sebastian. 1993. Openness, Trade Liberalisation, and Growth in Developing Countries. *Journal of Economic Literature* 31:1358–1393.

———. 2001. *The Economics and Politics of Transition to an Open Market Economy: Colombia*. Paris: Development Centre, OECD.

Edwards, Sebastián, and Roberto Steiner. 2000. On the Crisis Hypothesis of Economic Reform: Colombia, 1989–91. *Cuadernos de Económica* 37 (112): 445–493.

Emery, R. 1967. The Relation of Exports and Economic Growth. *Kyklos* 20 (4): 470–484.

Energy Information Administration. 2003. World Energy Areas to Watch. http://www.eia.doe.gov/emeu/security/hot.html#COL.

Esfahani, H. 1991. Exports, Imports, and Economic Growth in Semi-industrialised Countries. *Journal of Development Economics* 35 (1): 93–116.

Espectador, El. 2006. La Fiscalía tiene la palabra. April 16.

Etter, A., and W. van Wyngaarden. 2000. Patterns of Landscape Transformation in Colombia, with Emphasis in the Andean Region. *Ambio* 29 (7): 432–439.

Everett, M. 2001. Evictions and Human Rights: Land Disputes in Bogotá, Colombia. *Habitat International* 25 (4): 453–471.

FARC. 1993. Programa agrario de los gurrilleros de las FARC-EP. Proclaimed July 20, 1964, in Marquetalia, corrected by the 8th national conference of FARC, April 2, 1993. http://six .swix.ch/farcep/Documentos/plan_agrario.htm.

———. 1999. Secretariado del Estado Mayor Central de las FARC-EP Fuerzas Armadas Revolucionarias de Colombia—Ejército del Pueblo FARC-EP Colombia. May 27. http://six.swix.ch/farcep/Nuestra_historia/35_aniversario_de_las_FARCEP.htm.

———. 2000a. 36 Years for Peace and National Sovereignty. Secretariat of the Central General Staff, FARC–People's Army Mountains of Colombia. http://www.farcep .org/pagina_ingles.

———. 2000b. Discurso del lanzamiento del Movimiento Bolivariano por la Nueva Colombia. March 29.

———. 2000c. Manifiesto del movimiento Bolivariano por la nueva Colombia.

———. 2000d. Montañas de Colombia, Marzo 25 del año 2000 Pleno del Estado Mayor Central de las FARC-EP.

———. 2002. The self-defense forces: There's a big difference between the one and the other . . . *Resistencia* 30 (July–October). http://www.farcep.org/pagina_ingles/.

Farzad, Robert. 2007. Extreme Investing: Inside Colombia—An Improbable Journey from Crime Capital to Investment Hot Spot. *Business Week.* May 28.

Fearon, James D., and David Laitin. 2003. Ethnicity, Insurgency, and Civil War. *American Political Science Review* 97 (1): 75–90.

FIDA [Fondo Internactional de Desarrollo Agrícola]. 2003. Colombia.

Filippone, Robert. 1994. The Medellin Cartel: Why We Can't Win the Drug War. *Studies in Conflict and Terrorism* 17:323–344.

Franco, Saul. 2003. A Social-Medical Approach to Violence in Colombia. *American Journal of Public Health* 93 (12): 2032–2036.

Franko, Patrice M. 1999. *The Puzzle of Latin American Economic Development.* Lanham, Md.: Rowman and Littlefield.

Fundación Seguridad y Democracía. 2006. *Informe Especial Violencia Política en los Procesos Electorales de 1997, 1998, 2002 y 2006: Análisis Trimestral Enero–Marzo de 2006.* www .seguridadydemocracia.org.

GAD [Grupo de Apoyo a Desplazados (Support Group for Displaced People Organizations)] 1999. *Report of Forced Displacement in Colombia 1999.*

Galbraith, W. O. 1966. *Colombia: A General Survey.* London: Oxford Univ. Press, Royal Institute of International Affairs.

Gallie, W. B. 1956. Essentially Contested Concepts. *Proceedings of the Aristotelian Society* 56: 167–198.

Galvis Aponte, Luis Armando. 2001. La topografia economica de Colombia. Centro de Estudios Economicos Regionales no. 22. Cartagena: Banco de la Republica.

———. 2001a. ¿Qué determina la productividad agrícola departmental en Colombia? Centro de Estudios Economicos Regionales no. 19. Cartagena: Banco de la República.

García García, J., and G. Montes Llamas. 1988. Coffee Boom, Government Expenditure, and Agricultural Prices: The Colombian Experience. Research Report 68. Washington, D.C.: International Food Policy Research Institute.

George, Alexander L., and Andrew Bennett. 2005. *Case Studies and Theory Development in the Social Sciences.* Cambridge, Mass: MIT Press.

Gilbert, Alan. 2004. The Urban Revolution. In Gwynne and Kay 2004, 93–116.

Giovannucci, Daniele, Jose Leibovich, Diego Pizano, Gonzalo Paredes, Santiago Montenegro, Hector Arevalo, and Panos Varangis. 2002. Colombia: Coffee Sector Study. Documento 2002–15. Bogotá: CEDE, Universidad de los Andes.

Gleichen, E., R. C. Graham, et al. 1925. The Sierra Nevada of Santa Marta, Colombia: Discussion. *Geographical Journal* 66 (2): 106–111.

Goldberg, Pinelopi, and Nina Pavcnik. 2003. The Response of the Informal Sector to Trade Liberalization. *Journal of Development Economics* 72:463–496.

Gold-Bliss, Michael. 1993. Colombia: Understanding Recent Democratic Transformations in a Violent Polity. *Latin American Research Review* 28 (2): 215–234.

Gomez, Karoll, and Santiago Gallon. 2002. El impacto de la corrupción sobre el crecimiento economico colombiano, 1990–1999. *Lecturas de Economia* 57 (July–December): 49–85.

Gonzalez, Fernan. 2002. Colombia entre la Guerra y la Paz: Aproximación a una lectura geopolitica de la violencia colombiana. *Revista Venezolana de Economía y Ciencias Sociales* 8 (2): 13–49.

Gonzalez, Francisco, and Carlos Esteben Posada. 2001. Criminalidad, violencia y gasto publico en defensa, justicia y seguridad en Colombia. *Revista de Economía Institucional* 4:78–102.

Gootenberg, Paul, ed. 1999. *Cocaine Global Histories.* London: Routledge.

Griess, P. R. 1946. Colombia's Petroleum Resources. *Economic Geography* 22 (4): 245–254.

Guerrero Baron, Javier, and David Mond. 2001. Is the War Ending? Premises and Hypotheses with Which to View the Conflict in Colombia. *Latin American Perspectives* 28 (1): 12–30.

Guevara, Che. 1985 [1961]. *Guerrilla Warfare.* Lincoln: Univ. of Nebraska Press.

Gujarati, Damodar. 2003. *Basic Econometrics.* 4th ed. Boston: McGraw-Hill.

Gutiérrez Sanín, Francisco. 1999. Crimen e impunidad: Precisiones sobre la violencia. *Revista de Estudios Sociales* 3 (June): 133–136.

———. 2001. Inequidad y violencia política: una precisión sobre las cuentas y los cuentos. *Análisis Político* 43: 55–75.

Gwynne, Robert N., and Cristóbal Kay, eds. 2004. *Latin American Transformed: Globalization and Modernity.* London: Arnold.

Hallberg, K. 1991. *Colombia: Industrial Competition and Performance.* Washington, D.C.: World Bank.

Hansen, Brian. 2000. Colombia's Environment a Casualty in U.S. War on Drugs. *Environment News Service*. November 20. http://www.ens-news.com.

Hardy, Melissa A. 1979. Economic Growth, Distributional Inequality, and Political Conflict in Industrial Societies. *Journal of Political and Military Sociology* 7 (Fall): 209–227.

Harkavy, Robert E., and Stephanie G. Neuman. 2001. *Warfare and the Third World*. New York: Palgrave.

Hartlyn, Johnathan. 1989. Colombia: The Politics of Violence and Accommodation. In *Developing Countries: Latin America*, ed. J. J. Linz and S. M. Lipset, 290–334. London: Adamantine Press.

Hayes, Bernadette. 2001. Sowing Dragon's Teeth: Public Support for Political Violence and Paramilitarism in Northern Ireland. *Political Studies* 49:901–922.

Helmsing, A. H. J. 1986. *Firms, Farms, and the State in Colombia: A Study of Rural, Urban, and Regional Dimensions of Change*. Boston: Allen and Unwin.

Henao, M. L., N. Rojas, and A. Yaneth Parra. 1999. *El Mercado Laboral Urbano y La Informalidad en Colombia: Evolucion Reciente*. Documentos de Trabajo No. 5. Bogotá: Departamento Nacional de Planeación.

Henderson, James D. 1985. *When Colombia Bled: A History of the Violencia in Tolima*. Tuscaloosa: Univ. of Alabama Press.

———. 2001. *Modernization in Colombia. The Laureano Gómez Years, 1889–1965*. Gainesville: Univ. of Florida Press.

Heshusius Rodriguez, Karen. 2005. Medición del impacto de un programa de reforma agraria en Colombia. Documento 2005-28. Bogotá: CEDE, Universidad de los Andes.

Hofman, André A. 2000. *The Economic Development of Latin America in the Twentieth Century*. Cheltenham, UK: Edward Elgar.

Holmes, Jennifer S. 2001. *Terrorism and Democratic Stability*. Manchester: Manchester Univ. Press.

———. 2004. Drugs, Terrorism, and Congressional Politics: The Colombian Challenge. In *Contemporary Cases in U.S. Foreign Policy: From Terrorism to Trade*, ed. Ralph Carter. 2nd ed. Washington D.C.: Congressional Quarterly Press.

Holmes, Jennifer S., and Sheila Amin Gutiérrez de Piñeres. 2006. The Illegal Drug Industry and the Economy in Colombia: A Department Level Analysis. *Bulletin of Latin American Research* 25 (1): 104–118.

Holmes, Jennifer S., Sheila Amin Gutiérrez de Piñeres, and Kevin Curtin. 2006. Drugs, Violence and Development in Colombia: A Department Level Analysis. *Latin American Politics and Society* 48 (3): 157–184.

Holmes, Jennifer S., forthcoming. The State of the Contemporary Study of Terrorism. In *Sage Handbook of Comparative Politics*, ed. Todd Landman and Neil Robinson. London: Sage.

Howe, J. 2002. The Kuna of Panama: Continuing Threats to Land and Autonomy. In Maybury-Lewis 2002, 81–106.

Hoyos, Jose Fernando. 2006. El baile del Polo. *Semana*. May 28.

Howell, David. 2003. Beyond Unemployment: Toward a Summary Measure of Employment and Earnings Inadequacy. Working paper. http://www.csls.ca/events/cea2003/howell-cea2003.pdf.

Huggins, M. ed. 1991. *Vigilantism and the State in Latin America: Essays on Extralegal Violence*. New York: Praeger.

Human Development Report 2002. New York: Oxford Univ. Press.

Human Rights Watch. 2000. *World Report*.

———. 2006. Colombia: Uribe Must End Attacks on Media. April 17.

Hutchison, M., and N. Singh. 1992. Exports, Non-Exports and Externalities: A Granger Causality Approach. *International Economic Journal* 6 (2): 79–94.

Ibanez, Ana Maria, Andres Moya, and Pable Querubín. 2005. Towards a Proactive Policy for the Displaced Population in Colombia. Working paper, Sixth Global Development Network Conference, "Developing and Developed Worlds: Mutual Impact," Dakar, Senegal.

Intelligence Memorandum DCI Counternarcotics Center. 1992. Narco-Insurgent Links in the Andes. July 29.

International Confederation of Free Trade Unions. 2001. *Colombia: Annual Survey of Violations of Trade Union Rights (2001)*. Brussels.

International Monetary Fund [various years]. *International Financial Statistics Yearbook*.

International Monetary Fund, Western Hemisphere Department. 2001. *Colombia: Selected Issues and Statistical Appendix*.

International Press Institute. 2001. *2001 World Press Freedom Review*. http://www.freemedia.at/wpfr/world.html.

Iregui, Ana Maria, and Jesus Otero. 2003. On the Dynamics of Unemployment in a Developing Economy: Colombia. *Applied Economics Letters* 10:895–898.

Ireland, G. 1938. *Boundaries, Possessions, and Conflicts in South America*. Cambridge, Mass.: Harvard Univ. Press.

James, P. E. 1923. The Transportation Problem of Highland Colombia. *Journal of Geography* 22:346–354.

Jaramillo, Carlos Felipe. 2001. Liberalization, Crisis, and Change: Colombian Agriculture in the 1990s. *Economic Development and Cultural Change* 49 (4): 821–846.

Jiménez-Gomez, C. 1986. *Una procuraduria de opinión, 1982–1986: Informe al congreso y al país*. Bogotá: Editorial Printer Colombiana.

Jones, A. D. 1899. *The History of South America: From its Discovery to the Present Time*. London: Swan Sonnenschein.

Jones, Adam. 2004. Parainstitutional Violence in Latin America. *Latin American Politics and Society* 46 (4): 127–148.

Joyce, Elizabeth, and Carlos Malamud, eds. 1998. *Latin America and the Multinational Drug Trade*. New York: St. Martin's.

Jung, W., and P. Marshall. 1985. Exports, Growth, and Causality in Developing Countries. *Journal of Development Economics* 18 (2): 1–12.

Kay, Cristóbal. 2001. Reflections on Rural Violence in Latin America *Third World Quarterly* 22 (5): 741–775.

Kinross, Stuart. 2004. Clausewitz and Low-Intensity Conflict. *Journal of Strategic Studies* 27 (1): 35–58.

Kline, H. F. 1999. *State Building and Conflict Resolution in Colombia.* Tuscaloosa: Univ. of Alabama Press.

———. 2007. *Chronicle of a Failure Foretold: The Peace Process of Colombian President Andrés Pastrana.* Tuscaloosa: Univ. of Alabama Press.

Knoester, Mark. 1998. War in Colombia. *Social Justice* 25 (2): 85–109.

Kravis, I. 1970. Trade as a Handmaiden of Growth. *Economic Journal* 80 (320): 850–872.

Krueger, A. 1988. *Foreign Trade Regimes and Economic Development: Liberalization Attempts and Consequences.* Cambridge, Mass.: Ballinger.

Lambsdorff, Johann Graf. 2003. How Corruption Affects Persistent Capital Flows. *Economics of Governance* 4:229–243.

Laqueur, Walter. 1997. *Guerrilla: A Historical and Critical Study.* Edison, N.J.: Transaction.

Lazare, D. 1997. Drugs and Money. NACLA *[North American Congress on Latin America] Report in the Americas* 30 (6): 37–43.

Leal Buitrago, Francisco. 1984. *Estado y política en Colombia.* Bogotá: Siglo Vientiuno Editores de Colombia.

Le Billon, Philippe. 2001. The Political Ecology of War: Natural Resources and Armed Conflicts. *Political Geography* 20:561–584.

Lee, Rensselaer. 2002. Perverse Effects of Andean Counternarcotics Policy. *Orbis* (Summer): 537–554.

Lee, Rensselear, and Francisco Thoumi. 2005. Drug Effects. *Economist.* February 26.

Leech, Garry. 2004. Plan Petroleum in Putumayo. NACLA *Report on the Americas* 37 (6): 8–11.

Lemus, Gustavo Bell. 1998. The Decentralized State: An Administrative or Political Challenge. In *Colombia: The Politics of Reforming the State,* ed. Eduardo Posada-Carbó. New York: St. Martin's.

LeoGrande, William Mo, and Kenneth Sharpe. 2000. Two Wars or One? Drugs, Guerrillas, and Colombia's New Violence. *World Policy Journal* 17 (3): 1–11.

Leonard, David K., and Scott Straus. 2003. *Africa's Stalled Development: International Causes and Cures.* Boulder, Colo.: Rienner.

Lieberman, I. W., and J. C. Hanna. 1992. Colombia: Industrial Restructuring and Modernization. In Cohen and Gunter 1992, 119–155.

Lijphart, Arendt. 1971. Comparative Politics and the Comparative Method. *American Political Science Review* 65 (3): 682–693.

Llorante, María Victoria, Camilo Echandía, Rodolfo Escobedo, and Mauricio Rubio. 2001. Violencia homicida y estructuras criminals en Bogotá. *Análisis Político* 44:17–38.

López-Alves, Fernando. 2000. *State Formation and Democracy in Latin America, 1810–1900.* Durham, N.C.: Duke Univ. Press.

———. 2001. The Transatlantic Bridge: Mirrors, Charles Tilly, and State Formation in the River Plate. In *The Other Mirror: Grand Theory through the Lens of Latin America,* ed.

Miguel Angel Centeno and Fernando López-Alves, 153–176. Princeton, N.J.: Princeton Univ. Press.

Lupu, Noam. 2004. Towards a New Articulation of Alternative Development: Lessons from Coca Supply Reduction in Bolivia. *Development Policy Review* 22 (4): 405–421.

Macario, Carla, Regis Bonelli, Adriaan Ten Kate, and Gunnar Niels. 2002. Export Growth in Latin America: Policies and Performance. Boulder, Colo.: Lynne Rienner.

Mancuso, Salvatore. 2002. Letter to Luis Carlos Restrepo, Alto Comisionado para la Paz. September 27. http://www.colombialibre.org.

Mancuso, Salvatore, and Carlos Castaño. 2003a. Las verdaderas intenciones de las Autodefensas. Letter of April 4. http://www.colombialibre.org.

———. 2003b. Carta Abierta al doctor James Lemoyne Asesor Especial del Secretario General de la ONU para Colombia. Letter of May 18. http://www.bloquecacique nutibara.org/.

Mansilla, Armando Borrero. 2001. Defensa y seguridad nacional: Elementos para una política democrática. *Análisis Político* 42:26–40.

Manwaring, Max. 2002. *Nonstate Actors in Colombia: Threat and Response.* Carlisle, Penn.: Strategic Studies Institute.

Mao Tse Tung. 1961. *Guerrilla Warfare.* Translated by Samuel B. Griffith. Champaign: Univ. of Illinois Press.

Marcella, Gabriel. 2003. *The United States and Colombia: The Journey from Ambiguity to Strategic Clarity.* Carlisle, Penn.: Strategic Studies Institute.

Mark, Robert. 1986. Policing a Britain Under Threat. In *The Future of Political Violence,* ed. Richard Clutterbuck, 159–166. New York: St. Martin's.

Markham, C. R. 1913. The Putumayu and the Question of Boundaries between Peru and Colombia. *Geographical Journal* 41 (2): 145–147.

Marks, Thomas. 2002. *Colombian Army Adaptation to FARC Insurgency.* Carlisle, Penn.: Strategic Studies Institute, United States Army War College.

———. 2003. Colombian Army Counterinsurgency. *Crime, Law, and Social Change* 40:77–105.

———. 2005. *Sustainability of Colombian Military/Strategic Support for "Democratic Security."* Carlisle, Penn.: Strategic Studies Institute, United States Army War College.

———. 2007. A Model Counterinsurgency: Uribe's Colombia (2002–2006) vs FARC. *Military Review* 87:41–56.

Marquez, German. 2003. Transformación de ecosistemas, pobreza y violencia en Colombia: Aproximación empirica. Conference paper, Congreso Iberoamericano Desafios locales ante la globalización. FLACSO [Facultad Latinoamericana de Ciencias Sociales], Quito, Ecuador.

Marquez, Gustavo. 1999. Unemployment Insurance and Emergency Employment Programs in Latin America and the Caribbean: An Overview. Paper presented at the Conference on Social Protection and Policy. February 5. Washington, D.C.: Inter-American Development Bank.

Martinez, Hermes. 2002. Estudio Espacial de la Violencia en Colombia. Working paper, Universidad de los Andes, Bogotá.

Martz, J. D. 1992. Contemporary Colombian Politics: The Struggle over Democratization. In Cohen and Gunter 1992, 21–46.

Mason, T. David, and Dale A. Krane. 1989. The Political Economy of Death Squads: Toward a Theory of the Impact of State-Sanctioned Terror. *International Studies Quarterly* 33 (2): 175–198.

Maullin, R. L. 1973. *Soldiers, Guerrillas, and Politics in Colombia*. Lexington, Mass.: Lexington Books.

Maybury-Lewis, David, ed. 2002. *The Politics of Ethnicity: Indigenous Peoples in Latin American States*. Cambridge, Mass.: Harvard Univ. Press.

McGuire, Nancy. 2002. Combating Coca in Bolivia and Colombia: A New Perspective on the Forces that Drive Peasant Coca Farming. Working Paper, Council for Emerging National Security Affairs, Washington, D.C.

McIlwaine, Cathy, and Caroline Moser. 2003 Poverty, Violence and Livelihood Security in Urban Colombia and Guatemala. *Progress in Development Studies* 3 (2): 113–130.

McLean, Phillip. 2002. Colombia: Failed, Failing or Just Weak? *Washington Quarterly* (Summer): 123–134.

Medina Gallego, Carlos. 1990. *Autodefensas, Paramilitares y Narcotráfico en Colombia: Origen, desarrollo y consolidación; El caso de Puerto Boyacá*. Bogotá: Editorial Documentos Periodísticos.

———. 1996. *ELN: Una historia contada a dos voces*. Bogotá: Rodríguez Quito Editores.

———. 2001. *ELN: Una historia de los orígenes*. Bogotá: Rodríguez Quito Editores.

Meertens, Donny. 1997. *Tierra, violencia, y género: hombres y mujeres en la historia rural de Colombia, 1930–1990*. Rotterdam: Katholieke Universiteit Nijmengen.

Meertens, Donny, and Richard Stoller. 2001. Facing Destruction, Rebuilding Life: Gender and the Internally Displaced in Colombia. *Latin American Perspectives* 28 (1): 132–148.

Mendofilo, Medina. 1985–1986. Algunos factores de violencia en el sistema politico colombiano 1930–1986. *Anuario Colombiano de Historia Social y de la Cultura* 13–14: 281–297.

Metz, Steven. 2000. *Armed Conflict in the Twenty-first Century: The Information Revolution and Post Modern Warfare*. Carlyle, Penn.: Strategic Studies Institute.

Ministerio de Defensa Nacional. 2000a. *La fuerza pública y los derechos humanos en Colombia*. Bogotá.

———. 2000b. Los Grupos Illegales de Autodefensa en Colombia. Bogotá.

———. 2003. *Política de Defensa y Seguridad Democrática*. Bogotá.

Moloney, Anastasia. 2004. Displaced in Colombia. *NACLA Report on the Americas* 38 (2): 9–12.

Moreno Ospina, Carlos, and Libardo Sarmiento Anzola. 1989. *Impacto del conflicto armado y del narcotráfico sobre la producción agropecuaria en Colombia, 1980–1988*. Bogotá: Instituto de estudios liberals.

Moreno-Sanchez, Rocio, David Kraybill, and Stanley Thompson. 2003. An Econometric Analysis of Coca Eradication Policy in Colombia. *World Development* 31 (2): 375–383.

Morrison, S. 1997. The Dynamics of Illicit Drug Production: Future Sources and Threats. *Crime, Law, and Social Change* 27:121–138.

Mousseau, Michael. 2002–2003. Market Civilization and its Clash with Terror. *International Security* 27 (3): 5–29.

Muller, Edward. 1985. Income Inequality, Regime Repressiveness, and Political Violence. *American Sociological Review* 50 (1): 47–61.

Muller, Edward, and Mitchell Seligson. 1987. Inequality and Insurgency. *American Political Science Review* 81 (2): 425–451.

Muller, Edward, Mitchell Seligson, and Hung-der Fu. 1989. Land Inequality and Political Violence. *American Political Science Review* 83 (2): 577–595.

Murphy, John F. 2005. The IRA and the FARC in Colombia. *International Journal of Intelligence and Counter Intelligence* 18 (Spring): 76–89.

Nelson, R. R., T. P. Schultz, et al. 1971. *Structural Change in a Developing Economy: Colombia's Problems and Prospects*. Princeton, N.J.: Princeton Univ. Press.

Nitsch, Volker, and Dieter Schumacher. 2004. Terrorism and International Trade: An Empirical Investigation. *European Journal of Political Economy* 20:423–433.

Nuevo Herald, El. 2005. Uribe invite a guerrilleros del ELN iniciar un proceso de paz. June 8.

Ochoa, Pablo. 1998. Export Promotion Policies and Instruments in Colombia. *Integration and Trade* 4 (5): 133–145.

O'Donnell, Guillermo. 1999. A Latin American View. In *Counterpoints: Selected Essays on Authoritarianism and Democratization*. Notre Dame, Ind.: Univ. of Notre Dame Press.

Offstein, Norman. 2002. An extortionary guerrilla movement. Documento 2002–09. Bogotá: CEDE, Universidad de los Andes.

Organizacion de Panamericana de la Salud–Colombia. Indicatores de Pobreza 1995–1998. http://www.disaster-info.net/desplazados/informes/pobreza/mapa1.htm

Orozco, Cecilia. 2002. Interview with Castaño. In *¿Y ahora que? El futuro de la guerra y la paz en Colombia*. Bogotá: El Ancora Editores.

Ortiz, Roman. 2002. Insurgent Strategies in the Post–Cold War: The Case of the Revolutionary Armed Forces of Colombia. *Studies in Conflict and Terrorism* 25:127–143.

Ortiz Sarmiento, Carlos Miguel. 1990–1991. Violencia política de los ochenta: Elementos para una reflexión historica. *Anuario Colombiano de Historica Social y de la Cultura* 18:245–280.

Osterling, Jorge P. 1989. *Democracy in Colombia*. New Brunswick, N.J.: Transaction.

O'Sullivan, Patrick. 1983. Geographical Analysis of Guerrilla Warfare. *Political Geography Quarterly* 2 (2): 139–150.

O'Sullivan, Patrick, and Jesse W. Miller. 1983. *The Geography of Warfare*. New York: St. Martin's.

Ozak, Omer, and Oscar Mauricio Valencia. 2002. Impacto Macroeconomico y Distributivo del Impuesto de Seguridad Democratica. *Archivos de Economía* 209 (October 18).

País Libre. n.d. http://www.paislibre.org/

Pardo, Rafael. 2000. Colombia's Two Front War. *Foreign Affairs* 79 (4): 64–73.

———. 2005. Key Issues in the Negotiations Process. In *The Peace Process in Colombia with the Autodefensas Unidas de Colombia-AUC*, ed. Cynthia J. Arnson, 17–22. Woodrow Wilson Center Report on the Americas #13. Washington D.C.: Woodrow Wilson International Center for Scholars.

Paredes, M. T. V. 2001. La crisis económica en Colombia: Análisis sectoral. Working Paper, Latin American Studies Association.

Park, J. W. 1985. *Rafael Núñez and the Politics of Colombian Regionalism, 1863–1886*. Baton Rouge: Louisiana State Univ. Press.

Parra, Clara Elena. 1998. Determinantes de la inversion en Colombia: Evidencia sobre el capital humano y la violencia. *Planeación y Desarrollo* 29 (3): 163–187.

Pécaut, Daniel. 1992. Guerrillas and Violence. In Bergquist, Peñaranda, and Sánchez 1992, 217–240.

———. 1997. Presente, pasado y futuro de la violencia en Colombia. *Desarrollo Económico* 36 (144): 891–930.

———. 2001. *Guerra contra la Sociedad*. Bogota: Espasa.

Pérez, Manuel. 1999. El desplazamiento por violencia y los procesos de reconstrucción vital en Colombia. *Revista Javeriana* 67 (October): 663–676.

Peters, B. Guy. 1998. *Comparative Politics: Theory and Methods*. New York: New York Univ. Press.

Peterson, Sarah. 2002. People and the Ecosystems in Colombia. *Independent Review* 6(3): 427–441.

Petras, James. 2000. The FARC Faces the Empire. *Latin American Perspectives* 27 (5): 134–143.

Pizarro, Eduardo. 1991. *Las Farc, 1949–1966: De la autodefensa a la Combinación de todas las formas de lucha*. Bogotá: Tercer Mundo.

———. 1992. Revolutionary Guerrilla Groups in Colombia. In Bergquist, Peñaranda, and Sánchez 1992, 169–194.

Plan Colombia. 1999. http://www.usip.org/library/pa/colombia/adddoc/plan_colombia_101999.html.

Pombo, Joaquín de. 1992. Dynamics of the Colombian Agricultural Sector. In Cohen and Gunter 1992, 164–184.

Posada-Carbó, Eduardo. 1996. *The Colombian Caribbean: A Regional History, 1870–1950*. Oxford: Clarendon Press.

Programa agario de los guerrilleros de las FARC-EP. n.d. http://six.swix.ch/farcep/Documentos/plan_agrario.htm.

Prillaman, William. 2003. Colombia's Crisis: New Thinking on an Old Problem. *Orbis* (Fall): 737–746.

Pruitt, F. M. 1936. The Coffee Industry of Colombia. *Journal of Geography* 35: 68–72.

Rabasa, Angel, and Peter Chalk. 2001. *The Colombian Labyrinth: The Synergy of Drugs and Insurgency and Its Implications for Regional Stability*. Santa Monica, Calif.: Rand.

Rangel Suárez, Alfredo. 1998. *Colombia: Guerra en el Fin de Siglo*. Bogotá: Tercer Mundo.

————. 1999. Las FARC-EP: una mirada actual. In *Reconocer la Guerra para construir la Paz,* ed. Malcolm Deas and María Victoria Llorente, 23–51. Bogotá: CEREC, Ediciones Uniandes, Editorial Norma.

————. 2000. Parasites and Predators: Guerrillas and the Insurrection Economy of Colombia. *Journal of International Affairs* 53 (2): 577–601.

Rausch, J. M. 1984. *A Tropical Plains Frontier: The Llanos of Colombia, 1531–1831.* Albuquerque: Univ. of New Mexico Press.

————. 1999. *Colombia: Territorial Rule and the Llanos Frontier.* Gainesville: Univ. Press of Florida.

Red de Solidaridad. n.d. http://www.red.gov.co/portal/default.aspx

Renner, G. T. J. 1927. Colombia's Internal Development. *Economic Geography* 3 (2): 259–264.

Restrepo, Jorge, and Michael Spagat. 2004. The Colombian Conflict: Uribe's First 17 Months. Working paper. April, CEPR Discussion Paper No. 4570.

Restrepo, Jorge, Michael Spagat, and Juan Vargas. 2003. Dynamics of the Colombian Civil Conflict: A New Data Set. Discussion Papers in Economics, Royal Holloway, University of London.

Restrepo, Luis Alberto. 2001. The Equivocal Dimensions of Human Rights in Colombia. In Bergquist, Penaranda, and Sanchez 2001, 95–126.

Reyes, Alejandro. 1995. Drug Trafficking and the Guerrilla Movement in Colombia. In Bagley and Walker 1995, 97–120.

Richani, Nazih. 1997. The Political Economy of Violence: The war-system in Colombia. *Journal of Interamerican Studies and World Affairs* 39 (2): 37–45.

Robinson, Mary. 2002. Letter from High Commissioner Mary Robinson to President Uribe. http://www.hchr.org.co/estadosexcepcion/ex0200.html.

Rocha, Ricardo. 2000. The Colombian Economy after 25 Years of Drug Trafficking. United Nations Drug Control Program, Bogotá Country Office, http://www.undcp.org/colombia/rocha.html.

Rochlin, F. James. 2003. *Vanguard Revolutionaries in Latin America.* Boulder, Colo.: Rienner.

Romero, Mauricio. 2000. Changing Identities and Contested Settings: Regional Elites and the Paramilitaries in Colombia. *International Journal of Politics, Culture and Society* 14 (1): 51–69.

————. 2003. *Paramilitares y autodefensas, 1982–2003.* Bogotá: IEPRI.

Rosenbaum, H. Ron. 1974. Vigilantism: An Analysis of Establishment Violence. *Comparative Politics* 6(4): 541–570.

Rostow, Walt. 1962. Countering Guerrilla Attack. In *Modern Guerrilla Warfare: Fighting Communist Guerilla Movements, 1941–1961,* ed. Franklin Osanka. Glencoe, N.Y.: Free Press.

Rubén Sánchez, David. 1998. El Influjo de la violencia en las elecciones. *Revista Javeriana* 131 (646): 51–57.

Rubio, Mauricio. 2001. Violencia y Conflicto en los noventa. *Coyuntura Social* 22: 1–39.

———. 2002. Conflicto y Finanzas publicas municipales en Colombia. Documento 2002-17. Bogotá: CEDE, Universidad de los Andes

Safford, Frank, and Marco Palacios. 2002. *Colombia: Fragmented Land, Divided Society*. New York: Oxford University Press.

Salazar Pérez, Robinson. 2002. *Comportamiento de la Sociedad Civil Latinoamericana*. Montevideo: Libros en Red.

Sambanis, Nicholas. 2001. Do Ethnic and Nonethnic Civil Wars Have the Same Causes? *Journal of Conflict Resolution* 45 (3): 259–282.

———. 2004a. Expanding Economic Models of Civil War Using Case Studies. *Perspectives on Politics* 2 (2): 259–279.

———. 2004b. What Is a Civil War? *Journal of Conflict Resolution* 48 (6): 814–858.

Sánchez Torres, Fabio, Ana Maria Díaz, and Michel Formisano. 2003. Conflicto, Violencia y Actividad Criminal en Colombia: Un Analisis Espacial. Documento 2003-05. Bogotá: CEDE, Universidad de los Andes.

Sánchez, Gonzalo. 1992. The Violence: An Interpretative Synthesis. In Bergquist, Peñaranda, and Sánchez 1992, 75–124.

———. 1998. Colombia: Violencias Sin Futuro. *Foro Internacional* 38 (1): 37–58.

Sánchez, Gonzalo, and William Aviles. 2001. Introduction. *Latin American Perspectives* 28 (1): 5–11.

Sánchez, Gonzalo, and Peter Bakewell. 1985. La Violencia in Colombia: New Research, New Questions. *Hispanic American Historical Review* 65 (4): 789–807.

Sarmiento Gómez, Alfredo. 1999. Violencia y equidad. *Planeación y Desarrollo* 30 (3): 47–62.

Sarmiento Gómez, Alfredo, and Lida Marina Becerra. 1998. Análisis de las relaciones entre violencia y equidad. Working Paper #93, Departamento Nacional de Planeación. http://www.dnp.gov.co/paginas_detalle.aspx?idp=695.

Sarmiento, Libardo, and Carlos Moreno. 1990. Narcotráfico y sector agropecuario en Colombia. *Economía Colombiana* 226–227: 29–37.

Schock, Kurt. 1996. A Conjunctural Model of Political Conflict: The Impact of Political Opportunities on the Relationship between Economic Inequality and Violent Political Conflict. *Journal of Conflict Resolution* 40 (1): 98–133.

Schultz, Frederick. 2004. Breaking the Cycle: Empirical Research and Postgraduate Studies on Terrorism. In *Research on Terrorism: Trends, Achievements and Failures*, ed. Andrew Silke, 161–185. New York: Routledge.

Schultz, T. 1971. Rural-Urban Migration in Colombia. *Review of Economics and Statistics* 53 (May): 157–163.

Seligson, Mitchell. 1996. Agrarian Inequality and the Theory of Peasant Rebellion. *Latin American Research Review* 31 (2): 114–157.

Semana. 1999. Informe Especial: Marquetalia 35 años después. May 31–June 7.

———. 2000. Muerto en combate el máximo comandante del EPL. February 21.

———. 2001. La batalla: La cruenta confrontación entre el ELN y los paras en el sur de Bolívar tiene en la cuerda floja las negociaciones de paz con ese grupo subversivo. May 14.

———. 2003a. Uribe critica organizaciones de derechos humanos. September 7.

———. 2003b. La ira presidencial: El discurso de Alvaro Uribe contra las ONG indica que la línea más dura gana espacio en el gobierno. September 15.

———. 2006a. Habla "Jorge 40." March 4.

———. 2006b. Peligra el proceso. May 20.

Serletis, A. 1992. Export Growth and Canadian Economic Development. *Journal of Development Economics* 38 (1): 133–145.

Shifter, Michael. 1999. Colombia on the Brink. *Foreign Affairs* 78 (4): 14–20.

Sigelman, L., and M. Simpson. 1977. Cross National Test of Linkage between Economic Inequality and Political Violence. *Journal of Conflict Resolution* 21 (1): 105–128.

Silberfein, Marilyn. 2003. Insurrections. In *The Geographical Dimensions of Terrorism*, edited by Susan Cutter, Douglas Richardson, and Thomas Wilbanks, 67–73. New York: Routledge.

Simpson, Erin, and Michael Horowitz. 2005. Event Count and Zero-Inflated Models. http://www.people.fas.harvard.edu/~rtmoore/GMMC/EventCountandZeroInflated Models.pdf.

Small, Melvin, and J. David Singer. 1982. *Resort to Arms: International and Civil Wars, 1816–1980.* Thousand Oaks, Calif.: Sage.

Smith, A. C. 1930. Mountain Tops and Lowlands of Colombia. *Economic Geography* 6 (4): 398–407.

Smith, Eugene B. 2002. The New Condottieri and US Policy: The Privatization of Conflict and its Implications. *Parameters* 32 (Winter): 104–119.

Snyder, Richard. 2001. Scaling Down: The Subnational Comparative Method. *Studies in Comparative International Development* 36 (1): 93–110.

Soto, Martha E., and Orlando Restrepo. 2002. Carlos Castaño Afirma que Envió Instructores a las Autodefensas. *El Tiempo Bogotá.* June 27.

Sprinzak, Ehud. 1995. Right-Wing Terrorism in a Comparative Perspective: The Case of Split Delegitimization. *Terrorism and Political Violence* 7:17–43.

Steiner, Roberto. 1998. Colombia's Income from the Drug Trade. *World Development* 26 (6): 1013–1031.

———. 1999. Hooked on Drugs: Colombian-US Relations. In *The United States and Latin America: The New Agenda,* ed. Victor Bulmer-Thomas and James Dunkerley, 159–174. London: Institute of Latin American Studies, Univ. of London.

Steiner, Roberto, and Alejandra Corchuelo. 1999. Economic and Institutional Repercussions of the Drug Trade in Colombia. Working paper. Bogotá: CEDE, Universidad de los Andes.

Stohl, Michael, and George A. Lopez, eds. 1984. *State as Terrorist: The Dynamics of Governmental Violence and Repression.* Westport, Conn.: Greenwood.

Stokes, C. J. 1967. The Freight Transport System of Colombia, 1959. *Economic Geography* 43 (1): 71–90.

Tamayo, Juan O. 2000. U.S. Officials Tie Colombian Guerrillas to Drug Exports. *Miami Herald.* December 13.

Thies, Cameron. 2005. War, Rivalry, and State Building in Latin America. *American Journal of Political Science* 49 (3): 451–465.

Thompson, R. William. 2001. Identifying Rivals and Rivalries in World Politics. *International Studies Quarterly* 45 (4): 557.

Thoumi, Francisco E. 1995a. *Political Economy and Illegal Drugs in Colombia*. Boulder, Colo.: Rienner.

———. 1995b. Why the Illegal Psychedelic Drug Use Industry Grew in Colombia. In Bagley and Walker 1995, 77–96.

———. 2002. Illegal Drugs in Colombia: From Illegal Economic Boom to Social Crisis. *Annals of the American Academy of Political and Social Science* 582:102–116.

———. 2003. *Illegal Drugs, Economy, and Society in the Andes*. Washington, D.C.: Woodrow Wilson Center Press.

———. 2005. The Colombian Competitive Advantage in Illegal Drugs. *Journal of Drug Issues* 35 (1): 7–25.

Tilly, Charles. 1985. War Making and State Making as Organized Crime. In *Bringing the State Back In,* ed. Peter Evens, Dietrich Rueschemeyer, and Theda Skocpol, 169–192. Cambridge: Cambridge Univ. Press.

Torres Arias, Edgar. 1995. *Mercaderes de la muerte*. Bogotá: Inermedio Editores.

Trujillo, Edgar, and Martha Elena Badel. 1997. Los costos economicos de la criminalidad y la violencia en Colombia, 1991–1996. *Planeación y Desarrollo* 28 (4): 266–308.

UNDCP [United Nations Drug Control Program]. 1994. *Drugs and Development*. Technical Series No. 1.

———. 1998. *Economic and Social Consequences of Drug Abuse and Illicit Trafficking*. Technical Series No. 6.

———. 2004. *World Drug Report 2004*. Volume 2: *Statistics*.

———. 2005. *Coca Cultivation in the Andean Region*.

United Nations [various years]. *United Nations Monthly Bulletin of Statistics*.

United Nations Development Programme. 2003. *National Human Development Report for Colombia: Understand in Order to Transform the Local Roots of Conflict*.

United Nations Development Programme. 2004. *Democracy in Latin America: Towards a Citizens' Democracy*.

United States Institute of Peace. 2004. Civil Society Under Siege in Colombia. Special Report No. 114.

U.S. Congress. House. Committee on International Relations. 1996. *Overall U.S. Counternarcotics Policy toward Colombia: Hearing before the Committee on International Relations*. 104th Cong., 2nd sess., September 11. Washington, D.C.: Government Printing Office.

U.S. Department of State. Bureau of Democracy, Human Rights and Labor. 2000. *1999 Country Reports on Human Rights*.

———. Bureau of Democracy, Human Rights and Labor. 2004. *2003 Country Reports on Human Rights*.

U.S. Department of Agriculture. Foreign Agricultural Service. 2002. Rising Global Supplies Push Coffee Prices to 100-Year Lows. International Trade Report.

Van Der Veen, Hans. 2003. Taxing the Drug Trade: Coercive Exploitation and the Financing of Rule. *Crime, Law, and Social Change* 40:349–390.

Vargas, Ricardo. 2002. The Anti-Drug Policy, Aerial Spraying of Illicit Crops, and Their Social, Environmental and Political Impacts in Colombia. *Journal of Drug Issues* 2 (1): 11–60.

Vasquez Carrizosa, A. 1986. *Los No Alineados.* Bogotá: Carlos Valencia Editores.

Vélez, Carlos Eduardo, Mauricio Santamaría, Benedicte de la Breyere, and Natalia Millan. 2001. Inequality, Poverty and Welfare in Urban Colombia: An Overview of the Last Two Decades. Washington, D.C.: World Bank.

Vélez, María Alejandra. 2000. FARC–ELN evolución y expansión territorial. Documento 2000–08. Bogotá: CEDE, Universidad de los Andes. http://economia.uniandes.edu.co/esp/html/publicacion.php3?id=1321&tipo=4.

Vellinga, Menno. 2000. The War on Drugs and Why It Can Not Be Won. *Journal of Third World Studies* 17 (2): 113–128.

———, ed. 2004. *The Political Economy of the Drug Industry: Latin America and the International System.* Gainesville: Univ. Press of Florida.

Villamarín Pulido, Luis Alberto. 1996. El cartel de las FARC. Bogotá: Ediciones El Faraón.

Von der Walde, E. 2001. La novela de sicarios y la violencia en Colombia. *Iberoamericana* 3: 27–40.

Waldmann, Peter. 1997. Cotidianización de la violencia: El ejemplo de Colombia. *Ibero-Amerikanisches Archiv* 23 (3–4): 409–437.

Watson, Cynthia. 2000. Civil-Military Relations in Colombia: A Workable Relationship or a Case for Fundamental Reform? *Third World Quarterly* 21 (3): 529–548.

Weede, Erich. 1987. Some New Evidence on Correlates of Political Violence: Income Inequality, Regime Repressiveness, and Economic Development. *European Sociological Review* 3 (2): 97–108.

Weede, Erich, and H. Tiefenbach. 1981. Some Recent Explanations of Income Inequality. *International Studies Quarterly* 25 (2): 255–282.

Weinberg, Leonard, Ami Pedahzur, and Sivan Hirsch-Hoefler. 2004. The Challenges of Conceptualizing Terrorism. *Terrorism and Political Violence* 16 (4): 777–794.

Wilkinson, Paul. 1986. Maintaining the Democratic Process and Public Support. In *The Future of Political Violence,* ed. Richard Clutterbuck. New York: St. Martin's.

Wilson, James. 2001. Coffee or Poppies? Colombia's Growers under the Spotlight. *Financial Times.* October 25.

World Bank. 2007. Colombia 2006–2010: A Window of Opportunity. Policy Notes.

Worldmark Encyclopaedia of the Nation. 1984. Detroit: Gale.

Yaghmaian, B. 1994. An Empirical Investigation of Exports, Development and Growth in Developing Countries: Challenging the Neoclassical Theory of Export-led Growth. *World Development* 22 (12): 1977–1995.

Yau, Kelvin K. W., Kui Wang, and Andy H. Lee. 2003. Zero-Inflated Negative Binomial Mixed Regression Modeling of Over-Dispersed Count Data with Extra Zeros. *Biometrical Journal* 45 (4): 437–452.

Yunes, João, and Zubarew, Tamara. 1999. Mortalidad por causas violentas en adolescentes y jóvenes: un desafio para la region de las Americas. *Revista Brasileira de Epidemiologia* 2 (3): 102–171.

Zambrano, Carlos Vladimir. 1999. Diversidad y democracia: Riesgo y reto para una Colombia en el siglo XXI. *Revista Javeriana* 67: 165–172.

INDEX

Milton Keynes UK
Ingram Content Group UK Ltd.
UKHW030658220824
447225UK00001B/12